Theory for Beginners

Theory for Beginners

Children's Literature as Critical Thought

KENNETH B. KIDD

Fordham University Press
NEW YORK 2020

Copyright © 2020 Fordham University Press

All rights reserved. No part of this publication may be reproduced, stored in a retrieval system, or transmitted in any form or by any means—electronic, mechanical, photocopy, recording, or any other—except for brief quotations in printed reviews, without the prior permission of the publisher.

Every effort was made to obtain permission to reproduce copyrighted material in this book. If any proper acknowledgment has not been made, we encourage copyright holders to contact us.

Fordham University Press has no responsibility for the persistence or accuracy of URLs for external or third-party internet websites referred to in this publication and does not guarantee that any content on such websites is, or will remain, accurate or appropriate.

Fordham University Press also publishes its books in a variety of electronic formats. Some content that appears in print may not be available in electronic books.

Visit us online at www.fordhampress.com.

Library of Congress Cataloging-in-Publication Data available online at https://catalog.loc.gov.

Printed in the United States of America

23 22 21   5 4 3 2 1

First edition

Contents

Theory for Beginners

Introduction: Children's Literature Otherwise

In 1963, humorist Louise Armstrong and illustrator Whitney Darrow Jr. published a mock picturebook entitled *A Child's Guide to Freud*. Dedicated to "Sigmund F., A Really Mature Person," *A Child's Guide to Freud* is a send-up of Freudian ideas at their most reductive, pitched to adults and, in particular, readers of *The New Yorker* (Darrow being a *New Yorker* cartoonist as well as a children's book illustrator). "The feelings you have about Mommy and Daddy closing their door are called OEDIPAL," the book quickly explains (see Figure 1). "This means that you want to have a Meaningful Relationship with Mommy. If you think a lot about this, it is called a WISH. If you think about it in your sleep, it is called a DREAM. If you suck your thumb instead of thinking about it, it is called COMPENSATION." And so on. The joke here is that while Freud certainly had a lot to say about children, he did not usually talk to them, and we certainly have no business sharing Freud directly with them.

As I emphasize in my previous study *Freud in Oz*, another American picturebook appeared in 1963, this one produced sincerely for children and also inspired by Freudian ideas: Maurice Sendak's *Where the Wild Things Are*. While Sendak's book met some resistance at first, it quickly became popular largely because it gave creative expression to ideas about child anger, oedipality, and unconscious life—without naming those things explicitly. By the time the book appeared, Americans had come to expect that fairy tales and works of fantasy help children navigate psychological challenges. The idea was well-entrenched by the time Bruno Bettelheim capitalized on it with *The Uses of Enchantment*. It

FIGURE 1. Louise Armstrong and Whitney Darrow, Jr., *A Child's Guide to Freud* (1963).

was perfectly acceptable, even praiseworthy, to present Freudian or other adult ideas indirectly and in the form of a (sincere) picturebook. What makes *A Child's Guide to Freud* funny is its conceit of direct address to the child or the idea that Freud might be appropriate for children raw and unmediated. Never mind that Freud actually did talk to children sometimes, even if he did not write for them, and that he described children as little researchers and theorists, puzzling out the sexual and other secrets of adults. *A Child's Guide to Freud* is funny in that *New Yorker* sort of way because it acknowledges that children are indeed curious and that adults have the sometimes-uncomfortable task of enlightenment. The book alludes to the scenario of adults talking to kids about sexuality or evading such talk. (Of course, if we believe Freud, children do not need to read him or anyone else since they are already doing what Freud does himself, testing and revising ideas.)

Fast-forward to the 2017 publication by MIT Press of an English translation of Bini Adamczak's *Kommunismus*, titled *Communism for Kids.* Adamczak is a Berlin-based scholar who has published on communism and its discontents in the former Soviet Union. Published in Germany over a decade ago to little fanfare, the book tells the story of people suffering under feudalism, then capitalism, then more promising but finally disappointing models of communism. Competition between two factories leads to a crisis that workers try to solve six times, never successfully. Finally, the workers take control of the factories and form a new collective, and the book ends on an ambiguous note: Will they succeed in establishing a happier and more just society? And if so, how?

Adamczak's book met with howls of protest in the United States. The book was denounced as anti-American, anti-Christian, and antifamily; one reviewer even called it "the most dangerous book on economics ever written for kids" (Wenzel). One of its translators, Jacob Blumenfeld, observes in a *New York Times* piece that while "the narrative is full of suffering, defeat, and failure, the real scandal of the book lies in its optimism, its hope that another world is still possible in the womb of the old." Blumenfeld goes on to clarify that *Communism for Kids* "is not a children's book at all, but a book written for everyone in a language that, for the most part, children, too, could understand. The title we chose for the American edition was an elegant way to convey this aspect of the book."

Likely someone behind the project, whether Blumenfeld and his cotranslator Sophie Lewis or the powers at MIT Press, expected and even courted the controversy; the book has sold nicely thanks to such. I doubt many kids are reading this book. Its readers are likely curious and/or bemused adults. Regardless, Blumenfeld's comment underscores just how provocative is the rhetoric of address to children when it comes to a topic like communism. Of course, just as there are plenty of children's books with Freudian tonalities, so too are there a good many children's books with Marxist and/or socialist commitments. Scholars such as Kimberley Reynolds, Jane Rosen, Michael Rosen, Julia L. Mickenberg, and Philip Nel have written about and even reproduced some of them. These books do not hide their progressive ideas, but neither do they announce them so nakedly, much less declare the appropriateness of communism for kids. As with *A Child's Guide to Freud*, what makes the translation and repackaging of Adamczak's book so scandalous (on top of its perverse optimism) is the explicit designation of a child audience (sincere or not). The ideas of Freud or Marx can be acceptable if hidden inside a children's book, but to speak openly to children about Freud or Marx is apparently beyond the pale.

The idea that philosophy might be "for" children, however, has met with considerable public as well as academic success. That is especially true when philosophy is built into the narrative structure of children's books rather than spotlighted as a topic or concern, but even books for children about philosophy do not carry the same potential for scandal as do books about Freud or Marx. One of my topics in *Theory for Beginners* is the philosophy for children movement (acronym P4C), which got its start in the early 1970s in the United States and has since expanded globally. P4C developed its own materials for children and makes use of existing children's literature. Indeed, P4C has become increasingly reliant on children's literature over the decades. But P4C does not need to work undercover in a children's book; it can also announce itself openly. It may be that to the broader public, philosophy is not as threatening as the names Freud or Marx. Philosophy remains associated with Western culture and the search for wisdom rather than with sexuality or economics. Philosophy does not seem political or even cultural, although of course it is both. For whatever reasons, the prospect of philosophy for children has been quite palatable, even compelling. That does not mean that all philosophers deem P4C appropriate or even possible. Its early advocates were outliers, in a sense. But as time went on, P4C took root. Theory, meanwhile, probably does not ring a bell outside the academy, except in its general meaning of hypothesis or speculation. Theory is more narrowly academic as a discourse or genre and, when mentioned at all beyond academia, does not enjoy the approval rating of philosophy. But like philosophy, theory thinks about the child and even invests in children's literature. Theory has an even stronger interest in that cousin to the child—the beginner. Theory loves a beginner.

Theory for Beginners examines the relationship of children's and young adult (YA) literature to P4C and what I am calling theory for beginners.[1] Whatever else it may be—a mode of address, a literary heritage, a multigenre body of work, a publishing category, a field of professionalization—children's literature is a set of experiments in thinking and feeling. Children's literature can be narrowly prescriptive, of course, but much of the time it is imaginative, expansive, and surprising in its strategies of engagement and cultivation. It invites us all to dream, wonder, and explore. In helping children to read, it also helps them to "read"—to interpret, contextualize, understand.[2] It often does so self-reflexively, inviting would-be readers to engage materially as much as psychologically and emotionally. Literature for young children often takes picturebook form, and recent years have seen an upsurge in YA graphic novels. These materials are not simply "illustrated"; rather, they invite and even demand different sorts of interaction and manipulation. Aaron Kashtan makes the case that comics help us grasp the materiality of texts, and the same can be said for children's books, with their varying styles, sizes, shapes, and textures. Given all of this, it is no surprise that psychological discourse looks to children's literature for inspiration or that children's literature correspondingly has a psychological texture. I told that story of reciprocity in *Freud in Oz*. *Theory for Beginners* shifts focus to how philosophy and theory draw motivation and power from children's literature, conventionally understood, while also encouraging and even developing materials for beginners—what I am referring to as children's literature "otherwise," meaning in an alternative form or register. Like psychoanalysis, philosophy and theory are ostensibly adult projects that nonetheless concern themselves with childhood and make use of—and sometimes produce—texts for children and/or beginners. While *Freud in Oz* focuses on the psychological uses of enchantment, or the association of children's literature with psychological work, *Theory for Beginners* considers the intellectual uses of enchantment (alternatively, the uses of intellectual enchantment), or the association of children's literature with thought and thinking.

Children's literature scholars such as Deborah Thacker and Katharine Jones have rightly underscored theory's neglect of children's literature despite the opportunities the latter offers for thinking about language and culture.[3] But if we think expansively about what counts as children's literature, there is a record of engagement by theory, one that should excite theorists and philosophers as much as children's literature scholars. Children's literature broadly construed is a philosophical and theoretical as well as aesthetic and educational affair, one providing inspiration to philosophy and theory, as well as the reverse. While the term *children's literature* has descriptive value and convenience, I do not treat it as clearer or more stable than the terms *philosophy* or *theory*. All three terms enjoy a certain amorphousness that is generally helpful, if also sometimes frustrating. Writing on modernist studies and "weak theory," Paul Saint-Amour proposes that an academic field's strength increases as consensus about its central term weakens (451).[4] This has been true of children's literature studies. The more we question and expand the conceit of children's literature, the more productive have been our analyses. It is not that there is no such thing as children's literature but that there are many such things.[5] We can affirm the legitimacy and legibility of children's literature without assuming that it is a (lowly) thing apart. Even now, children's literature is too often imagined in narrowly functional terms. What if children's literature encompasses not only literature at large but also philosophy and theory?

Granted, psychoanalysis has a particularly intense involvement with childhood, whereas philosophy and theory are less obviously child-centric, having other emphases. Philosophy, in fact, is sometimes framed as something to be taken up only or especially later in life. And yet, philosophy is also imagined as especially appropriate for novices and/or children, most centrally in the P4C movement. As I show in Chapter 1, P4C builds on the philosophical foundations of children's literature while also revising that tradition by reimagining children's literature as philosophy in creative form. P4C does not represent all philosophy, but it is an important initiative, one partaking of both analytic and continental traditions. Theory, meanwhile, despite its reputation for complexity and difficulty, has mined classic children's books for wisdom and also self-positioned as for beginners especially, giving priority to new methods and perspectives over mastery and established knowledge. Beginners, of course, are not always children, any more than children are always beginners, but there is overlap between the categories. I suggest in Chapter 2 that theory for beginners resembles children's literature in its methods of education and its enthusiasm for learning. In presenting for and identifying with the beginner, theory participates in a kind of children's literature, even when it does not also (as it sometimes does) invoke established children's titles.

P4C is a well-documented phenomenon, while theory for beginners is more challenging to track. I understand theory for beginners as both descriptive and aspirational. It is descriptive in that some theorists have already framed theory as undertaken on the behalf of beginners, designed with their education and engagement in mind. I identify a tradition of sorts within theory that is beginner oriented. But my use of the term is also aspirational in that I affirm and amplify this perspective. Recognizing the importance of complexity and expertise, I nonetheless believe that more theory should be for beginners. Theory for beginners shares some territory with other programs of alt-theoretical articulation that find inspiration in nonelite cultural materials, such as Houston Baker Jr.'s vernacular theory (drawing on blues music), Jack Halberstam's low theory (animation), and Jane Gallop's anecdotal theory (anecdotes).[6] Theory for beginners can and already does take various forms, among them theory introductions as well as shortish academic books of cultural criticism such as those in the Object Lessons series of Bloomsbury Publishing or the Avidly Reads series of NYU Press. Meanwhile, as I emphasize in the third and final chapter, children's literature as conventionally recognized is arguably philosophical and/or theoretical as much as literary. Like the first two chapters, Chapter 3 argues for an expansive approach to children's literature, imagining such as a literature for minors and experimenting with the idea that some children's books can function as queer theory for kids.

If this book aims to put philosophers and theorists in conversation with scholars of children's literature, I hope it will also be useful for childhood studies. Childhood studies has largely been a social science undertaking, with only more recent momentum in the humanities.[7] And yet it is obvious to anyone in children's literature studies that childhood studies has long been practiced from within. Reflecting on the panel "The Case for Childhood Studies" at the 1997 Nashville Conference on Modern Critical Approaches to Children's Literature, Richard Flynn remarks that "childhood studies is being done all the time. And nowhere is it done more skillfully than by the scholars of children's literature whose primary concerns have included defining and historicizing representations of childhood and exploring childhood as a notion constructed by politics, rhetoric, and human institutions" (144). As Flynn emphasizes, the study of children's literature has much to contribute to childhood studies, given its focus on matters of language, representation, and cultural ideology. *Theory for Beginners* underscores the importance of children's literature for childhood studies while also recognizing that children's literature is even more interdisciplinary than typically acknowledged, engaged not only with education and library science (as is often recognized) but also with philosophy and theory. P4C represents an especially rich subject for childhood studies, as it brings together education, children's literature, and children's rights. Theory for beginners may seem less immediately useful for childhood studies, but the beginner is often paired with the child, with consequences that childhood studies can help illuminate.

The Philosophical Turn

If philosophy is for children, and theory for beginners, children's literature has also become more adult-associated with its links to philosophy and theory. At least since Jacqueline Rose raised the issue with her 1984 study *The Case of Peter Pan, or The Impossibility of Children's Fiction*, presenting it as something of a scandal, children's literature studies has struggled with and apologized for the presence of the adult in writing for children, what Maria Nikolajeva calls its "aetonormativity" (*Power*).[8] Yet children's literature is largely produced and sometimes also consumed by adults. It has never been definitively separate from so-called literature for adults or adult literature. In a landmark article, Felicity Hughes underscores that until the 1880s the English novel was generally considered "family reading" (543) and that only later did authors and critics try to decouple the genre from child readers. In *Books for Children, Books for*

Adults: Age and the Novel from Defoe to James, Teresa Michals explains that the Anglophone novel was launched for a mixed-age readership of children, servants, and women. Children's literature was not an offshoot of adult literature; rather, specialization "by age for adults occurred much later in the history of the novel" (2). There is a case to be made that children's literature came first and that adult literature emerged in relation to such.[9] The Victorians enjoyed what Claudia Nelson calls "age inversion" in literature, such that children's books circulated "for the pleasure of adult readers" even as adult works employed "strategies more usually associated with children's fiction" (164).[10] And if, by the early twentieth century, gatekeepers of elite-aspirant American literary culture had repressed this history of entanglement, casting children's literature as a thing inferior and apart, the repression was never complete and now the lines blur again.[11] Rachel Falconer points to the acceleration of the "crossover novel" and cross-generational reading in the period of 1997 to 2007, bound up with the success of *Harry Potter* but also evidenced by the inclusion of children's books in more book prizes, greater media interest in children's literature, and the production of dual editions of the same title (one targeting children, one adults). Falconer attributes this phenomenon to a general tilt toward youth culture and soft capitalism's "mythology of self-discovery through play/work" (41).

As children's literature is drawing nearer adult fiction, resembling such in complexity and aesthetic sophistication, it is also drawing nearer adult critical discourse.[12] Scholars have not stood apart from this development but rather encouraged and enabled it. It was only a matter of time before we made a virtue of necessity and accepted and thought carefully about adult presence in children's literature. In *The Hidden Adult*, Perry Nodelman responds to Rose by proposing that adult investments are both obvious and acceptable because they make children's literature a critical as much as a creative enterprise. Emphasizing the need for more "energetic" practices of analysis, David Rudd reminds us that theory lives inside all texts, such that "works like Lewis Carroll's *Alice* have proved a playground for philosophers, mathematicians, logicians, chess players, and of course, psychoanalysts—let alone countless other creative writers" (4).

Scholars of children's literature are increasingly keen to emphasize the continuity and even parity of children's literature and adult critical discourse. A typical example is Dean A. Kowalski's contribution to Jacob Held's edited volume *Dr. Seuss and Philosophy*, titled "Horton Hears You, Too! Seuss and Kant on Respecting Persons." "Kant never wrote books for children," writes Kowalski. "In fact, his prose is complex and foreboding; however, some of his ideas—like Dr. Seuss's—are immanently intuitive, bordering on common sense. Indeed, the moral messages of Dr. Seuss and Kant tend to converge" (119). The idea that Dr. Seuss could be on equal footing with Kant would have seemed ludicrous until recently. Or consider Andrea Schwenke Wyile's 2013 essay "'Astonishment Is Thinking': Graphic Metaphor and Its Philosophical Consequence in Mahler's *Poèmes* and Lemieux's *Stormy Night*." Citing Seymour Chatman and Ludwig Wittgenstein, Wyile argues that these two picturebooks juxtapose the verbal and the visual to generate the "astonishment" fundamental to thinking in Wittgenstein's formulation (277). Wyile anticipates the arguments now being made about comics and imagetext experiments in theory. In 2015, Annette Wannamaker called Janne Teller's YA novel *Nothing* "as much a work of philosophy or critical theory as it is a work of fiction, though perhaps these genres have a great deal more in common than is often acknowledged" (83).[13] Lisa Sainsbury has done much to advance this perspective from within children's literature studies. Her terrific *Ethics in British Children's Literature* (2013) frames post-1945 British children's literature as a series of provocative experiments in ethical thinking and relation. Sainsbury examines "the ways in which children's literature might be considered philosophical" (9), inviting children "to think about the very categories that define them" (48).[14] In a more recent article, she proposes that children's literature often employs thought experiments in both "narrative" and "paradigm" form. Sainsbury traces the formal properties of the thought experiment (conversational mode, double engagement, modal positioning) in Carroll's *Alice* and more contemporary titles for children ("'But'"). For Joe Sutliff Sanders in *A Literature of Questions: Nonfiction for the Critical Child* (2018), children's nonfiction proffers an invitation to critical engagement and thereby fosters critical literacy. The "critical child" has a history, of course, just like the "creative child" before her.[15] And it can be tricky to identify what "critical thinking" looks like or involves.[16] But an important takeaway is that children's literature is no longer seen as separate from adult intellectual discourse. Rather, for these and other commentators, children's literature *is* critical thinking, just in different dress.

Not only that, but children's writers sometimes got there first, according to some scholars. Carl F. Miller brilliantly reads Dr. Seuss's picturebook *Horton Hears a Who!* as "a popular expression of [Alain] Badiou's philosophy almost forty years in advance" (84). Educational theorist Tyson E. Lewis goes one step further, finding the philosopher Giorgio Agamben lacking in comparison to picturebook master Maurice Sendak. Drawing on Agamben's conception of the "anthropological machine" out of which human exceptionalism is manufactured, Lewis concludes that Sendak "surpasses Agamben and makes an invaluable contribution to the field of the philosophy of childhood" ("King" 288), showing how the "passionate attachment to the human" brings Max back safely from the land of the wild things.[17] Reflecting on its success, Falconer describes contemporary crossover fiction as metacritical, writing that it "excels at increasing a reader's awareness of the areas of overlap as well as the differences between children's and adult fiction. It prompts a reader to interrogate everything that happens in these in-between territories. . . . [It] calls into question the boundaries which used to define children's fiction" (27). Cross-reading, meanwhile, "highlights how children's literature has never existed in a truly separate sphere" (9). Philosophers are also getting into this newish subfield of children's literature studies, contributing to volumes such as Peter R. Costello's *Philosophy in Children's Literature* and various handbooks of philosophical introduction based on popular children's titles and media franchises. The attitude is again that the source materials are philosophical or at least proto-philosophical.

Scholars are not the only people invested in this idea. In the popular press, we see faith in the wisdom of Dr. Seuss, for instance, and more generally in the philosophical power of both childhood and children's literature. Popular philosophy especially now finds its reflection in children's literature, in and around the success of P4C. Across the world, children's picturebooks, chapter books, and young adult novels are used in P4C. Any number of children's and YA texts might be mined for their philosophical and/or theoretical insights, often because they were inspired or at least informed by philosophy and/or theory. Teller's *Nothing* reads like philosophy because it was designed to pose difficult, perhaps unanswerable questions about art and life. Granted, most of the children's books that interest P4C advocates are not explicitly about philosophers or philosophical categories and terms. Jostein Gaarder's young adult novel *Sophie's World* (1991) is an exception, as it is both a philosophical novel and a novel about philosophy. Another exception is the European Plato & Co. picturebook series published by Diaphanes, which "introduces children—and curious grown-ups—to the lives and works of famous philosophers." Each volume "features an engaging—and often funny—story that presents basic tenets of philosophical thought alongside vibrant color illustrations."[18] There are thirteen titles so far, including *Diogenes the Dog-Man*, *Dr. Freud, Fish Whisperer*, *Kierkegaard and the Mermaid*, and *Wittgenstein's Rhinoceros*. The series is published in German, English, and French. In any case, faith that children's books can be philosophical, with or without attention to philosophical specifics, is now widespread. In 2013, for example, Matthue Roth and Rohan Daniel Eason published an illustrated book of three retold Franz Kafka stories called *My First Kafka: Runaways, Rodents, and Giant Bugs*. While funny, *My First Kafka* is not a joke book for adults like *A Child's Guide to Freud*; rather, it is a book "for all ages" in the tradition of writers like Sendak, Edward Gorey, and Daniel Handler. In her entertaining review of *My First Kafka* alongside the edited academic volume *Philosophy and Kafka*, Rebecca Schuman writes that it is unfair to compare them, "as these are works in vastly different categories. One is a philosophically original exploration of often underrepresented aspects of Kafka's oeuvre that may have a lasting impact on the genre—and the other is a book of critical essays."

Children's literature scholars are both recognizing and helping to promote the philosophical turn. Miller hears Badiou in *Horton Hears a Who!* because Dr. Seuss shares territory with the philosopher and because it is increasingly acceptable to pair them. While no one has commented on the philosophical turn per se, Sanders does remark that scholars seem "particularly anxious about the issue of critical engagement because the history of children's literature has been dominated by books, writers, publishers, reviewers, and educators who have seen the primary purpose of children's literature to be conservative moral indoctrination" (295). Sanders makes these remarks not in *A Literature of Questions* but in an earlier essay about China Miéville's novel *Un Lun Dun*. In a section of that essay titled "Why Children's Literature Longs for the Left," Sanders speculates that many children's literature scholars long for leftist texts that will counter that conservative moral indoctrination. He notes that the term *critical* "can mean both 'intellectually engaged' and 'inclined toward antagonist readings'" (294).

But it is not just a matter of scholarly longing; there is also a robust tradition of progressive and radical children's literature internationally, literature that links progressive politics with critical thinking. Mickenberg's *Learning from the Left* and Reynolds's *Left Out* are important monographs on American and British material, respectively, and both Mickenberg and Reynolds have collaborated on anthologies of radical children's literature—Mickenberg with Nel, in *Tales for Little Rebels*, and Reynolds with Jane and Michael Rosen, in *Reading and Rebellion*. Essays in Claudia Mills's collection *Ethics and Children's Literature* make observations echoing those of Sainsbury concerning the ethical and intellectual boldness of writing for young people. Contributors to *Beyond Babar*, edited by Sandra L. Beckett and Maria Nikolajeva, emphasize how European children's classics promote progressive ideology and aesthetic experimentation. In her contribution, Beckett discusses the French writer Michel Tournier as a "failed" philosopher, noting that "he would like to have taught philosophy to children" (174) but instead became a children's author and "taught" philosophy to children indirectly.[19] Harald Bache-Wiig, meanwhile, addresses Gaarder's *Sophie's World*, which has been translated from Norwegian into multiple languages and sold millions of copies. Bache-Wiig explains that presenting philosophy in the format of a novel rather than a textbook is crucial to the lesson that one must "adopt an enquiring and open-minded attitude to life without letting oneself be subdued by learned authority and seemingly ready-made solutions" (270).[20] As these examples suggest, a good amount of European and American children's literature is bound up with philosophy and theory as well as with progressive politics.

The question of how critical children's literature might or should be is beyond my scope. I am somewhat skeptical of the "critical" upsurge, especially insofar as the critical child seems to have displaced the desiring child of psychoanalysis. Queer theory restores the latter child to some degree, as does some children's literature, against the more rationalist idea of the critical child we see in much P4C. But if we could learn from a genealogy of the critical child, I am persuaded enough that contemporary children's literature often models and invites critical engagement.

If philosophy and theory have encouraged a certain rigorousness in children's literature studies, they have also brought a commitment to play, creativity, and counterfactual thought, aligning with children's literature. It is important to remember that philosophy and theory model and encourage wonder, as well as analytical thought. *Theory for Beginners* honors that dual commitment while observing and historicizing the philosophical turn. The turn is observable not only in the material I cite but also in the broader investment in theory within children's literature studies. For decades, children's literature specialists have drawn on and contributed to traditions including deconstruction, feminism, psychoanalysis, reader-response theory, Marxism, postcolonial theory, queer theory, and posthumanism. That history is well-known. Rather than rehearse it here, I concentrate on other ways in which philosophy, theory, and children's literature have become linked inside and outside the academy. My case studies are selective rather than comprehensive, giving priority to more recent as well as more neglected texts and contexts.

Chapters in Brief

Chapter 1, "Philosophy for Children," for example, could start with educational philosophy in the eighteenth century or with John Dewey and progressive education in the early twentieth century—both relevant to the broader topic, but also both extensively researched. Instead, the chapter examines the P4C movement, which helped promote the idea that both children and children's literature have philosophical tendencies. P4C proposes that philosophy can begin almost anywhere, most especially in the routines and experiences of everyday life, and that children are both natural and inventive philosophers. For P4C, to think philosophically means both to think critically—to engage in logic and critique—and to think creatively or imaginatively, to "wonder" and speculate. This vision of philosophy aligns with a similar understanding of theory as both interrogative and generative, rigorous and fanciful. P4C got its start in the United States and has since spread to other countries and continents. It has footholds in Australia, Europe, North America, South America, and Asia, with growing momentum in Africa. At its height, before federal funding for such was cut in the early 1990s, there were reportedly five thousand P4C programs in the United States alone. P4C has since enjoyed a resurgence and continues to be influential worldwide, thriving especially in the United Kingdom, thanks to the Society for the Advancement of Philosophical Enquiry and Reflection in Education (SAPERE), which in 2016 alone trained some 4,500 teachers in P4C methods. I do not study contemporary P4C programs but rather focus broadly on the evolving use of children's literature in P4C as a way of understanding the growing mutualities of children's literature and at least some versions of philosophy. As I show, working alongside but usually separately from children's literature scholarship, P4C has helped to establish children's literature as philosophical and ethical engagement, linking it with progressive education and children's rights. It also promises to keep philosophy fresh for practitioners and the larger public. Contemporary P4C or PwC (philosophy with children) also gives priority to picturebooks and is beginning to think about how imagetexts are particularly conducive to philosophical work.

There's nothing quite so cohesive when it comes to theory for beginners. Chapter 2 first considers the tendency of certain strains of theory to present for children or beginners and then turns to graphic or imagetext guides to theory. Like theory at large, what I am calling theory for beginners is a set of practices, speculations, and relations, as much as a set of ideas, always performative and sometimes deliberately fanciful. Theory is concerned with the beginner in part because theory needs beginners; theory cannot otherwise reproduce. Theory thus addresses the adult beginner and folds her into the project. In other words, as with children's literature, the education of beginners becomes part of the apparatus. As Chapter 2 emphasizes, theory is not merely interested in but also self-presents *as* a beginner. A governing principle is that theory, however demanding and of whatever provenance, breaks with tradition and recalls us to the play of ideas. Theory involves critique but is not reducible to such; it has additional functions, including that of enchantment. "What is called 'theory,'" notes Rita Felski in her critique of critique, "consists of many language games, not just one" (20).

Theory is for beginners not only because it is accessible but also because it is demanding,[21] re-enacting in the adult learner that mix of desire and dread attendant to literacy acquisition. This orientation within the theoretical canon itself dovetails with the pedagogical material surrounding and explicating such. The task is to explain while maintaining the allure and respecting the challenge. Thus, Scott Carpenter opens *Reading Lessons: An Introduction to Theory* with "Remember when reading pained you? This book aims to make reading hard again, to restore some of the impenetrability of texts while rekindling the delight we took in discovery" (2).[22] As mentioned above, an imagetext literature for the beginners of theory and assorted cultural topics has emerged in and around theory more properly. There are two lines of these guides, also described as documentary comic books: the For Beginners series and the Introducing series. Hundreds of titles are in print. While *Philosophy for Beginners* exists as a multimodal guide—in fact, it is the top best-selling For Beginners title—as yet there is no multimodal *Theory for Beginners*. I use "theory for beginners" to indicate theory that is friendly to beginners and also materials that introduce theory or make it more accessible. If theory can refer to a set of more or less canonical writings by theorists, theory for beginners includes some such writings but also other materials, such as less-canonical source texts and overviews designed for introduction or orientation. I want theory for beginners to underscore a tendency in some theoretical writing and to align said tendency with texts outside theory as conventionally understood and institutionalized.

P4C and theory for beginners share roots in political critique and social progressivism. The acknowledged founder of P4C, Matthew Lipman, was concerned by the lack of political awareness and critical thinking skills among his undergraduate philosophy students, especially in the wake of the Vietnam War. P4C connects reasoning and philosophical ability to ethical and civic development. The contemporaneous reception of "French theory" in the United States began with elite universities, Yale in particular, but the theory itself is sometimes skeptical about knowledge claims and traditional philosophical practice (if not also fancy academic culture). Not a little such theory appeals to the beginner and/or the childlike. The graphic guides to theory have many influences but emerged most immediately from the anticolonial and Marxist labor of Mexican activist and author-illustrator Eduardo del Río, a.k.a. Rius. Rius's *Cuba Para Principiantes*, or *Cuba for Beginners* (1970), kicked off the For Beginners series, emphasizing the self-teaching of political critical awareness. The genre gradually went mainstream, losing its political edge and becoming a kind of intellectual self-help literature. P4C likewise lost its progressive energy with the expansion/mainstreaming of its apparatus. Even so, P4C and theory for beginners still hope to reach people outside the academy. They participate in what Dale Jacobs calls "literacy sponsorship," developed from Deborah Brandt's introduction of the concept.[23]

We might expect a literature for beginners to take imagetext form, given the example of picturebooks and other visual materials for child learners. And in fact, theory for beginners does take imagetext form with the guides, even ahead of P4C's turn to picturebooks. But as W. J. T. Mitchell reminds us in *Picture Theory*, "the interaction of pictures and texts is constitutive of representation as such: all media are mixed media" (5). Mitchell's aim, as he explains, is not to produce a theory of pictures but rather "to *picture theory* as a practical activity in the formation of representations" (6). Theory can take graphic form or can have imagetext coordinates. Famous examples include A. J. Greimas's semiotic rectangle and Jacques Lacan's Borromean knot, as well as Fredric Jameson's provocative engagements with both.[24] Working with more representational materials, Mitchell points to Foucault's essay on Magritte's famous painting *The Treachery of Images* (*Ceci n'est pas une pipe*), which for Mitchell underscores how Foucault's work is concerned with even as it performs "the dialectic of the visible and the sayable" (71). The graphic guides do not just illustrate, in other words; they carry forth and embody the visual and material aspects of theory. The guides picture theory and help us to do the same.

Chapter 3 entertains the idea that children's literature more conventionally construed can be productively understood as a literature for minors, and even as a minor literature as conceptualized by Gilles Deleuze and Félix Guattari in their book on Kafka. Children, of course, are legally minors, but adults can be minors too, culturally if not also legally. Such an understanding of children's literature might broaden our sense of its purpose or commitment. For Deleuze and Guattari, a minor literature is a literature produced inside a dominant discourse, one that attempts to deterritorialize said discourse. In this case, the dominant discourse would be (adult) literature and culture, inside which children's literature is produced and against which at least some children's literature is positioned. Obviously, such an understanding of children's literature is selective if not idealistic. But it is a popular view all the same, and this chapter traces as much as affirms belief that children's literature tends toward both theory and oppositionality, or toward resistance and critique. I begin with Walter Benjamin's attention to childhood and children's forms as a baseline for critical thinking. Resistant to the idea of children's literature as a specialization, Benjamin nonetheless saw children's books as a resource for experiments in thinking and even composed his own materials for the young. He was arguably one of our first theorists of children's literature in an expansive sense. I then trace the reception history of Lewis Carroll's *Alice*, the Anglophone children's classic that most closely approaches recognition as theory. Finally, I propose that some children's literature not only runs parallel to the academic formation called queer theory but also functions as queer theory for kids. With its singular characters, odd kinships, eccentric plots, fantastical settings, and funky temporalities, children's literature is not just fabulous material to analyze. It also performs for young readers some of the tasks that queer theory performs for adults. Not all children's literature works this way, of course, but I am interested in material that does. Chapter 3 concludes with a reading of Alison Bechdel's second graphic memoir, *Are You My Mother?*, seemingly for adults but preoccupied with queer childhood. I suggest that such material returns sexuality to the critical child, bringing psychoanalysis back into contact with philosophy and theory.

Term Limits

When I say that philosophy is for children and theory for beginners, I do not mean all theory or philosophy, just certain strains or articulations. On the philosophy side, I am focusing on P4C, a mix of analytic and continental philosophy; on the theory side, I mean mostly poststructuralist and posthumanist theory, although some thinkers I discuss have been associated with "high" theory. If theory appeals to beginners, it is also very much designed for experienced practitioners, "theoretical sophistication" being nearly a redundancy, says Joseph Litvak (*Strange Gourmets* 2–3).[25] Philosophy, too, is a complicated affair and often imagined as appropriate for only advanced users. I mean no disrespect in emphasizing beginner-friendly iterations of both.

And though they share considerable territory, theory and philosophy are hardly identical. I cannot be sufficiently responsible to the complexities of either, much less to their relation (and never mind their relation to literature).[26] I opt for some crude but useful generalizations. Philosophy is sometimes considered the longer tradition, even credited with bringing theory into the world, although some argue that theory was nascent from the start as a technique or orientation within philosophy. The Greek *theoria* predates *philosophein* or philosophizing, true, but matters are not so simple either, as D. N. Rodowick notes in *Elegy for Theory* (xiii). In *Keywords*, Raymond Williams holds that philosophy retains "its earliest and most general meaning . . . the love of wisdom, understood as the study and knowledge of things and their causes," although he notes the expansion of the term into more applied or "managerial" areas (236). Williams's gloss on theory is longer and emphasizes the term's relationship to "practice" and "praxis" (317). Even now, philosophy claims some association with wisdom seeking, as well as with system building, while theory is more consistently linked, on the one hand, with contemplation and speculation (also spectacle) and, on the other hand, with critique (often Marxist or materialist). Theory's meanings have been expanded such that the theoretical still means something different from the practical even as it designates a kind of practice.[27] But even "critical theory" retains a sense of the speculative; it does not just mean applied.

Citing Fredric Jameson, Andrew Cole sees theory as "the move away from philosophy within philosophy itself," originating with Hegel (xi). Theory, like the notion of the dialectic with which it is entangled, is now understood "as a kind of critical thinking in opposition to a postulated unity or grand philosophical system" (xxx). Drawing on Lyotard, Gregg Lambert proposes that the theorist emerged from and against analytic philosophy, with the theorist becoming a new kind of philosopher who does not pretend to be a detached metaphysician but rather embraces limitations and positionality. Whatever we think of particular accounts, we do associate theory with critique and with self-reflexivity. Building on Jonathan Culler's description of theory as "an unbounded group of writings about everything under the sun" (*Literary Theory* 3), Brian McHale understands theory as a "postmodern phenomenon" (69). Literary theory is a subgenre of critical theory, even if it exercises some influence on the latter.[28] As these accounts suggest, theory functions simultaneously as a content, a form of cultural capital, and a mode of dissemination.

Theory can also be shorthand for particular schools or moments (Frankfurt, Birmingham) or for the institutionalization of critique, whether at large or with respect to the American research university.[29] In *Cultural Capital*, John Guillory reminds us that the syllabus of theory has joined the syllabus of literature as part of the ongoing modernization of the vernacular canon. François Cusset calls theory "this weird textual object," peculiarly American and "definable today as a strange breed of academic market rules, French (and more generally continental) detachable concepts, campus-based identity politics, and trendy pop culture" (xi). For Cusset, theory names in particular denationalized and Americanized French and German philosophy.[30] Derrida identified theory as a "purely North American artifact" ("Some" 71) even as he came to personify theory; Douglas Kellner stresses the more contemporary globalization of theory. While he does not talk explicitly about it, Michael Trask would probably situate theory as a continuation of the "ironic social style" typical of the academy from midcentury forward, marked by a fondness for "the theatrical, the synthetic, the artificial" and "improvisational reality" (1–2, 20). Commenting on Pierre Bourdieu's discussion of the academic *habitus*, Trask remarks that the cultural capital of literature is not just the "prestige associated with canonical forms of knowledge but also the prestige associated with a fundamental suspicion of such forms," embodied in the "hermeneutics of suspicion and its equally powerful fetish for demystification" (21). Theory can offer both ironic style and cultural critique.

Whereas philosophy long "tended to bypass the problems of coming to terms with its own textual or rhetorical constitution," observes Christopher Norris, literary theory "has made these problems its peculiar concern, and in this sense has moved into regions of enquiry closed off to 'philosophy' as such" (11). Put another way, philosophy long struggled to suppress rather than acknowledge its "philosophical imaginary," to quote Michèle Le Doeuff, while theory has been comparatively happy to be seen with and even as literature.[31] Granted, a certain strain of philosophy—renegade, wild—has moved toward theory and art for some time. Nietzsche, of course, recast philosophy as an act of creation or construction, and others followed in his wake, especially in the continental tradition. Against loftier visions, Wittgenstein insisted that philosophy was not a theory or a subject but an activity, one concerned with the often frustrating attempt to express the inexpressible.[32] Jean-François Lyotard asserts that philosophy "is not a discrete terrain in the geography of disciplines. Everybody knows that" (*Postmodern* 100). In *What Is Philosophy?*, Deleuze and Guattari define philosophy the way others define theory, as the self-reflexive making and mobilization of concepts. "Philosophy is always meanwhile," they assert, and it needs "nonphilosophy" (159). Analytic philosophy played a role in the twentieth-century remodeling of philosophy toward theory, as did Richard Rorty's neopragmatism and elaboration of the "edifying philosopher" (Cascardi 53). Bernard Stiegler recasts philosophy as desire, as impossible in terms of satisfaction, better understood as a perpetual state of perplexity, as well as "an experiment, indeed a way of life" (109). (Theory, meanwhile, is a "specific form of attention" [109].) Theory and philosophy seem nearly to name a kind of intellectual restlessness or desire. In his recent account of philosophy in the English-language tradition, Jonathan Reé suggests that rather than see philosophical texts "as candidates for inclusion in some ultimate compendium of knowledge, we might do better to treat them as individual works of art forming a tradition as intricate and unpredictable as, say, Yoruba sculpture, Chinese poetry or the classical string quartet" (5).

In this account, I am glossing over differences between theorists and philosophers, as well as differences among those in each ensemble. As Marah Gubar emphasized in her response to an earlier version of this introduction, the relationship between theory and philosophy is one not only of cheerful overlap but also of mutual suspicion and rivalry. When literary critics at University of Cambridge wanted to give Derrida an honorary degree, she reminded me, the philosophers there forbade it on the grounds that Derrida's work was so much drivel. Derrida was a philosopher but in the continental more than the analytic tradition (despite his attention to language) and hence a "theorist" to many, thanks especially to his American packaging. Analytic philosophers, who dominate Anglo-American philosophy departments, are not overly fond of theory's methods or style. The theorist is often dismissed as shallow and foreign and flamboyant, and it is not a stretch to understand theory-phobia not just as resembling but as deriving from both homophobia and xenophobia. Discussing the transition from midcentury liberalism to New Left politics, Trask observes that in "renouncing the Cold War establishment, the New Left assimilated the inauthentic liberal to the effeminate pervert whose bad habits liberals had themselves treated as the abject foil to the academic style" (3). Theorists, meanwhile, have complained that analytic philosophers are unimaginative and worse. I do not mean to oversimplify the relationship between theory and philosophy. I want only to emphasize that certain strains of philosophy have helped to legitimate if not also moved toward theory, building on a commitment to wonder and shuttling between a classically humanist and a more antifoundationalist sensibility.

In P4C, to be philosophical means not only to think critically but also to embrace wonder and even perplexity. P4C advocates Matthew Lipman and Gareth Matthews were trained as analytic philosophers but pioneered a child-centered philosophical practice that was both more classically humanist and more theory-friendly. They pivoted away from the norms of their discipline to engage with and compose stories for the young, recalling philosophy to its more public aspirations. P4C has increasingly absorbed the theory-friendly language of postmodern or posthumanist philosophy even as it maintains a humanistic, child-centered agenda. Contemporary P4C experts Joanna Haynes and Karin Murris, for instance, stress philosophy's capacity "to redescribe, to imagine the possibility of things being otherwise" (142).[33] Picturebooks, they propose, help show the way. If philosophy retains its associations with enlightenment, it increasingly shares theory's identity as a practice of critical thinking and making, as illustrated by P4C.

In emphasizing theory's beneficial tendencies, I also recognize its elitism as a Eurocentric discourse. In *Figures in Black*, Henry Louis Gates Jr. documents how Western literary theory depends upon a long tradition of historical and philosophical racism. Drawing inspiration from Houston Baker Jr.'s work on the blues as vernacular theory, Gates develops a countertheory rooted in the black vernacular tradition and emphasizing the practice of "Signifyin(g)." Contemporary black theorists such as Saidiya Hartman, Christina Sharpe, Fred Moten, and Alexis Pauline Gumbs continue this work but also find new themes, forms, and methodologies for theory. "The question for theory," writes Sharpe in *In The Wake*, "is how to live in the wake of slavery, in slavery's afterlives, the afterlife of property, how, in short, to inhabit and rupture this episteme with their, with our, knowable lives" (50). Theory critique and elaboration is rich and ongoing. Other traditions of alt- or revisionist theory that reorient theory's concerns or registers include crip theory (Robert McRuer), queer theory (assorted figures), low theory (Halberstam), anecdotal theory (Gallop), picture theory (Mitchell), outsider theory (Eburne), and weak theory (assorted). Sometimes alt-theory is positioned against problems with theory—contesting theory's identity as high/elitist, or strong/paranoid, or ableist, and so forth—and sometimes it just designates a particular lens. The more we look at theory, the more heterogenous it seems, but that does not mean that theory cannot ossify or embody privilege.

Whose Child Is This?

There is a rich body of scholarship on the material and discursive history of the child, including analysis of the child as a negotiation of the normative and the nonnormative or "misfit"[34] and as a vehicle for adultist projection even in critical discourse.[35] We have learned from the historian Carolyn Steedman (among others) that the child has functioned as a metaphor for human interiority at least since the nineteenth century, well ahead of psychoanalysis. In a series of provocative articles, Joanne Faulkner situates the child of contemporary theory in the context of historical and philosophical investment in the child—more particularly, in the sovereign boy-child. In "Humanity's Little Scrap Dealers," for instance, Faulkner proposes that the boy's potential for growth and full sovereignty was a positive one in the Enlightenment but then turned more anxious or ambivalent, such that we continue to see the child as radically other to the adult and as full of potential—as inhabiting a pure realm of play and innocence—but in order to guard against anxieties about mortality, sexuality, and decay. In "Innocents and Oracles," Faulkner explores the child more generally as a figure of both knowledge and critique.

Feminist theory has been especially attentive to the ideological manipulation of childhood in the context of family life and gendered violence.[36] For this reason perhaps, feminist theory has contributed to children's rights advocacy but has not often prioritized the child as a vehicle for theoretical expression or renewal. (Neither has Marxist theory, which approaches the child in the context of generational labor, although some Marxist writing shows interest in the beginner.) Instead, feminist theory tends to be critical of theoretical uses of the child.[37] Like children's literature, theory has been criticized for making unethical or uncritical claims for, as well as on, the child. Karín Lesnik-Oberstein, for instance, extends Rose's critique of children's fiction to children's literature criticism, to broader rhetorics of child ownership, and (in a sequence of essays, the first coauthored with Steven Thomson) to queer theory's child.[38] Claudia Castañeda offers an expansive and often persuasive critique of theory's child in her *Figurations: Child, Bodies, Worlds*. Therein she warns that oppositional theorists like Foucault, Deleuze and Guattari, and Lyotard appropriate the child as a natural-theoretical resource and even self-position as the child.[39] Erica Burman offers a less cautionary assessment of what she calls "pedagogies of post/modernity," looking specifically at Walter Benjamin and Jean-François Lyotard. Her perspective resonates more with that of Faulkner, who makes a similar case for Agamben in both "Innocence, Evil, and Human Frailty" and "Negotiating Vulnerability." "It seems that recourse to the child as a utopian or dystopian figure is irresistible," she writes, "even to theorists whose accounts speak to the significant disenchantment with the project of social development and revolutionary change" (63). Burman finds Benjamin the more forward-looking of those two, in that he "offers an account of childhood . . . not as some prior, integral life stage, but as the encounter with the cultural-political, as the engagement with artefacts, in the pleasures and constraints of their consumption" (69). She emphasizes that for both Benjamin and Lyotard, "a thoroughly modern notion of childhood is invoked as a state of potentiality, of possibility" (81). Examining the association of childhood with metaphors of development,

Burman holds that such thinkers draw strategically rather than naively on childhood as a metaphor for dependence and interdependence and even as an aspirational condition.[40]

That sense of childhood as potentiality persists in even the most antifoundational thinking, taking some interesting turns. Chris Jenks, for instance, faults sociology and developmental psychology for insufficiently understanding the child as Other in their "overattentive elaboration of the compulsive processes of integration" into adulthood (4). Even sociology that dedicates itself to the critique and challenge of the existing social order "seems unable to mobilize the potentiality of the child as an agent of such change," he writes (46). Jenks urges and tries to model "a more radical conception of the child as a vision and a potential" (47), recommending to that end historical, comparative, and phenomenological[41] research on childhood—all hallmarks of childhood studies, he notes. Along with Allen Prout and Allison James, Jenks was a key player in the new sociology of childhood developed in the United Kingdom in the 1990s, which tried to balance a social constructionist perspective on childhood with a commitment to that "more radical conception," laying a foundation for childhood studies. James notes that said sociology emerged out of the Ethnography of Childhood workshops organized by Judith Ennew and held in Cambridge in the 1980s (215), which explains Jenks's faith in ethnography as a counterpoint to developmental essentialism (in an otherwise poststructuralist account). As Tyler Bickford puts it, this framework "provides a strong enough basis to maintain that childhood, like gender, is the performative accomplishment of actual children" (23).

I follow Burman and Faulkner in thinking that theorizing on, for, and even as the child has benefits that outweighs the risks.[42] The psychoanalytic term *infans* might seem miles away from the "inner child" of popular psychology, but both conceits are rooted in the coevolution of child and self. If we should scrutinize theoretical uses of the child, we also should recognize when those uses are productive and acknowledge that none of us stands outside the discursive domain of childhood. For me, as for Bickford, "it is more important to affirm that childhood is philosophically difficult, and that difficulty can be intellectually productive," pointing as it does to how "necessity, dependence, and intimacy are often key values of human life and community" (27). There may be some wishful thinking in theoretical work on childhood, but there is more to such than abuse. Wishful thinking has its place (and is not much thinking wishful?).[43]

Work on theory's child could take cues from recent emphasis in children's literature studies on adult-child collaboration. Philosophy and theory address the young and the uninitiated and in that sense are designed on their behalf. But they are also collaborations, especially in the case of P4C. They also identify with and depend on those figures. The child and the beginner perhaps serve as what Deleuze and Guattari, in *What Is Philosophy?*, call conceptual personae, embodying and animating critical thinking. P4C, theory for beginners, and children's literature conventionally understood are concerned with real people even as they are speculative, imaginative, theoretical projects, designed to foster speculative, imaginative, theoretical thinking. When they romanticize childhood, they do so strategically. P4C began as and largely remains an Enlightenment project, rarely evincing the sort of skepticism toward education or progress we see in Benjamin and Lyotard. P4C happily presents the child as a natural/born philosopher, in turn suggesting that the philosopher remains a child at heart. Philosophy begins in wonder, the story goes, and wonder begins in childhood, hence the wondering/wonder child.

The term *wonder* has a surprising usefulness across domains and contexts, including environmentalism, popular science, and medicine. Recall, for example, Rachel Carson's *The Sense of Wonder* (1965), which recounts how Carson's nature walks with her nephew led to her own renewed appreciation for nature's vitality. Lauren Greyson's *Vital Reenchantments: Biophilia, Gaia, Cosmos, and the Affectively Ecological* (2019) shows how works of popular science published in the 1970s and 1980s (by the likes of E. O. Wilson, James Lovelock, and Carl Sagan) cultivate "affective wonder" as a strategy of scientific re-enchantment with the natural world and its possibilities. Drawing on material by diverse thinkers and artists (among them Charles Le Brun, Martha Nussbaum, Gilles Deleuze, Jane Bennett, Howard Parsons, and Jakob von Uexküll), Greyson describes affective wonder as "a sudden attunement to affects that one had not been attuned to before," "a sensitivity to new becomings" (76).[44] Much of P4C's rhetoric of the wonder child materialized at the same time and seems strategically rather than naively wondering, aimed at playing up the child's agency and abilities in the service of education, progress, and ethical citizenship. The architects of P4C emphasized the child's critical powers alongside the adult's renewed capacity for wonder and surprise.

One of the founding figures of P4C, Gareth Matthews, is assertively skeptical about skepticism. He takes on Jacqueline Rose directly in his *Philosophy of Childhood*: "I think we should be suspicious of the idea that all, or even most, writers of children's stories have more complex or more questionable motivation than writers of other types of fiction" (103). "Neither Lobel's *Frog and Toad Together* nor Steig's *Yellow and Pink* is phony,"

Matthews asserts. "Nor are their authors manipulative. With great poetic simplicity these stories raise questions, including fascinating philosophical questions, that are well worth reflecting on, whether one is a child or an adult" (110). In addressing children and beginners, philosophy and theory aim to keep wonder alive, just like children's literature. And if there's risk in romanticizing the child, it is a risk worth taking.[45]

1 / Philosophy for Children

In 1970, with the help of an NEH grant, philosophy professor Matthew Lipman wrote his philosophical novel for children *Harry Stottlemeier's Discovery* and then taught it as a field experiment in fifth- and sixth-grade public school classrooms in Montclair, New Jersey. *Harry Stottlemeier's Discovery* runs about the length of a standard middle-grade novel, at ninety-six pages with seventeen chapters. Published in stapled-cover format, the novel was reprinted several times, although it was never picked up by an established publishing house. Lipman believed strongly in the Socratic dialogue as a pedagogical model, and *Harry Stottlemeier's Discovery* is a series of dialogues, ostensibly realistic and designed to inspire dialogue among real-world students. Harry and his friends are fifth graders pursuing philosophical questions in their daily lives, involving logic, epistemology, and ethics. Discussion often gravitates to the workings of thought and of language and to their relation. Harry, for instance, muses on the reality of thoughts, concluding that in some ways "'they're even more real than things. Because when things aren't around, we can't be sure they're still there, but our thoughts we always carry with us'" (15). Assigned to write a theme paper on "The Most Interesting Thing in the World," Harry and his classmates muse over the multiplicity of "thing," their teacher Mrs. Halsey prompting "'Yes, a thing can be an object, like a tennis racket, something you can see and touch and measure, or it can be something rather vague and hard to define, like an activity.'" "'Like doing your thing?' asked Fran, with a grin" (16). Harry decides that The Most Interesting Thing in the World is thinking: this is his great discovery.

In the original experiment and in its replications, pupils saw measurable gains in both reasoning and reading ability.[1] Success with the book and Lipman's pilot P4C program helped lead to the 1974 establishment of the Institute for the Advancement of Philosophy for Children (IAPC), headquartered at Montclair State College, where Lipman was then appointed. Articles about Lipman's novel and project appeared in *Time*, *Newsweek*, *Ladies' Home Journal*, *The New York Times*, and *The Boston Globe* (Pritchard 4). Under Lipman's supervision, the IAPC produced pedagogical materials used widely in school settings, beginning with six additional novels plus accompanying teacher's manuals.[2] Lipman wrote the novels solo but collaborated on the manuals with IAPC colleagues. Lipman also wrote books about philosophy and/as education, designed graduate-level programs in P4C, and founded *Thinking: The Journal of Philosophy for Children*, which ran from 1979 to 2011. By 1976, P4C programs were in place in elementary schools in Newark, New Jersey; Baltimore; East Lansing, Michigan; Denton, Texas; and Hastings-on-Hudson, New York (Bynum 1). These were typically under the supervision of university faculty. A number of colleges and universities developed P4C programs or modules, among them Montclair State, Washburn University of Topeka, University of Nebraska, University of Cincinnati, University of Delaware, University of Massachusetts, Yale, Johns Hopkins, and Lehigh. The Subcommittee on Pre-College Philosophy of the American Philosophical Association was then working on an APA statement of standards, and professional journals on the topic were beginning to materialize. A national organization of philosophers, teachers, and parents was formed, the National Forum for Philosophical Reasoning in the Schools.[3]

Lipman is acknowledged as P4C's founder, but another pivotal figure was Gareth B. Matthews, a philosophy professor at the University of Massachusetts Amherst and author of *Philosophy and the Young Child* (1980), *Dialogues with Children* (1984), and *The Philosophy of Childhood* (1994). After producing scholarship on more conventional philosophical topics, Matthews turned his attention to childhood. His interest in P4C, he explains, was sparked by dialogues with his young daughter, whose questions recalled those not only of his college students but of the great philosophers being studied.[4] Unlike Lipman, who wrote his own material for children, Matthews embraced existing children's literature, especially canonical works of fantasy and imaginative realism, from *Alice* and *Winnie-the-Pooh* to *Frog and Toad Together*, *Charlotte's Web*, and *Tuck Everlasting*. "There is an important strand of children's literature that is genuinely philosophical," he remarks in *The Philosophy of Childhood*. "I am fond of telling anyone who will listen that, for example, Arnold Lobel's

Frog and Toad Together, which is so simple in its vocabulary as to count as an 'I can read book,' is also a philosophical classic" (4). While Lipman prioritizes logical thinking, and creates his own children's books to model such, Matthews searches existing children's literature for examples of what he calls "philosophical whimsy," a writing style that "consists in raising, wryly, a host of basic epistemological and metaphysical questions familiar to students of philosophy . . . not at all unusual in children's literature" ("Philosophy" 9). Friends and occasional collaborators, Lipman and Matthews went about P4C differently, and over time, Matthews's brand of P4C became more dominant, even though Lipman's materials are still in circulation. The two men agreed, however, that the purpose of P4C is not to teach philosophy as a subject but to encourage philosophical thinking. Both felt that kids are natural-born philosophers needing guidance and hoped P4C would foster a thoughtful, ethically engaged citizenry.[5]

P4C helped to accelerate philosophy's attention to childhood and especially to children's literature.[6] Peter Costello credits psychoanalysis for the initial push, writing that it was "not until philosophers begin to take up the insights of psychoanalysis that philosophy texts undertook rigorous study of childhood on its own terms, i.e., as a mode of existence worthy of its own description" (xiv). Costello points to the work of Merleau-Ponty and to Simone de Beauvoir in particular, and of course psychoanalysis has long attended to fairy tales, picturebooks, and other genres categorized as being for children. Another factor was the gradual easing of tension between philosophy and literature more generally. Philosophers came to understand that literature is not necessarily sophistry and thus a corruption of philosophy, and more gradually even accepted that philosophy has its own literary tendencies and figurative language, or what Le Doeuff identifies as the "philosophical imaginary."[7] But as this chapter emphasizes, we also have P4C to thank for philosophy's growing attention to children's literature and especially for the idea that children's literature can function as a philosophical project.

Whatever its successes as an educational enterprise, P4C put the spotlight on children's literature not simply as a tool or curriculum but as an arena of philosophical engagement and opportunity. P4C proposes that philosophers write for children while recognizing that children's authors philosophize. Beginning with Matthews especially, P4C understands children's literature as a parallel enterprise, carried out by writers hoping to encourage the imaginative and intellectual lives of children. That approach to children's literature dovetails with and perhaps helps to legitimate the rise of children's literature criticism within literary studies. The Children's Literature Association (ChLA) was formed in 1972, two years after Lipman's *Harry Stottlemeier's Discovery* appeared, and Matthews engaged directly with literary scholarship from the 1970s forward, even presenting a paper ("Philosophy as Child's Play") at the 1990 ChLA conference. In recent years, P4C has come to emphasize the particular usefulness of picturebooks, with Karin Murris leading the way.

If P4C has not exercised much influence on academic philosophy, meaning philosophy as practiced in university settings, it has played an important role in educational philosophy and popular or outreach philosophy, dedicated to the notion that philosophy applies to and should be accessible to everyone. The 1920s saw the rise of middlebrow institutions like the Book-of-the-Month Club and the publication of various "outlines" such as Will Durant's *The Story of Philosophy* (1926). Ever since there has been a waxing and waning market for popular philosophy primers, and they are now again on the upswing. I am thinking of books like *Plato and a Platypus Walk into a Bar . . .* (2008), *If You Can Read This: The Philosophy of Bumper Stickers* (2010), *Breakfast with Socrates* (2011), and *Philosophy on Tap* (2011). Since the year 2000, Open Court Publishing Company has published a series of applied philosophy casebooks on popular culture, including children's and young adult literature, with 123 titles and counting. These volumes are playful and even styled after their source texts. *Harry Potter and Philosophy*, for instance, mimics the experience of being at Hogwarts, opening with everyone gathered in the great hall for sorting into theoretical houses (Baggett and Klein). The introduction to *Dr. Seuss and Philosophy* takes the form of a Seussian poem. While these primers exploit the popularity of children's culture, they acknowledge children's authors as philosophers and appeal to both child and adult readers. Obviously this boom in pop philosophy has a lot to do with convergence culture, but P4C is in the mix too.

P4C and the Wonder Kids

That philosophy should be addressed and taught to children, and in the form of a children's book, is not a new idea, even if P4C gave it new life. Anglo-European children's literature is rooted in the philosophical ideas of John Locke and Jean-Jacques Rousseau about education and child-rearing, even if it has not continually embraced the radical politics of the early philosophical novel.[8] It is not just that Western philosophy helped inspire children's literature; children's literature is in part a narrative engagement with philosophical as much as educational principles. As Samuel Pickering reminds us, Locke was a popularizer, writing *Some Thoughts Concerning Education* (1693) in deliberately accessible prose, with no Greek or Latin references. His emphasis on the malleability of childhood and the power of education inspired authors such as Maria Edgeworth and Sarah Trimmer to write fiction based on Lockean precepts. Much of this early literature encouraged critical thinking on the part of the child, both independently and in dialogue with adults. That emphasis continued in Victorian authors such as Carroll, Stevenson, and Nesbit, as Marah Gubar (in *Artful Dodgers*) and Victoria Ford Smith especially have shown. P4C maintains the general link between philosophy and children's literature while moving toward the idea that children's literature is not only a form of applied philosophy (as with Lipman) but also a philosophical form in its own right (as for Matthews).

A more troubling but persistent philosophical-literary tradition leading up to P4C is the Robinsonade. Adopted early into the canon of children's literature, the Robinsonade offers a happier version of the thought experiment of social isolation than the story of the feral child, typically a kind of test case about the human condition (or rather about human conditioning).[9] The Robinsonade is a kind of literary version of sovereign boy-child philosophy as discussed by Faulkner. Aware of the philosophical possibilities of children's literature, and working just as P4C was getting underway, the influential French novelist Michel Tournier rewrote Daniel Defoe's *Robinson Crusoe* twice, first for adults as *Friday* (1967) and subsequently for children as *Friday and Robinson* (1972).[10] "Although he rewrote his first *Friday* in order to make it less explicitly philosophical and abstract," observes Sandra Beckett, "he insists that the shorter version [for children] retains an important, but implicit, philosophical element. If he had become a philosopher, Tournier says that he would like to have taught philosophy to children" (174). Such was his ambition with his books; he calls them "philosophical books for ten-year-old children."[11] Tournier was a friend of Gilles Deleuze, and Deleuze even wrote an essay about *Friday*, which was included as an afterword in later editions (Beckett 175). It was no accident that Tournier turned to the Robinsonade, long of critical interest and long linked with Rousseauian dreams of self-sufficiency and sovereignty.[12] It is interesting to think about the appeal of the genre to children's writers especially.[13]

In any case, P4C shares some territory with the Robinsonade and related philosophical-literary genres but also revises them and makes use of other materials. P4C plays up the idea of child sovereignty and intellectual independence. But it also leans heavily in favor of the social contract by encouraging and fictionalizing Socratic-style child-adult dialogue and a peer-based "community of inquiry." P4C's roots in the social movements of the 1960s, as well as the broader tradition of progressive education, helped to ensure that the child thinker was not isolated literally or metaphorically. No child is an island, and P4C is uninterested in the thought experiments of the Robinsonade. Instead, P4C emphasizes the power of dialogue and community. To its credit, P4C has turned to a rich variety of children's texts over time, capitalizing on and further developing a diverse set of scripts for subjectivity and exchange.

P4C merges analytic with continental philosophy, combining a focus on language and logic with an appreciation for curiosity and speculative thought. Some P4C contexts and programs are more analytic than others. But as I mentioned in the introduction to this book, a key concept for P4C across the board is "wonder," aligned with the terms *play* and *enchantment*. In *Theaetetus*, Plato puts these words in the mouth of Socrates: "I see, my dear Theaetetus, that Theodorus had a true insight into your nature when he said that you were a philosopher, for wonder is the feeling of a philosopher, and philosophy begins in wonder" (155 c–d). In *Metaphysics*, Aristotle remarks that wonder first led men to philosophize (982b12). The idea that philosophy begins in wonder, or *thaumazein*, has become a core element of the Platonic legacy, taken up by thinkers as diverse as Hegel, Kierkegaard, Heidegger, and Whitehead. It is a serious academic idea, as well as an idea asserted by the broader public, sometimes against academic philosophy.[14] Wonder has a double construction with respect to philosophy. It is both the source for philosophy and a corrective to or caution against its excesses or abuses; wonder ostensibly keeps philosophy true or pure. Wonder is not reducible to reason or thought. Plato calls wonder a feeling, while Aristotle speaks of astonishment. Modern definitions underscore both wonder's proximity to thinking and its ostensibly healthy distance from such. As a noun, *wonder* suggests "a feeling of surprise mingled with admiration, caused by something beautiful, unexpected, unfamiliar, or inexplicable"; "the quality of a person or a thing that causes wonder"; "a strange or remarkable person, thing, or event." As a verb, it suggests the desire to know but not absolutely or without doubt; it is a more speculative, less invested sort of desire.[15] Wonder, it seems, leads to philosophy but also exceeds, survives, even redeems it. Wonder seems nearly to affirm something like the unconscious of philosophy. Wonder makes space within philosophy for resistance to knowledge as much as its pursuit. To think philosophically means not only to seek insight but to welcome doubt.

In some formulations, wonder gestures toward the spiritual or metaphysical, "signifies that the world is profounder, more all-embracing and mysterious than the logic of everyday reason had taught us to believe"—even leads us to "a deepened sense of mystery . . . [to] the knowledge that being, qua being, is mysterious and inconceivable" (Pieper 115).[16] In such formulations, wonder evidences and also becomes that mysteriousness we can never quite grasp. Increasingly, wonder has been associated with childhood. If philosophy begins in wonder, the thinking runs, wonder begins in childhood. Consider, for instance, psychiatrist Neel Burton's 2014 *Psychology Today* article "A Study of Wonder," which urges readers to open themselves to wonder rather than fear it. "To wonder is also to wander," he writes, "to stray from society and its norms and constructs, to be alone, to be free—which is, of course, deeply subversive and why even organized religions need to tread a fine line with wonder." Burton opines that children "brim with wonder, before it is leached out of them by need and neurosis." If Burton's formulation seems simplistic, other articulations of wonder and the wonder child are more nuanced.

The conceit of the wonder child has many sources, among them romanticism as filtered through progressive education and also gifted education, two overlapping if also opposing movements. Dewey's influential conception of the child, as Richard Hofstadter points out, "was more romantic and primitivist than it was post-Darwinian" (363), showing the influence of G. Stanley Hall and especially Francis Wayland Parker. Parker might be even described as an early advocate of P4C, conceiving of the child as "omnivorously curious, as having a natural interest in all subjects, as being a sort of savant in the making, and a born artist and handicraftsman as well" (Hofstadter 366). Dewey shares this conception, postulating that "education is growth" and pitting the natural and curious child against ostensibly artificial society. As Hofstadter emphasizes, such a conceit ("one of the most mischievous . . . in the history of modern education" [373]) makes the very project of education difficult if not impossible.

In the nineteenth century, bright or accomplished children were called prodigies and seen as accidents of nature or culture. The German *wunderkind* (wonder child) dates back to this period and has generally been used to describe child prodigies. In the early twentieth century, encouraged by increased demand for intellectual sorting in an overburdened public school system, a group of psychologists created and normalized the category of "gifted children," capitalizing on the priceless rhetoric and implying that gifted children were themselves gifts to humanity. Leta S. Hollingworth, Lewis M. Terman, and Henry H. Goddard led the way, designing influential studies and intelligence tests. Terman adapted Alfred Binet's intelligence test for US schools, hence the Stanford-Binet. Granted, giftedness has always been an exercise in white, middle-class exceptionalism if not outright racism, as Leslie Margolin stresses in her study of the movement.[17] At the same time, and without downplaying its problems, giftedness discourse does make space for the smart and curious child, and in this sense paves the way for P4C and for less harmful constructions of the wondering/wonder child. Determined to combat hostility toward bright children, gifted child advocates stress that such children are well-adjusted leaders and problem solvers. In *Gifted Children: Their Nature and Nurture* (1926), Hollingworth speculates that "their intellect enables them to adopt the philosophical point of view to an unusual degree" (18). While elitist, such comments do convey respect for children's intellects.[18]

P4C affords a more encouraging test case, assuming that all children are gifted without dividing them into classes or categories. In P4C there is no line between the philosophical and the nonphilosophical child. All children are philosophical, the logic runs: they were born that way. P4C thus has more in common with progressive pedagogy than with gifted education proper, still an elitist project favoring white kids. At the same time, P4C is not a discourse of child normality or normalization. P4C insists that all children are philosophical and special at the same time.

The wonder child conceit is core to P4C, even when "wonder" is not a keyword. The child ostensibly recalls us to the wonder that is philosophy and that exceeds philosophy as a strictly academic (and adult) enterprise. Especially for Matthews, the child is not merely a capable practitioner of philosophy but rather the most exemplary one.[19] Lipman is not as rhapsodic about the child as Matthews, preferring to talk about curiosity and its indulgence through the exercise of logical reasoning. His creative writing for children is strictly instrumentalist. All children are curious, Lipman believes, and all children can learn to think philosophically. Matthews, however, courts a romantic understanding of the child as natural philosopher, aligning himself with creative writers for children. Matthews portrays the child as intuitively philosophical, implying that philosophy is not so much taught to as drawn out of the child. Lipman and Matthews tend to downplay the more uncomfortable dimensions of wonder. The child of P4C is rarely anxious or uncomfortable.

The child-philosopher association bolsters all parties; the child rejuvenates the philosopher, and the philosopher enables the child to reach full potential.[20] The child, writes Matthews in a typical passage in *Philosophy and the Young Child*, "has fresh eyes and ears for perplexity and incongruity" (85). Children "have not yet learned to reject as queer and misbegotten the many questions that philosophers have taught themselves to rescue from the wastebin of inquiry" (92). Children let themselves wonder. In a later work, *Socratic Perplexity and the Nature of Philosophy*, Matthews refines his take on wonder into a theory of philosophical "perplexity," underscoring that philosophy is based in astonishment and even aporia (and emphasizing the latter's centrality to Greek discourse). Moreover, perplexity implies a state of passivity or not-mastery. Wonder and perplexity keep us open to possibility and also balance overconfidence about what we think we know.[21]

Wonder child discourse can run minoritizing or universalizing but applies to all children theoretically.[22] The attribution of wonder even seems to be migrating down to babies, if psychologist Alison Gopnik's bestselling *The Philosophical Baby* (2009) is any indication. Therein, Gopnik urges respect for the imaginative life of babies, saying that we have long misread their play as "evidence of children's cognitive limitations rather than evidence of their cognitive powers" (29–30) and emphasizing the power of children's "counterfactuals," a term borrowed from philosophy that Gopnik glosses as "the woulda-coulda-shouldas of life, all the things that might happen in the future, but haven't yet, or that could have happened in the past, but didn't quite" (18). It is a short step, she holds, from the imaginary friends of childhood to the creative worlds of adults.[23]

Kathryn Bond Stockton proposes that children "queered by innocence" "share estrangement from what they approach: the adulthood against which they must be defined. That is why 'innocent' children are strange" (31). We might say something similar of the philosophical child, the child queered by wonder, who likewise approaches adulthood but also must be shielded from it. She must grow while retaining the capacity for wonder. In P4C, wonder often functions as a counter-normative disposition, almost an altered state. Yet P4C rarely embraces or exploits the radical potential of the wonder child, unlike poststructuralist and posthumanist thinkers. P4C encourages some "queerness" of mind and disposition, in the context of mainstream society, but remains wedded to traditional ideas about growth and development. P4C does not comment on the queerness of bodies or sexuality. Rather, it hopes that children will lead mindful lives and then grow up to be mindful adults.

P4C meanwhile expects adults to grow down, as it were, to maintain or reclaim a situation of curiosity and receptivity. In formulations of this theme, adults can only be wise and just if they remain wonder-struck. P4C is thus as urgent for adults as it is for children. Lipman and his colleagues lament that adults often struggle to think and reason. "Indeed, this must be one of the most paradoxical characteristics of our culture," they write, "the acquisition by adults of an incapacity not generally found in children. The indisposition of adults to learn reasoning contrasts so sharply with the readiness of children to learn it (along with language) that we must face the fact that getting older is in some respects not growth but diminishment" (Lipman et al., *Philosophy in the Classroom* [1977] 5). P4C guards against that diminishment. The adult recalls and reinvigorates her philosophical childhood in a retrospective act of identity construction reminiscent of the "backwards birth" of queer children as discussed by Stockton (6). If P4C does not seem interested in the queerness of sexuality, it arguably queers time as much as identity in insisting that the adult learns from the child. We can see this insistence in P4C's cultivation of the wonder child, its elevation of children's literature as a sister enterprise, and its reassertion of philosophy as a project for all.

Matthew Lipman's Dialogues

In 1958, the American Philosophical Association prepared a report entitled "The Teaching of Philosophy in American High Schools." That report served to document as well as encourage experiments in high-school-level philosophy instruction. A decade later, the Carnegie Foundation funded a three-year study of the feasibility of introducing philosophy to high school students, in Chicago specifically, the success of which in turn led the National Endowment for the Humanities (NEH) to fund the establishment of the Center for High School Philosophy at the University of Massachusetts Amherst, where Matthews was appointed. P4C took a cue from precollege philosophy programs and more general inspiration from progressive education. In *Philosophy Goes to School*, Lipman points out that until the Reformation philosophy was part of the education of adolescent princes and princesses but was then abandoned in favor of science and business (12). He acknowledges the broader contribution to what he calls "reflective education" of figures such as Michel de Montaigne, John Locke, Maria and Richard Edgeworth, Samuel Taylor Coleridge, I. A. Richards, Charles Peirce, G. H. Mead, Jerome Bruner, and especially Dewey, who did so much to redefine education "as the fostering of thinking rather than as the transmission of knowledge" (4). However, not even Dewey, observes Lipman, thought to promote philosophy in elementary education.

While studying at the Sorbonne on a Fulbright fellowship, Lipman had learned that it was "possible to discuss profound philosophical ideas with ease and clarity," as he reports in an unpublished piece entitled "Dramatizing Philosophy" (cited in Johnson and Reed 224). There he "resonated" (his words) to Diderot and other encyclopedists attempting to bridge the gap between expert and man on the street. "Diderot," writes Lipman, "did much to shape my convictions about the role of philosophy in the public sphere" (225). While in Paris he also read an article by Bernard Groethuysen entitled "The Child and the Metaphysician," which likens the thinking of children to that of philosophers, with Kierkegaard as case study. Lipman's path was thus set. In 1969, he won a grant from the NEH to write "a story telling, almost as a child would relate it, of the discovery by a group of children of how their own thought processes work" and to use the book in "a true field experiment" (17). He composed *Harry Stottlemeier's Discovery* quickly and used it at the Rand School in 1970–1971. His work at the school involved the collective reading of this novel and discussion of the philosophical problems it raises. There was no homework and indeed no written work at all; there were also no grades involved. Even so, a series of reasoning quizzes administered over the nine-week period revealed a marked improvement in the students' ability to engage in logical reasoning. Lipman provides an extensive analysis of the study (discussing its hypothesis, definitions, treatments, randomization, statistical design, and results), which convinced Lipman "that philosophy can and should be a part of the entire length of a child's education" ("Philosophy" 39).

With help from the philosophy department at Columbia, he continued the project, writing the first teacher's manual and beginning work on a children's workbook. Lipman designed the P4C apparatus in the hopes of increasing the child's intellectual freedom and capacity for discovery. The child's whole school experience, he writes in *Philosophy Goes to School*, "should be chockfull of opportunities for surprise, with the tension of exciting possibilities, with tantalizing mysteries to be wondered at as well as with fascinating clarifications and illuminations" (9). Like other wonder advocates, he sees routine as the enemy of personal and cultural growth. Lipman also reminds us that philosophy does not begin in adulthood, even if we are not used to recognizing children's thoughts and activities as philosophical. "Having observed few children eager to browse through Kant or even to peruse the livelier passages of Aristotle," Lipman and his colleagues drily observe, "having met with little success in our efforts to convey directly the impact and urgency of the greatest happiness principle, we have been led to draw the irresistible inference that there is an unbridgeable chasm between the disciplined reflection that is philosophy and the unbridled wondering characteristic of childhood" (*Philosophy in the Classroom* [1980] 42). Not so, in their view. We just need to see philosophy otherwise.

In the rationale for the NEH grant and pilot project, reproduced in his contribution to *Metaphilosophy*, Lipman proposes that "Johnny can't reason" because he is not taught to think logically and philosophically. Lipman challenges the primacy of reading and mathematics in the curriculum, suggesting that while those disciplines "contribute usefully to good thinking, they cannot *suffice* to produce it" ("Philosophy" 18). Only guided practice in thinking can produce good thinking, hence the need for P4C. Mathematics and science do help children learn inference, and some schools offer limited training in problem solving, but Lipman otherwise finds K–12 curriculum sorely lacking. We teach the child "about" a vast array of subjects, he notes. "But we do not teach him to think about thinking" (21). Lipman and his colleagues felt strongly that philosophy has the potential both to coordinate all the subjects in the K–12 curriculum and to increase performance across all of them. Lipman calls philosophy "the discipline that prepares us to think in disciplines" (*Philosophy* 143).

Lipman attributes some of the resistance to teaching children to think about thinking to the emphasis of Jean Piaget's developmental or stage theory, a critique oft made in P4C.[24] It is not that Piaget did not think logical reasoning ability is important; rather, he thought children will naturally develop such ability. "The *inevitability* of logical development," writes Lipman, "which Piaget seems to imply in his descriptive (but rarely pedagogical) studies tends to lull many readers into believing that it is not necessary to *push* the child up the inclined plane of improved reasoning in the way we acknowledge we must push him in other disciplines" ("Philosophy" 21). College-level instruction in the scientific method and in formal logic cannot sufficiently revive the child's natural tendency to wonder—a tendency insufficiently encouraged by both Piagetian psychology and the K–12 curriculum, in Lipman's view. "Formal logic can, and should, be taught much earlier," he avers (24). Lipman advocates the use of dialogues, saying that while improvisational discovery has its place, students need a more structured experience of "discovery-in-practice" (26). He calls the Socratic dialogues of Plato "the greatest portraits of the discovery of understanding" (27) and models *Harry Stottlemeier's Discovery* upon them. Stiegler reminds us that teaching is "not simply the first question asked by philosophy; it is philosophy's practice," at least in the classical tradition. And "it really is a *battle* for intelligence" (107). Hence the emphasis in P4C on such skills as "drawing perceptual, logical, and causal inferences; making associations and analogies; forming hypotheses; making significant distinctions; considering alternatives; and searching for reasons, explanations, and assumptions" (Bynum 4).

The most important aspect of Lipman's novels is their dialogue format and modeling of a "community of inquiry," a central conceit for P4C and for philosophy more generally, put forth by pragmatist philosophers C. S. Peirce and Dewey. Lipman believed strongly that only collaborative dialogue could improve thinking. Citing the work of Lev Vygotsky (*Mind in Society*) and George Herbert Mead (*Mind, Self and Society*), he writes that we can find "both philosophical and psychological support for the thesis that *thinking is the internalization of dialogue*" (*Philosophy in the Classroom* [1980] 23; emphasis added). The classroom is a ready-made community of inquiry. Lipman and his associates also assumed that students would identity with and emulate the characters in the novel, although they do not offer theories as to how or why that happens (or proof that it does).

Lipman implies that traditionally prepared teachers can stand in the way of thinking and learning. "'We do learn to think,'" remarks Mark in *Harry Stottlemeier's Discovery*, "'but we never learn to think for ourselves. These teachers don't want to admit it, but I have a mind of my own. They're always trying to fill my mind with all sorts of junk, but it's not the town junkyard. It makes me mad'" (24). Lipman also rejects the traditional textbook, which he calls "a didactic device that stands over against the child as an alien and rigid *other*" (*Philosophy* 21). "To replace the secondary text with primary texts would be like rolling the stone away from the mouth of the cave and allowing the sunlight in," he asserts in *Philosophy Goes to School* (23). Lipman's dialogues take inspiration from both the classical dialogues of Plato, many of them addressed to youth, and later dialogues of religious and scientific instruction for children, such as Jeremiah Joyce's *Scientific Dialogues* (1809).[25] So too with P4C. As for the Platonic models, when the child philosophers of Lipman's dialogues are occasionally stumped, they do not experience the confusion and self-doubt on display in the Platonic dialogues. Unlike the adult, who must be taught to re-examine and give up his cherished beliefs, the child has little if any intellectual baggage and needs only to be encouraged in his wonder. The child may make mistakes but is quick to correct herself and learn from the error. Lipman and company go so far as to remark that just as "philosophy as a subject for study had to await the *Dialogues* of Plato," philosophy for children begins as an educational subject "only when it develops a special genre of literature of its own: the philosophical children's novel" (*Philosophy* [1977] 26).

Harry Stottlemeier's Discovery is largely dialogue, a series of conversations among children in group settings, often but not exclusively at school. As noted earlier, adults are mentors, but they are also sometimes antagonists. When Harry asks Mark what kind of school he would like to attend, Mark's response sounds like a description of A. S. Neill's Summerhill School or similar ventures in left-progressive schooling:

> "I'll tell you what kind of school I'd like to go to. You wouldn't have to go to class unless you wanted to. So they'd have to make the courses real interesting in order to get you interested enough to attend. And,

just like in the museum, any time you wanted to know more about something, all you'd have to do is press a button, and a movie would go on, or a teaching machine would start up. And all the science courses would be taught like science fiction." (24)

In the absence of such options, they innovate. Kids, opines Harry, "'need to be free to think for themselves just as much as grown-ups, maybe more so'" (47). As mentioned earlier, Lipman believes that adults need to listen to kids, or at least not be so ready to supply answers to their questions. They even need to be willing to learn from their students. Thus, at the beginning of chapter 11, Milly Warshaw remarks of an exemplary (English) teacher: "'Imagine Mrs. Halsey saying *she* learned something from *us*! I never heard a grown-up say that before. Whenever I ask Daddy or Mummy anything, they've got an answer ready before I've even finished with my question. It's funny—the moment Mrs. Halsey said that, I felt like more of a person. I felt as if I knew who I was a little better! I wonder why?'" (53).

Discussion gravitates more generally to the relations of thought and language, as I have already shown. Here is another, extended example. Harry's friends Laura O'Mara and Fran Wood are sleeping over at Jill Portos's house. They have stayed up late talking about dreams, death, and Disney's *The Sorcerer's Apprentice*. Fran wonders aloud:

"But what's a 'mind'? And how do you know you have one?"

Laura yawned and somehow managed to stretch out and wiggle her toes under the bedclothes at the same time. "I know I've got a mind," she replied. "Just like I know I've got a body."

Jill's father knocked at the door and told the girls it was past midnight and time they were asleep. The girls promised to stop talking (at least Jill did; the others just giggled). But before long they were back on the same subject.

Fran insisted that a person could see and touch his body, but he couldn't see or touch his mind, and how could anyone know his mind was real if he couldn't see or touch it? "When you say 'mind,'" Fran concluded, "all you're talking about is your brain."

"There are lots of things that are real, even though we can't see or touch them," Laura objected. "For example, if I go for a swim, is there really some kind of thing called a swim? If I go for a walk or a ride, are there really things called walks or rides?"

"So, what are you saying?" Fran asked.

"What I think Laura is saying," said Jill, "is that what we call thinking is something we do, like swimming or walking or riding."

> "That's right," Laura agreed, "that's just what I mean. When I said before I had a mind, I meant that I mind things. I mind the telephone, or my baby sister, or just my own business. But 'having a mind' is nothing but 'minding.'"
>
> But Fran wasn't happy with the solution Jill and Laura had arrived at. "I agree," she said, "that maybe the mind isn't quite the same thing as the brain. I know I said before it was, but I've changed my mind." Everyone giggled for a while, then Fran went on. "What I mean is, you can't see electricity, but it's real. So why couldn't our thoughts be something electrical in the brain?" (*HSD* 27–28)

Jill's mom then comes in to shush them but gets drawn into the discussion. She proposes that "sometimes I think [the mind is] nothing but language." When pressed, she explains that when children first begin to talk, they talk to other people, but when people are not available for dialogue, children begin talking to themselves, "more and more quietly until they can't make sounds at all. That's called thinking." Here we get the closest thing to an explanation of how dialogue is internalized or interiorized. Fran asks Mrs. Portos if she means that "'the thoughts in our minds are really just the traces of things in our memories?'" to which Mrs. Portos replies, "Oh my, Fran, I don't know, I never thought of it quite like that" (*HSD* 27–29). Remarking on this passage, Tony W. Johnson notes that no final answer on the mind question has been reached, but progress has been made all the same on the challenging topics of mind and thinking, and even the adult begins to see things a little differently (23).[26] It is the kind of incremental but meaningful progress that analytic philosophy promises.

Lipman published additional novels in dialogue: *Lisa* (1976), *Suki* (1978), *Mark* (1980), *Pixie* (1981), and *Kio and Gus* (1982). Each is paired with an IAPC instruction manual.[27] The title characters in each book make appearances in subsequent ones: Kio, two years old in *Harry Stottlemeier's Discovery*, is seven in *Kio and Gus*. Lipman and the IAPC thought of each book-manual pair as a module, focused on a particular area of inquiry while supporting the overarching project of teaching logical reasoning. *Pixie* focuses on language and mind, *Kio and Gus* on nature and science—more specifically, zoology and ecology, disciplines emphasizing observation and experimentation, according to Lipman and Anne Margaret Sharp's accompanying manual, *Wondering at the World*. The last in the series, this manual emphasizes other concerns of philosophy besides logic, such as epistemology, metaphysics, ethics, and aesthetics.

Lipman and his collaborators saw their project as supporting child agency. For them the adult-produced dialogues are a kind of necessary evil, designed to jumpstart thinking and counter top-down education. In *Philosophy in the Classroom*, a handbook for teachers first published in 1977 and updated in 1980, Lipman, Sharp, and Oscanyan acknowledge that "children's literature is generally written *for* children rather than *by* children" and argue that if "adults *must* write for children, then they should do so only to the extent necessary to liberate the literary and illustrative powers of those children" ([1977] 17–18). Their purpose, they explain, "is not to establish an immortal children's literature, but to get children thinking. If this purpose is attained, the instrument can self-destruct, as a match burns up once it has lit the fire" (18). Existing children's literature is not up to the task, in their view. Lipman, like Bruno Bettelheim, knew little about children's literature. In any case, *Harry Stottlemeier's Discovery* was disposable enough; it has never attracted any attention as a literary work, having none of the playful, imaginative, and managed style of the so-called classic fantasies. But it certainly lit the fire of P4C. "If our approach is correct," they continue, "the textbook written by professional scholars may eventually give way to children's books written by teachers and children themselves, yet incorporating the imagination and insight and understanding which such children acquire at each stage of their development" (*Philosophy in the Classroom* [1977] 18). "What is important is that the imagination be de-professionalized: that children be encouraged to think and create for themselves" (18). Until then, however, "the least we can do is write books for them that will promote their creativity rather than diminish it" (19). Lipman and his colleagues see no irony in having Harry speak so passionately about thinking for himself. In another teacher's manual, called *Wondering at the World*, Lipman and Sharp describe Lipman's novels as "lures to the children, aimed at catching their attention and provoking them to discussion and debate" and modeling reflexive discussion (6). While some "effort has been made to show these [fictional] children as not altogether implausible," they explain in a curious turn of phrase, what is important is the modeling of a "philosophical sensibility" (6).

In emphasizing the positives of P4C, I have said less about P4C's leveraging of childhood toward a reform of philosophy, but that is also part of the Lipman agenda. Lipman believed that philosophy had of necessity become a specialized knowledge industry and thereby relinquished "virtually all claims to exercising a socially significant role." "Even the most celebrated professors of philosophy," he writes, "nowadays would be likely to admit that, on the vast stage of world affairs, they appear only as a bit players or members of the crowd" (*Philosophy* 11). Philosophy chose to distance itself from childhood so that it could be taken seriously, but now childhood holds the key to philosophy's success. For Lipman, P4C has the potential to restore philosophy to its broader social function and greater cultural status. Lipman and Sharp explain that his child protagonists "know nothing of the lexicon which post-Aristotelian philosophers inherited; they are much more akin to the pre-Socratic philosophers whose aphorisms betrayed little awareness of philosophy (and its subcategories) as a unique, professional discipline" (6). Even so, Harry and company "return to the very roots of philosophy and of human cognition generally, putting aside the masks and personae into which the philosophical systems and schools have forced us" (6).[28] Lipman's dialogues aim not only to lure children into thinking but to revitalize philosophy.[29]

Gareth Matthews and Philosophical Whimsy

In his introduction to the 1976 special issue of *Metaphilosophy* devoted to P4C, Bynum observes that while the IAPC materials designed by Lipman remain the most promising, "it is at least conceivable" that children's literature might also suffice (3). "The primary need seems to be for stories, poems, and other creative works that have intrinsic interest and value for children," writes Bynum, "that stimulate imagination and generate wonder, and especially that encourage thoughtful discussion of questions of importance to children" (3). In fact, it was more than conceivable that children's literature would suffice, as Matthews makes clear. Like Lipman, he was a fan of Socratic dialogue. His book *Dialogues with Children* reports on his Socratic-style work with a small class of eight- to eleven-year-old children in a Scottish music school. But unlike Lipman, Matthews embraced existing children's literature and especially texts with "philosophical whimsy." Whereas Lipman designed his children's books as a delivery system for philosophy, Matthews felt that existing children's literature was already engaged with philosophical questions, if sometimes obliquely. While he never said so, Matthews seems to have agreed with Bettelheim that the "enchantment" of the children's book should happen unconsciously. Certainly, he preferred materials that playfully stage philosophical issues to materials that explicitly model philosophical processes (e.g., *Harry Stottlemeier's Discovery*) or introduce philosophical thinkers (e.g., *Kierkegaard and the Mermaid*). For Matthews especially, P4C banks on the child-philosopher's curiosity, creativity, and capacity for wonder and whimsy.

Matthews introduces these ideas in his 1976 special issue contribution. "Philosophy and Children's Literature" begins with a summary of Frank

Tashlin's children's book *The Bear That Wasn't* (1946), showing how its "philosophical whimsy" adumbrates big philosophical topics and themes, among them the nature of reality vis-à-vis dreaming and appearances, and the question of being/nonbeing. Matthews gives other examples of "masters of philosophical whimsy": L. Frank Baum, James Thurber, and A. A. Milne. Matthews goes so far as to compare the various puzzles of *Winnie-the-Pooh* to Wittgenstein's questions in *Philosophical Investigations* ("Philosophy" 11). "Time," he points out, "is perhaps the single topic most frequently dealt with philosophically by children's writers" (12). He clarifies that these books are not, strictly speaking, works of philosophy. Rather, they are children's stories that use philosophical whimsy, or a style that "consists in raising, wryly, a host of basic epistemological and metaphysical questions familiar to students of philosophy. . . . That style of writing is not at all unusual in children's literature" (9). Matthews's ideas speak to the more general belief that children's materials should not be explicitly didactic and should engage children in both story and style. Tournier thus fashioned his children's Robinsonade to be "less explicitly philosophical and abstract" (Beckett 174). Claudia Mills notes this shift in expectation in her introduction to *Ethics and Children's Literature*, pointing out that contemporary children's books are still engaged with ethical questions or dilemmas but less obviously so—there is usually no moralizing narrator, for instance, and readers are encouraged to reach their own conclusions. Bettelheim had already made the point that fairy tales work at the unconscious level. The prevailing attitude now is that children's books should work their enchantments behind the scenes. Some of the Anglophone classics are loved precisely for their restraint and suggestiveness—especially A. A. Milne's highly stylized Winnie-the-Pooh books.[30] Philosophers and psychologists have long been drawn to Pooh, Matthews included.[31]

Having established that some children's writers practice a philosophical style, Matthews then proposes that children have their own tendencies toward philosophical whimsy. As evidence he cites transcripts of "uninhibited conversation of rather reflective children," not those of Piaget—"The bits of conversation that, say, Jean Piaget lards some of his works with won't do" ("Philosophy" 13)—but rather of psychologist Susan Isaacs, in her groundbreaking 1930 study *Intellectual Growth in Young Children*, based on her 1920s research with children at the Malting House School in Cambridge, United Kingdom. Matthews chooses four examples from among the hundreds provided by Issacs, examples affirming that "philosophical whimsy is for at least some children, some of the time, a natural style of conversation" ("Philosophy" 14). Because it is not typically taught prior to college, and is not an easy undertaking, philosophy is often regarded as "some sort of intellectual aberration—perversion, even—that takes hold of certain people late in their intellectual life, in their intellectual senility, one might say" (15). Evidence of philosophical whimsy, thinks Matthews, refutes that notion.[32]

Like Lipman, Matthews challenges the developmental psychology of Piaget, on intellectual as well as ethical grounds. He objects to Piaget's stage theory of cognitive development, challenging not only the theory itself (with its three stages of thinking) but also Piaget's method for stage placing his subjects. Piaget does not ask the right questions of children, holds Matthews, nor does he really listen to their answers.[33] Matthews takes the critique much further than Lipman, writing that "any developmental theory that rules out, on purely theoretical grounds, even the possibility that we adults may occasionally have something to learn, morally, from a child is, for that reason, defective; it is also morally offensive" (*Philosophy of Childhood* 67).[34] Matthews's procedural criticism of Piaget is especially interesting:

> Piaget proposes to validate his claims about developmental stages by finding the same patterns of response in all children. Such a finding is to be considered a guarantee that the thinking of children really does develop in this fashion. The unusual response is discounted as an unreliable indicator of the ways in which children think. . . . But it is the deviant response that is most likely to be philosophically interesting. The standard response is, in general, an unthinking and un-thought-out product of socialization, whereas the nonconforming response is much more likely to be the fruit of honest reflection. (*Philosophy and the Young Child* 39)

Matthews, in contrast, cultivates the deviant response, the fruit of honest reflection. He talks up the child's "romancing," or hypothesis making—testing out theories playfully, provisionally. There are echoes here of the child researcher as envisioned by Freud, who theorizes about birth, sex, and so forth in the absence of information. Matthews seems nearly opposed to the notion of development in general.[35] For Matthews, philosophy comes naturally to the child—but not necessarily to the typical or normal child. Here he departs from Lipman and we see a contradiction in P4C. Whereas Lipman assumes all children to be little philosophers in the making, Matthews seems more interested in the imaginative, exceptional child, which suggests that P4C is not really for everyone. With Matthews, P4C becomes a kind of theory for beginners program, one in which feeling and intuition have equal importance to thought (and in which enchantments remain enchantments). In her book in progress, *How to Think about Children*, Marah Gubar describes Matthews's brand of P4C as a strategy for listening to the child and signal boosting her insights. She pairs Matthews with the psychiatrist Robert Coles, who likewise emphasizes and models a practice of humane and egalitarian child-adult relation that anticipates what Gubar calls a "kinship model of childhood."

Matthews's essay for *Metaphilosophy* appeared the same year as Bettelheim's *The Uses of Enchantment*, which argues for the developmental usefulness of fairy tales. Matthews's faith in the "philosophical whimsy" of children's literature is akin to that of Bettelheim, even if the latter did not know much about children's literature and is not so appreciative of the richness of language. Like Bettelheim, Matthews is interested in how child readers engage with the literary text. Whereas for Lipman, literariness is irrelevant to (even a distraction from) the business of dialogue, for Matthews literariness is a key part of the philosophical.[36] What matters is not only what the authors of philosophical whimsy say but also how they say it. Matthews understands that the complexities of language are part of philosophical exploration. In a chapter entitled "Naiveté" in *Philosophy and the Young Child*, he muses on "strong words" and remarks that once we learn the "literal-figurative distinction" of language, "we lose much of our natural curiosity about the wonderfully intricate ways in which the meanings of a word are related to each other" (93). He does not seem to endorse Lipman's assumption that philosophical dialogue taking place within a community of inquiry will naturally be transformed into thinking. For Matthews, dialogue and thus thinking is about language play as well as the play of ideas.

Matthews remarks as early as 1976 that "children's literature should not be condescended to" ("Philosophy" 16). Children's authors are gifted individuals, and children's materials "excite in young minds (and a few old ones, too) perplexities that can't be assuaged merely by passing on information, even information of a very sophisticated sort. These perplexities demand to be worried over, and worked through, and discussed, and reasoned out, and linked up with each other, and with life" (16). It is hard to imagine a more respectful statement about children's literature. "Perhaps identifying philosophical whimsy as a bone fide style of writing in children's literature," he concludes, "will help us find important new respect for children's poems and stories, and for children—indeed, for the child in each of us" (16).

Whereas Lipman self-presents as an educator, Matthews seems more identified with the whimsical children's author. Matthews recognizes the children's author as an ally in philosophical work, to the extent that Matthews cultivates an iconoclastic, literary persona, not simply quoting but imitating the wisdom of children's authors. As he refined his brand of P4C, Matthews began writing creatively and collaboratively with his child subjects, using short anecdotes or "story-beginnings" and moving into dialogues. He sometimes wrote dialogues with the kids, or rewrote them in response to discussions in the previous session, a more dynamic practice than anything Lipman envisioned. In general, his practice of P4C can be described as more whimsical than professional or systematic. In *Philosophy and the Young Child*, he describes his method as reading a story to young children and then, "in a very low-pressure way, discuss[ing] with the children any philosophical issues the story might suggest" (11). Actually, this is the method he teaches his college students to use when working with children. Matthews seems nearly to make fun of questions of method, explaining that he asks his students to undertake "a certain amount of 'lab work'"; here and elsewhere, "lab work" is in quotation marks, to underscore its playfulness and flexibility (11). In chapter 5, he returns to the question of what gives certain texts "philosophical whimsy," writing "I could perhaps call them 'intellectual adventure stories.' What I have in mind is that they invite us to consider situations different from our everyday experience, even worlds unlike the familiar one about us—that is, to participate in what philosophers call 'thought experiments'" (74). He notes in *Dialogues with Children* that even very young children engage in counterfactual thinking, anticipating Gopnik on counterfactual thinking in babies. Matthews in turn presents his own work as thought experiments, cultivating his own style and steering clear of the IAPC apparatus. At the same time, Matthews seems nearly a child analyst, his P4C emerging from and emphasizing contact with individual children, including his own, as with the work of Melanie Klein and other early child analysts, who wrote about their own children (if not so openly).[37] He assumes something like psychological expertise, organizing chapters of *Philosophy and the Young Child* around topics like "play," "fantasy," "anxiety," and "naiveté."

Chapter titles of *Philosophy and the Young Child* appear in giant font, as if for beginning readers, and a playful, pro-child tone obtains throughout. But Matthews's later work *The Philosophy of Childhood* is an imaginative, often moving plea for children's rights as much as a meditation on P4C. Responding to Rose's argument in *The Case of Peter Pan, or The Impossibility of Children's Fiction*, Matthews holds that children are not so easily taken in by what they read and that adults writing for children do not have "more complex or more questionable motivation than writers of other types of literature" (103). He does not see adult involvement as automatically tainting P4C, and he offers examples of narrative complexity in *Frog and Toad*.[38] In *The Philosophy of Childhood*, he builds a case for childhood as a rich intellectual, emotional, and aesthetic time of our lives, even questioning the concept of childhood itself, in his words "philosophically problematic in that genuinely philosophical difficulties stand in the way of saying just what kind of difference the difference between children and adult human beings is" (8). He reclassifies his own work as "*a* philosophy of childhood," through which he hopes to secure "a place in the philosophy curriculum of the future for *the* philosophy of childhood as a genuine area for academic research, writing, and teaching" (9). Matthews offers fascinating chapters on children's literature, childhood and death, and children's art. The last of these ventures into the politics of children's art and the "devaluation of the goods of childhood," which he sees as "embodied . . . in the very structure of our social institutions" (119). Rethinking children's art, he proposes, may help us rethink "the nature and significance of adult art, indeed, of art in general" (122). Matthews suggests that all of these pursuits might liberalize and even liberate society. And if philosophy can be good for childhood, the implication goes, childhood can be good for philosophy.[39] Albeit in different ways, Lipman and Matthews look to childhood to revitalize philosophy, drawing on childhood as a natural, renewable resource for adults. If, as Gubar suggests, Matthews advocates for a "kinship model" of child-adult relation, he also stresses the kinship of childhood and philosophy.

That is not to say that Matthews got everything right. He shared with Lipman a dissatisfaction with academic philosophy that bordered on the phobic. And unlike Lipman, who studied in Europe and admired continental thinkers, Matthews associates Piaget's ostensible limitations with the "Swiss and French culture in which he grew to maturity." "Philosophy on the continent," opines Matthews in the final pages of *Dialogues with Children*, "has tended to be more pretentious and more systematic than it has in English-speaking countries. By contrast, the styles of analytic philosophy that have dominated the English-speaking world have been characteristically unpretentious" (117–18). Such styles, he continues, are closer to the natural reflective styles of young children, as opposed to the "ambitious styles that Piaget took for a model" (118). Given his general fondness for play, creativity, and literary style, one might think that Matthews would prefer continental to analytic philosophy, but apparently not. However they position themselves in relation to modes of philosophy, Matthews and Lipman agree on the failings of psychology (Piaget and Bettelheim in particular), mostly because it does not give children sufficient credit for their abilities and potential, but maybe also because they recognize psychology as a disciplinary rival for P4C.

In any case, Matthews paves the way for the now-dominant attitude about children's literature in P4C, even within programs using IAPC materials: not as mere vehicle, or even as curriculum, but as a parallel project. Contemporary practitioners draw heavily on existing children's literature not only because that literature is widely available but also because they regard it as a creative equivalent to P4C. Lipman's novels in dialogue compare unfavorably to contemporary children's literature, as well as to the classics that Matthews champions. *Harry Stottlemeier's Discovery* is deadly earnest and not whimsical in the least. Most children would find it hard going, and it never took off as literature. Johnson and Reed concede that it is lacking as a literary work (they even call it "contrived and overly simplistic"). But they defend it as a vehicle for P4C (224). Much as I hate on principle to side with literariness, I am persuaded that philosophy in the form of a children's book should make the most of the children's book's aesthetic potential.

Consider briefly two texts from different moments in the arc of P4C that touch on this question. One of the most interesting—and probably most famous—examples of literary P4C is the YA novel *Sophie's World* (1991), by philosophy teacher Jostein Gaarder. Subtitled *A Novel about the History of Philosophy*, the book became a bestseller in Norway and has been translated into almost sixty languages. Gaarder was a high school philosophy teacher and wrote the novel for use with teens. His novel focuses on Sophie Amundsen, who, nearing her fifteenth birthday, embarks upon a philosophy correspondence course with a mysterious stranger named Alberto Knox, a philosophy professor and father surrogate. The book stays compelling as a mystery even as it delivers a history of Western philosophy. The historical presentation is conventional in terms of key figures and movements, even as the mystery story gets curiouser and curiouser. (Allusions to *Alice* are everywhere.) Sophie is tutored in philosophy not by a teacher—school, we are told, is boring and irrelevant—but by a private tutor whom she does not know. Many P4C principles are delivered at various points in the novel—for instance, the foundational mantra that (and this is in all caps) "THE ONLY THING WE REQUIRE TO BE GOOD PHILOSOPHERS IS THE FACULTY OF WONDER" (15). (The next sentence, not in caps, is another emergent lesson: "Babies have this faculty.") The book is very deliberately positioned as for young people (although not children); Sophie is keenly aware that had she not been plunged into her adventure at this critical point in her life, she might have lost her ability to wonder and think. Here is a core principle of P4C: catch them youngish. Another such principle evident in the novel is the idea that philosophy is not an ivory tower undertaking but rather the practice of everyday life. *Sophie's World* merges the Lipman and Matthews modes, since it is a series of dialogues that has been taught in schools but also a puzzling metafictional work full of surrealist and fantasy elements. Harald Bache-Wiig calls it "a kind of historical-philosophical space odyssey in a universe where there are no firm boundaries between the simulated and the real" (256). The paternal relation between Sophie and her teacher/father(s) in the novel further recalls the family practice aspects of early P4C, if with an interesting gender twist, and emphasizes the pleasure and value of adult-child collaboration beyond the traditional dialogue. Not surprisingly, *Sophie's World* became a kind of textbook and has its own SparkNotes discussion guide—appropriate for a novel that self-presents as "in reality a textbook on philosophy" (538) and one in which, as teacher/father Alberto puts it, all the dialogues "are in reality one long monologue" (358).[40]

We might think that its metafictional elements merely make more palatable otherwise boring lessons. But Bache-Wiig thinks that *Sophie's World* unites philosophical knowledge and aesthetic experience through the metafictional framework, preferring mystery and wonder over knowledge acquisition. The book may have a didactic form, in other words, but that form is interrogative and not aimlessly metafictional. Philosophy, argues Bache-Wiig, is not cumulative after all; "philosophers have not become more certain of their true knowledge just because they have placed themselves on the shoulders of their predecessors" (264). Rather than maintain the illusion of steady and growing knowledge, or (more painfully) despair over the futility of philosophical investigation, *Sophie's World* opts to celebrate "wondering doubt" or "philosophical amazement" (Bache-Wiig 264, 269). That is why existential philosophers get the last word in Gaarder's novel, he thinks. The takeaway for Bache-Wiig is the novel's celebration of collaborative inquiry and its resistance to top-down authority. "Teaching philosophical knowledge cannot take place with any success if it is regarded as a *vertical* impartment of knowledge from a knowing teacher to an ignorant student" (271). Slavishness to philosophy the subject can kill philosophy the activity. Granted, *Sophie's World* is not your usual YA novel, although many YA novels engage in philosophical questions more indirectly. In any case, Gaarder's novel registers a simultaneous shift toward a more collaborative practice *with* children alongside a growing preference for philosophical questions over answers. It probably does still appeal for the philosophical knowledge it promises as for the intellectual adventure story that it tells.

A more typical work of contemporary P4C in children's book form is Shinsuke Yoshitake's whimsical picturebook *Can I Build Another Me?*

(2014), translated from Japanese.[41] Young Kevin—named Kevin Young—is tiring of chores and decides he needs a clone. He buys a robot and instructs the robot to become another Kevin by watching and imitating him. The book explores all the big questions of ontology and epistemology but most centrally, what, if anything, makes a person that person? In tutoring the robot, Kevin thinks and talks about his physical self, his likes and dislikes, his abilities and inabilities. He knows he leaves traces of himself: "You can tell where I've been even when I'm not there." In different places he becomes different people, he thinks. Kevin also imagines how others might see him—his parents, his friends, his doctor, and his teacher, even a visiting alien. He muses that he is a human machine: poo-making, hair-growing, song-playing, giggling. Somehow, he muses, he stays the same no matter how much he changes. "There are lots of versions of me," he tries to explain, "but all of them are me!" "I think all my younger selves are still inside me," he says earlier. "So who am I?" he tries to conclude. "The harder I think about it, the more questions I come up with!" Good thing the journey matters most. "Thinking about yourself isn't always easy but it can be fun." At the end, the robot assumes Kevin's identity at home, but mom is not fooled. "Who on earth are you?" she asks. (Good question.) The answer, then, is that we cannot build another us. Not so much because we are special—"I'm quite ordinary, really," Kevin insists; "There are plenty of other kids like me"—but because we are distinct, because we build ourselves even as we come prebuilt.

Can I Build Another Me? checks many of the boxes for philosophical whimsy and P4C work. It encourages curiosity about and reflection on the problem of identity. It asks readers to think about but also outside themselves, to adopt the perspectives of others (indeed, to recognize others as others, as part of seeing oneself). Without using philosophical terms, or introducing philosophical thinkers, the book is philosophical, with an episodic structure and a minimal plot. Kevin does not have a collaborator, as the robot is passive, unless we think of the reader as Kevin's coinvestigator. There is no adult presence, save that of the author-illustrator, who remains offstage. Unlike some P4C-affiliated picturebooks, and unlike *Sophie's World*, *Can I Build Another Me?* does not transgress the boundaries of page or otherwise tamper with form; the focus is on philosophy by a child in everyday life.

Philosophy with Children (with Picturebooks)

Lipman and Matthews both died in 2011, but P4C lives on, more a phenomenon than a movement. It has footholds not only in North America but also in Europe, South America, and Asia, with growing momentum in Africa. The 2007 UNESCO report *Philosophy: A School of Freedom* identifies three levels of P4C institutionalization worldwide: cases where it has been promoted by educational authorities, as in France; cases where official experiments have been conducted, as in Norway; and cases where P4C has been institutionalized and is part of the primary school curriculum, as in Australia (25).[42] Sometimes P4C represents a new direction in educational theory and practice; sometimes it merges with native curricula or philosophies.[43] Despite a downturn in federal funding in the 1980s,[44] a number of American universities sponsor philosophical work in K–12 schools, most prominently Montclair State, the University of Chicago, and the University of Washington. IAPC, described on its website as "the world's oldest organization devoted to young people's philosophical practice,"[45] is still headquartered at Montclair State and still sponsors a range of programs, from professional development forums to consulting operations with universities and public schools to P4C conferences and symposia. It offers partnerships with primary and secondary schools called "Philosophy in the Schools," with two tiers of engagement. Teachers can earn professional development hours in either tier (there is a fee for IAPC involvement, to cover materials and travel and per diem expenses for IAPC staff). IAPC materials, supplemented by children's books, continue to circulate globally and in various languages. The IAPC in turn inspired the formation of the International Council of Philosophical Inquiry with Children (ICPIC), based in Denmark. As noted in the book's introduction, a similar organization exists in the United Kingdom called the Society for the Advancement of Philosophical Enquiry and Reflection in Education (SAPERE). Lizzy Lewis, SAPERE's development manager, shared with me by email that some 40,000 teachers have been trained in the United Kingdom by the organization, 4,500 in 2016 alone.[46] These numbers suggest that SAPERE is fast approaching what the IAPC accomplished in the United States at the height of first-wave P4C. In addition, P4C has a presence in community education and homeschooling programs.

For all its benefits, P4C is built around some paradoxes: children are natural/born philosophers but must be lured into philosophical conversation and taught how to conduct such; teachers should follow where children lead but should provide appropriate materials and environments; philosophy is everyone's concern but should be overseen by those properly trained in P4C methods. We can also detect some ambivalence around the notion that all children are philosophical. Presumably, the goal of P4C was to make the child philosopher the normative type of child—

or to use Matthews's term, to make the deviant response (more) standard. Though democratic in tendency, endorsing the idea that all children are at least proto-philosophical, P4C seems sometimes to depend upon the exceptional child, the child who loves to think and think about thinking. This picture of the wondering child appeals especially to intellectual types, I am guessing, but what if we do not agree that thinking is the Most Interesting Thing in the World or the most significant? As Karin Murris points out, Lipman's dialogues start with the "abnormal child, the thinking child—the adult philosopher's child" ("Philosophy for Children Curriculum" 17). David Kennedy concurs, noting that Lipman's dialogues are "presented in such a way that they appear completely normal—until one realizes that they aren't at all. . . . Here are children talking about mind and body . . . about inquiry itself, in a completely believably unbelievable—or vice versa—way" ("From" 61). Also, P4C is child-centered, but it never became "children's philosophy," meaning philosophy produced by children. However, it never aspired to such. In any case, Lipman and Matthews both struggled with the problem of adult production, with Matthews distancing himself from educational programming and especially large-scale projects.

Contemporary P4C grapples with these complexities. It rejects the more rigid rationalism of Lipman and emphasizes after Matthews the importance of children's literature as philosophical coinquiry between adults and children. The Matthews emphasis on nurturing "philosophical whimsy" dovetails with and helps legitimate a practice of P4C rooted in children's literature, as well as philosophically based children's literature criticism and ethical arguments for children's rights. P4C gained momentum, after all, amid a vibrant 1970s dialogue on child agency and children's rights, taking place in public forums and in publications such as Paul Adams et al.'s *Children's Rights: Toward the Liberation of the Child* (1971), David Gottlieb's *Children's Liberation* (1973), Mark Gerzon's *A Childhood for Every Child* (1973), and Richard Farson's *Birthrights* (1974). As one might guess from such titles, there was a growing commitment to child liberation and not simply child protection, in the wake of advocacy for women's rights and gay rights. Leslie Paris elaborates on the shift from a protectionist to a liberatory model of children's rights, pointing out that the latter framed child protection as insufficient and even unethical. Farson thus claims that increased understanding of childhood has led not to children's rights but to the "sophisticated domination" of children by parents (3).[47]

P4C focuses on the liberation of the child's mind more than her body. That liberation can happen, according to its advocates, through a narrative-based community of inquiry, ideally a community of peers but potentially a classic Socratic community of adult mentor/child mentee. P4C kids do not take to the streets. But they do exercise independence of mind and will. P4C makes the fairly transgressive claim that children are capable of critical thinking from a young age. As we have seen, Lipman and Matthews challenge developmental theory that implies otherwise, in particular the stage theory of Jean Piaget. And as P4C evolved over the next several decades, it moved closer and closer to children's rights discourse and to emancipatory childhood studies. For many, P4C has evolved into philosophy *with* children or PwC.

Consider along these lines Jana Mohr Lone's *The Philosophical Child*, written for parents and teachers. Like Matthews, Lone is a philosopher who found her way into the field through her experiences as a parent, and she acknowledges Matthews and Lipman as mentors. An advocate of active listening and collaborative ("reciprocal") learning, she describes children as "co-inquirers" into life. She argues for the cultivation of "philosophical sensitivity" and draws on Howard Gardner's notion of "existential intelligence" (24). "People sometimes joke," she writes, "when I tell them about these kinds of conversations with children, that the kids must be having an existential crisis. In many ways it's true, but it's not a joke" (10). Lone finds PwC to be emotionally and professionally satisfying, unlike academic philosophy. PwC, she holds, can change lives, family relations, even the world. Lone works with a diverse if largely Anglo-American set of literary texts for young readers, among them (and this is a very partial list): Natalie Babbitt's *Tuck Everlasting*, Lincoln Barnett's *The Universe and Dr. Einstein*, Wolf Erlbruch's *Duck, Death and the Tulip*, Mordicai Gerstein's *How to Paint the Portrait of a Bird*, Crockett Johnson's *Harold and the Purple Crayon*, Michele Lemieux's *Stormy Night*, Leo Lionni's *A Color of His Own*, Arnold Lobel's *Frog and Toad*—now canonical in P4C—Claudia Mills's *Standing Up to Mr. O*, Margery Williams's *The Velveteen Rabbit*, and Markus Zusak's *The Book Thief*. None of these was written by a philosopher; none explains philosophy as a field or practice.

P4C practitioners vary in how much they know about children's literature and how much they think we should know in turn. They cannot always identify what makes children's literature philosophical. Lone notes (after Matthews) that "children's authors are aware of children's philosophical propensities in ways that most of the rest of us are not" (8).[48] She emphasizes the particular power of picturebooks, although limits their relevance to questions about aesthetics.[49] In *Big Ideas for Little Kids*, Wartenberg writes that "the reason that children's books provide such a good means for initiating philosophical discussions is that they present philosophical issues in a way that engages children that naturally leads to animated conversation" (22).[50] Such books are readily available (the supply is "virtually unlimited" [40]), and all teachers need to do, he says, is to "restructure the language-arts lessons they already teach" (7). Wartenberg takes the familiar position that you do not need to know philosophy to facilitate its practice because kids bring philosophy with them. His method involves using a "read-aloud" from a picturebook or chapter book and then moving into guided discussion.[51] While respecting children's literature, Wartenberg takes as axiomatic its teaching usefulness, pairing topics with texts.[52] He does speculate that literary texts are useful because they "pose but do not resolve philosophical questions" (21).

In *Picturebooks, Pedagogy, and Philosophy*, Joanna Haynes (United Kingdom) and Karin Murris (South Africa) reflect on the narrative turn in philosophy and in particular on the shift toward children's literature within P4C evidencing that turn. They advance considerably the critical conversation about children's literature and/as philosophy, drawing on an array of thinkers including Martha Nussbaum and Hans-Georg Gadamer. Murris has a background as a children's librarian and Haynes as a primary school teacher. They identify as "philosophers in education." Murris trained under Lipman and holds a PhD in the philosophy of childhood. In their collaboration, *Picturebooks, Pedagogy, and Philosophy*, Haynes and Murris criticize Lipman on several fronts[53] and accuse Matthews of being too wedded to the delivery of classical philosophy. Haynes and Murris propose a picturebook-based approach in which a postmodern style merges with an expanded understanding of what counts as thinking. Some philosophy can best be practiced in alternative forms like literature, argues Nussbaum in *Love's Knowledge* (1990), and Haynes and Murris claim such status for the modern and especially metafictional picturebook. That genre, they say, raises difficult questions about desire, identity, language, authority, and community. In recent years, similar arguments have been made on behalf of comics and graphic novels, and my next chapter extends that perspective to graphic guides about theory.[54]

Their attention to the picturebook signals not only growing respect for imagetext genres but a radical revision of P4C. Although picturebooks have been the site of psychological and aesthetic experimentation since at least the early twentieth century, P4C has only recently paid special attention to them. Lipman ignored the visual register altogether, eschewing illustrations in his own materials for kids and arguing against the use of pictures in P4C on the grounds that images hamper the imagination. In *Dialogues with Children*, Matthews does reflect on the question of whether we think in pictures, but he does not develop the line of thought and his notion of "philosophical whimsy" is verbal only. In *Words about Pictures*, Perry Nodelman points out that words and pictures in picturebooks "necessarily have a combative relationship; their complementarity is a matter of opposites completing each other by virtue of their differences" (221). In his view, the relationship between pictures and texts trends ironic, and not only in metafictional examples. Drawing on additional picturebook scholarship by David Lewis, as well as Evelyn Arizpe and Morag Styles, Haynes and Murris show how metafictional picturebooks challenge received wisdom about pretty much everything. P4C, they explain in their collaboration, is not a detached intellectual exercise (as it mostly is for Lipman) but a practice that involves the child's full body as well as brain. In their view, P4C necessarily engages with affect or emotion—with desire and sexuality—as well as with rational thought. Hence the usefulness of contemporary picturebooks that unsettle expectations about form and content as well as child-adult relation. Haynes and Murris argue that earlier P4C proponents confused imagery with the imagination when they recommended against pictures in P4C. Imagination is not only visualization, they assert (66–67). They explain that picturebooks have all the benefits of metafictional narrative more generally while offering some additional advantages to younger (beginning) readers. The gaps between words and pictures invite children to bring their own experiences into the reading process, they argue, and on top of that, children "pick up more visual cues than older adults," which facilitates a more egalitarian and collaborative relationship between adult and child (108). Indeed, Haynes and Murris recommend the use of select picturebooks precisely because such books "require open-minded *self*-reflection and *self*-correction" on the part of adults (37). Increasingly, P4C seeks to unschool the adult as much as school the child.

It is no surprise that Haynes and Murris also seek to deprivilege adult philosophy as the reference point for P4C and to give priority instead to the philosophy of child practitioners. "We are particularly interested," they write, "in children's philosophical perspectives and what they can bring to academic philosophy as a discipline" (61). It is important to listen to children; in fact, listening is a form of thinking, they insist, playing off Lipman's faith in dialogue. Haynes and Morris also expand upon the children's rights focus in Matthews's work, confirming a general pattern in which arguments for philosophy training for children facilitate a liberationist philosophy of childhood.

Murris continues these themes in her solo effort *The Posthuman Child*, embracing a "relational materialist conception of philosophy" and objecting to both individualism and human exceptionalism. To combat "onto-epistemic injustice"—especially that "done to children when they are wronged specifically in their capacity as a *knower*"—she recommends the Deleuzian solution of "listening without organs" (130). Drawing on Plato's description of Socrates as a stingray, Murris reminds us that Socrates was self-stinging, declaring himself just as perplexed by his inquiries as anyone else. The moral is that adults should never assume they know better than the children they presume to teach (all the more so, she says, with young people who "might also live in poverty and do not have English as their home language" [247]). Recommending a "rhizomatic intra-active pedagogy" featuring "philosophical listening," she writes that "*picturebooks* themselves . . . demand such philosophical listening. Their force and energy *in relationship with the reader* requires an intra-active pedagogy that positions people of all ages as able materialdiscursive meaning-makings and problem-posers" (201). She also believes that picturebooks are especially effective at destabilizing boundaries since they can show, for instance, a "gorilla who has a cat as a pet" or "a monster with human feet" or "a tree that can talk" (208). Murris is not alone in her enthusiasm for imagetext "provocations," as she puts it (204). In this book's introduction I mentioned the European picturebook series Plato & Co., which introduces children to the ideas of famous philosophers. But an interesting twist on picturebook P4C comes with the Spanish publisher Traje de Lobo SL's Wonder Ponder: Visual Philosophy for Children series, which "introduces readers aged six and over to philosophy's big questions playfully and appealingly" not through picturebooks but "wonder boxes," part book and part game and including notecards, blank cards, and posters.[55]

We have come a long way from Lipman, though Murris is quick to build bridges, describing Lipman's practice as "a radical democratisation of academic philosophy" realized through a transmutation of "Paulo Freire (democratic dialogue) and John Dewey (education as enquiry) into the *community of enquiry* pedagogy" (*Posthuman Child* 155). Haynes shares this view of Lipman with David Kennedy, who describes P4C as anticolonial. In 2002, Haynes had already linked P4C to particular articles on the Convention on the Rights of the Child (CRC) adopted by the UN General Assembly in 1989 (*Children as Philosophers* 2), and Haynes, Murris, Kennedy, and other P4Cers continue to support a child rights agenda. Ndofirepi Amasa and Mathebula Thokozani affirm P4C as a program for cultivating citizenship and promoting children's rights in postapartheid South Africa, amending Lipman's "community of inquiry" to "the community of inquiry for democracy," with community "including the disabled, the hypersensitive and children in difficult situations or those who struggle at school" (139). P4C has nurtured what ethicist John Wall terms "childism," playing up the ethical obligation of adults to educate children through respectful, even egalitarian collaboration and dialogue.[56] Meanwhile, children's literature scholars continue to explore the picturebook's facilitation of child rights and democratic principles.[57]

Even at its more conventional, P4C is full of reminders that children think and say the darndest things and that committing to philosophical work with children requires a new ethic of child-adult relation. "Kids are unrelenting in their inquiries," warns Marietta McCarty (xi). "If we really want to give our children the freedom they want and deserve, including the freedom to pursue their philosophical interest and to develop their argumentative skills," advises Wartenberg in *Big Ideas for Little Kids*, "then we have to reckon with young children who are more assertive, more intellectually independent, and less pliable than children have traditionally been taken to be by their teachers and parents" (139).

Thanks in part to P4C, legal scholars are increasingly turning also to children's literature in support and illustration of children's rights. Citing Barbara Bennett Woodhouse on the imaginative literature of children's rights,[58] Jonathan Todres and Sarah Higinbotham frame their 2016 study *Human Rights in Children's Literature: Imagination and the Narrative of Law* as a response to Article 42 of the CRC, which calls participants "to make the principles and provisions of the Convention widely known, by appropriate and active means, to adults and children alike" (UN General Assembly xvi).[59] In their view, stories with human rights themes are much more likely to have an impact on child readers than legal statues or decisions (xvi) and children's literature "is filled with human rights scenarios" that dramatize the cultural workings and limitations of law (1).[60] Some quibbles aside, the book is a significant contribution to scholarship on the ethical power of children's literature, something that P4C recognized decades ago.

The heterogeneity of contemporary P4C seems vital to its success. Murris et al. note that P4C "houses a complex mixture of educational ideas and philosophical traditions as practitioners situate the approach in their own cultural context" (1). "In a profound sense," they observe, "what P4C *is*, can be experienced only in practice." Borrowing from Wittgenstein, they suggest that the varied practices of P4C worldwide are unique but share a family resemblance (1). Murris even recommends "disequilibrium" in the enterprise, concerned that when P4C is implemented there is a danger "that the patriarch will be tempted to clone, rather than to tolerate real diversity in his family" ("Philosophy with Children" 672).

P4C aims not merely to transform educational experience for kids but also to insist on their intellectual powers and citizenship rights. In the process, it promises to rejuvenate philosophy, keep it fresh for professional practitioners as well as for the broader public. In this sense, P4C is for adults, too. In moving closer to children's literature, P4C has also moved closer to theory for beginners in its respect for the mysteries of language and thought and in its skepticism about mastery. We see that skepticism in Murris, certainly, but it is there from Matthews forward. "When now I teach Aristotle or Aquinas to university students," Matthews writes in *The Philosophy of Childhood*, "I try to locate the questioning child in me and my students. Unless I do so, the philosophy we do together will lose much of its urgency and much of its point" (14). Sounding like Lyotard or other theorists for beginners, the subject of my next chapter, Matthews continues:

> Descartes taught us to do philosophy by "starting over." Instead of assuming the correctness of what my teachers have taught me, or what the society around me seems to accept, I am to make a fresh beginning to see if I can show by some means of my very own that I really do know whatever it is I claim to know. . . . In a certain way, then, adult philosophers who follow Descartes in trying to "start over" are trying to make themselves as little children again, even if only temporarily. (18)

2 / Theory for Beginners

The preceding chapter explored how P4C helped to develop the idea that children's literature is a philosophical undertaking. This chapter considers how philosophy and especially theory create something akin to children's literature in identifying and aligning with the beginner both abstractly, in the form of theoretical reflection, and more instrumentally, in the form of imagetext or graphic guides. First, I review some theoretical texts that give priority to the child and the beginner and in connection with the task of theory introduction. Then in the longer part of the chapter, I examine the guides, which launched in the 1960s and are still going strong. That material is theory-adjacent at the least and perhaps even qualifies as theory itself. In my view, theory does not stand apart from but rather is constituted partly through its summary, reproduction, and modification.

Taking creative as well as critical form, the graphic guides to theory seek to encourage and amplify curiosity as much as to impart knowledge. Part of the American outline and digest tradition, the guides also had origin in leftist comic book writing in Mexico. The first such title was *Cuba Para Principiantes*, or *Cuba for Beginners* (1970), by the Mexican political cartoonist and comic book artist Eduardo del Río, pseudonym Rius. Born in 1934, Rius has written over a hundred books on assorted topics. Other titles by Rius soon followed, and over time the guides proliferated and diversified, undertaken by other writers and illustrators and focusing on a range of subjects. Constituting a multimodal literature for beginners with links to imagetext genres for children and young adults, the guides raise fascinating questions about knowledge production within and outside academe.[1] Understanding their history and function helps us enrich the story of theory's career, especially in the United States.

Beginner and Child

Theory does not often traffic in children's texts. More typically, it concerns itself with the figure of the child and the beginner, not only speaking up for those figures but also identifying with them. Jyotsna Kapur emphasizes that childhood was "one of the promises to emerge from social labor, was imagined as the exact opposite of alienated labor" (15). "Childhood, Marxism, and psychoanalysis, all grounded in the nineteenth century, are united by their hope for the possibility of the nonalienated life" (101).[2] Benjamin is an important early figure in the theoretical recognition of childhood's nonnormative promise, as is Marcel Proust. Thinkers as differently situated as Benjamin and Jean-François Lyotard have understood childhood as an oppositional ideal worth cultivating and exploiting.[3] And interest in "infancy" (from the Latin *infans*, or without language) as "an unspeaking state beyond the limits of language and pregnant with potentiality has captivated philosophers since the time of Saint Augustine," notes Sara Pankenier Weld in the opening sentence of her excellent book on the infantilist aesthetic of the Russian avant-garde. Weld observes further that Wittgenstein carried forward the tradition. Building on this trope and perhaps also on classical psychoanalysis, more contemporary theory positions the child as a test case for or limit of the human. Infancy and natality have been important to thinkers such as Hannah Arendt (*The Human Condition*), Giorgio Agamben (*Infancy and History*), and Christopher Fynsk (*Infant Figures*).[4] Agamben associates infancy with "not yet" "potentiality" and the possibility of community. In *The Inhuman* and elsewhere, Lyotard positions infancy and/as childhood as that which comes before the human but also exposes the human as impossible. Picking up on such discussion in her introduction to *Human, All Too Human*, Diana Fuss remarks that the child offers an even more vexed and therefore productive limit case of humanity than the object or animal since the child's alterity is temporal. In "On the Unrelenting Creepiness of Childhood," Avital Ronell notes that in contemporary philosophy, the child assumes the discursive role formerly played by the idiot. "Much can be said," she writes, "about the induction of wild children, savages, idiots, and infants into the realm of philosophical speculation, and it would be important to investigate more fully the peculiar yet crucial status of these minorities as philosophy conducts its adult raids" (101). And despite philosophy's careful management, the child nonetheless "constitutes a security risk for the house of philosophy. It crawls in, setting off a lot of noise" (102). In its many iterations, then, the child makes philosophy work; it constitutes and enables thought.

Without commenting on the child per se, Theodor Adorno reflects on the interplay of naïveté and sophistication in section 46 of *Minima Moralia* ("On the morality of thinking"), noting they "are concepts so endlessly intertwined that no good sense can come of playing one off against the other" (73). He goes on to say that we cannot side with either naïveté or sophistication—rather, we must balance them in our thinking. "The morality of thought," Adorno continues, "lies in a procedure that is neither entrenched nor detached, neither blind nor empty, neither atomistic nor consequential" (74). In his provocative *Strange Gourmets: Sophistication, Theory, and the Novel*, Joseph Litvak approaches Adorno (and theory more generally) as a kind of conduct literature.[5] Stressing Adorno's remarks on "sophisticated naïveté," Litvak reminds us that "sophistication" is rooted in "sophistry," an aberration from philosophy connoting perversion. Sophistication thus carries with it a perverse, regressive dimension linked with childhood. In Litvak's view, Adorno courts childhood and naïveté because they are generatively perverse. Litvak sees much the same operation (which he calls "an almost Pee-Wee Herman-like travesty—or transvestism" [125]) in Proust and in Barthes, who wrote extensively, and unconventionally, about childhood. Proust's "sophisticated intelligence," writes Litvak, "is bound up with an insistent, incorrigible humanity. . . . [His] regressive practice in fact enables his most powerfully sophisticated effects" (17). In Litvak's view, Adorno recommends neither growing up nor remaining a child but rather a third option, "that of *becoming a child*" (124). Litvak reads theory's ventriloquism of childhood not as bad faith but as a legitimate strategy for responding to the ills of mass culture. In his view, Adorno, Proust, and Barthes ironize more than colonize childhood.[6]

Theory's beginner is cousin to the child. We can trace this association at least to Nietzsche, who calls the child "innocence and forgetfulness, a new beginning, a sport, a self-propelling wheel, a first motion, a sacred Yes" (55).[7] And to Freud, of course, who cultivated the child as a little theorist and childhood as a baseline for insight (hence Frantz Fanon's declaration that "I believe it is necessary to become a child again in order to grasp certain psychic realities" [146]). In theory for beginners, the child and the beginner are interlocked and sometimes interchangeable.

The beginner is of particular importance to "French" theory. In his early (beginning) study *Beginnings: Intention and Method* (1975), Edward Said notes that the French critics "have made the problem of beginnings the beginning—and in a sense, the center—of their thought" (281). There is Derrida, most obviously, with his prologues and prefaces and introductions, always beginning again; there is also Roland Barthes, preparing to write the novel, theorizing the joys of beginning and especially the beginning of writing in midlife. And there are examples outside the French tradition. Said holds that with the decline of philology's influence, literary critics could no longer see themselves as part of a coherent and ongoing (his word is "dynastic") enterprise and instead came to understand their work as discontinuous with what came before—that is, as beginning anew rather than continuing something. The modern critic, Said writes, is something "of a wanderer, going from place to place for his material, but remaining . . . essentially *between* homes" (8). "Thus," he writes, "when one begins to write today one is necessarily more of an autodidact, gathering or making up the knowledge one needs in the course of creating" (8). "A beginning," concludes Said, "is what I think scholarship ought to see itself as, for in that light scholarship or criticism revitalizes itself" (380). Said's sentiments reflect a general belief in theory as countercultural and bound up with progressive politics.

Theory is of course for advanced practitioners too. Attending to the institutionalization of theory in the American academy, Jeffrey Williams emphasizes the two dimensions of theory—both "an institutionally circulated and governed body of knowledge . . . very much a professional device, a body of professional lore that functions to distinguish those inside the profession" and "a dynamic and rejuvenating product development unit or even market concept," one spawning new materials and generally refreshing the discipline ("Packaging" 284). Theory needs both experienced practitioners and new readers. For that reason, it is introduced in multiple ways and on multiple levels.[8] The challenge of beginning—its necessity—has become an internal feature of theory and a mode of address. Theory has made a virtue of the necessity of beginning, particularly in the tradition of poststructuralism. Psychoanalysis, of course, inspires some of this preoccupation with beginnings or returns. "Psychoanalysis gives us a chance," writes Lacan in *My Teaching*, "a chance to start again" (76), and while he means specifically the chance to reboot psychoanalysis, his description speaks to the idea that nothing is ever finished.[9] And as psychoanalysis reminds us, to become a child again (or to receive things as a child might) involves a return not only to wonder but also to complexity and frustration, to the condition of dependence. Philosophy and especially theory can reanimate forgotten fears and wishes. That is why "theory kindergarten" is both a "fun fair of experiments" and a horror show.[10]

Difficulty and ease are intertwined in theory for beginners. Theory is for beginners, but that does not make it easy. Theory leads us to understanding but also pushes against such, incorporating and figuring resistance.[11] Jonathan Culler reminds us that "good philosophy" and, by extension, good theory may require "bad writing"—that is, writing that respects and performs difficulty, writing that refuses mastery and even understanding (and certainly the claim of "clear" explication) ("Bad Writing"). Meanwhile, the beginner is not only the subject eager to learn but also a figure of resistance and even aporia. And experienced readers of theory can also be beginners of theory, as Williams suggests above. Theory often makes beginners out of experienced thinkers, even experienced readers of theory. While some may be newer than others to theory, or to particular iterations, we should not assume a sharp divide between beginners and nonbeginners. We might be better served by thinking of the beginner less as a type and more as a role. Theory presumes a beginner in that theory is designed to surprise, shake things up, make us think otherwise.

In *Le Postmoderne expliqué aux enfants*, shortened in the English translation to *The Postmodern Explained*, Lytoard declares that childhood "is the monster of philosophers. It is also their accomplice. Childhood tells them that the mind is not given. But that it is possible" (100). This comment comes in a letter to Hugo Vermeren, "Address on the Subject of the Course of Philosophy." Lyotard holds that philosophizing and reading are autodidactic activities and that we are always beginners in such. "You need to recommence. You cannot be a philosopher (not even the teacher of philosophy) if your mind is made up on a question before you arrive, if in class it does commence, if it does not resume the course from the beginning" (100–1). "If it is true that philosophizing, alone or in class, responds to a demand for a return to the childhood of thought," Lyotard asks in that letter, "what would happen if thought no longer had a childhood? If those who pass for children or adolescents ceased to be the milieu of human uncertainty, the very possibility of ideas? If interests were already fixed?" (105). He continues: "Maybe there is more childhood available to thought at thirty-five than at eighteen, and more outside a degree course than in one. A new task for didactic thought: to search out its childhood anywhere and everywhere, even outside childhood" (107).

Explaining the postmodern to children might seem a good joke, and maybe it is to some degree, especially since the child address often works more as a provocation, as with the examples I discussed in the book's introduction (*A Child's Guide to Freud* and *Communism for Kids*). But the original title of Lyotard's *Le Postmoderne expliqué aux enfants* (lit. "The Postmodern Explained to Children") is also, if not mostly, in earnest. A collection of letters addressed to the children of Lyotard's friends and colleagues, the book came into being at the urging of editors Julian Pefanis and Morgan Thomas, ostensibly despite Lyotard's reluctance. The team that translated the book into English explains in a preface that "the promise of the French title to 'explain to children' what adults find obscure is surely ironic and not to be taken literally" (Lyotard, *Postmodern Explained* x). They do not mean the "to children" tag but the "explained" part, noting that the book does not so much explain the postmodern as approach the questions raised by postmodernity "with patience and with the mind of the child. For childhood is the season of the mind's possibilities and of the possibility of philosophy" (x). They take that line from Lyotard, in the process affirming the foundation of P4C. They drop "to children" in the English title, shortening it to *The Postmodern Explained*. But audience is key, and the book as a whole, like each individual letter, participates in a long tradition of "translation" for beginners, often for the purpose of religious instruction.[12] What it means for something to be explained to children is not simple or self-evident.

In "Gloss on Resistance," addressed to David Rogozinski and responding to Claude Lefort's commentary on George Orwell's *1984*, Lyotard emphasizes writing as having the potential to make useful trouble for the forces of normalization and worse. Writing keeps "the event" alive or resonant. He continues:

> Let us recall—in opposition to this murder of the instant and singularity—those short pieces of Walter Benjamin's *One Way Street* and *A Berlin Childhood*, pieces Theodor Adorno would call "micrologies." They do not describe events from childhood; rather they capture the childhood of the event and inscribe what is uncapturable about it. And what makes an encounter with a word, odor, place, book, or face into an event is not its newness when compared to other "events." It is its very value as initiation. You only learn this later. It cuts open a wound in the sensibility. You know this because it has since reopened and will reopen again, marking out the rhythm of a secret and perhaps unnoticed temporality. This wound ushered you into an unknown world, but without ever making it known to you. Such initiation initiates nothing, it just begins.
>
> You fight against the cicatrization of the event, against its categorization as "childishness," to preserve initiation. This is the fight fought by writing against bureaucratic Newspeak. (*Postmodern Explained* 90–91)

The new narrative forms of science and technology can "bear witness to what really matters: the childhood of an encounter, the welcome extended to the marvel that (something) is happening, the respect for the event. Do not forget that you were and are this yourself: the welcomed marvel, the respected event, the childhood shared by your parents" (97). Jonathan Bignell remarks that for Lyotard and Benjamin both, childhood "shields the event from its containment in narrative and the dead weight of customary thinking, and thus childhood represents the possibility of the production of the event" (118). Lyotard invites his readers to imagine childhood as a state of possibility for living and thinking. In that sense, Lyotard shares much territory with P4C and especially PwC.

In *The Future of Theory*, Jean-Michel Rabaté combines an advocacy for "weak" theory with an account of theory as both hysterical and adolescent-rebellious. "Theory can never be pure because it is always lacking," he writes, "and this weakness is in fact its strength" (9). Rabaté proposes that Hegel and especially Lacan present knowledge as hysterical in drive. To Freud's three "impossible" tasks, writes Rabaté, Lacan added a fourth, to theorize, or to "'understand' fully by traversing an experience like that of psychoanalysis, then making sense of it by creating powerful concepts that are adequate to the vision, all the while keeping the *libido sciendi* alive, in a desiring dialectic best exemplified by the discourse of the Hysteric" (15). In this account, theory generates knowledge by way of that desiring dialectic; theory "should move, seduce, entrance, keep desire in motion; in other words, it should be 'sexy'" (16). And it should be hysterical, paranoid, melodramatic. Whatever we make of Rabaté, he presents theory as unequivocally for beginners (and in relation to philosophy):

> The hystericization effect I have described explains what kind of philosophy I mean: it is a philosophy for non-philosophers, a philosophy for those who want to walk on the streets without falling into a manhole, a philosophy for those who do not plan to be taken as professionals. First, life is too short, then often *really interesting problems strike beginners with more clarity than jaded experts*, and finally new issues tend to appear in the divides, hinges, margins of the domain. . . . The hystericization of Theory insists upon its "now." . . . I am not just calling for a return to philosophy as a more stable site of discourse after all others have failed, but I am suggesting that Theory should work through philosophy relentlessly, destabilizing it in the name of other discourses, among which literature will only provide one strategy, and not a particularly privileged access. (149–50; emphasis added)

Theory, in his view, aims to keep intellectual problems fresh. His theory is not a select tradition but a destabilizing force. And as he emphasizes, one version of the beginner is the child. He writes that in his ideal world, theory, "in spite of all the anti-Platonic gestures multiplied by French or American theorists, would look back to Plato's Socrates, who loved nothing like wonder and seduction, and who, moreover, believed that any untaught slave or child could rediscover the principles of science provided the right questions were asked" (150).

Some strains of theory and philosophy register in and through the child and the beginner (sometimes also the idiot) an ambivalence about their power or authority. The child is sometimes a name for the resistance(s) to theory even within theory.[13] The beginner, in other words, can be a figure of resistance to and even rejection of mastery. Rhetorics of mastery, after all, are in part what theory struggles against, even as theory enacts its own dramas of knowledge and reproduction.[14] Theory for beginners encourages exposure, familiarity, sometimes even fluency, but not mastery. It is ambivalent toward developmentalism; it encourages trial and error, repetition, misrecognition, circularity. It offers entry into critical discourse, not completion. And that entry is typically more like first contact than a proper introduction. Beginning is an ongoing process. We are always beginning theory.

Introducing the Graphic Guides

Theory is also for beginners when it supports learning and helps to generate or takes the form of introductory materials. It is not so easy to distinguish between theory proper and theory for beginners. Lacan's *My Teaching* and Jonathan Culler's *Structuralist Poetics* might qualify as the latter, for example, as theoretical works presenting complex ideas clearly and accessibly. Materials that are more obviously auxiliary, meanwhile, can inspire theory as well as explain it and may have theoretical tendencies of their own. Theory introductions are arguably part of the broader discourse of theory, not mere passport or gateway drug. And that discourse, as Elizabeth Bruss emphasizes, makes for a "more openly didactic form" than literature, "able to instruct its would-be readers more explicitly and at greater length in the mysteries required of them" (80).[15]

So far, the story of theory in America is largely a story of French theory, told ably by François Cusset. In his account, the work of a small group of mostly French intellectuals (themselves drawing on German thinking) found both audience and consolidation in American research institutions, elite ones especially.[16] Other scholars have been quick to point out that theory was implicit in earlier American philosophical and educational practices even if not articulated as theory per se.[17] "There was never a time when English as a twentieth-century university discipline in the

United States was 'untheoretical,'" writes Evan Watkins, and English "always foregrounds theory in one way or another . . . because it is *always in the business of recruiting*" (9; emphasis added).[18] Nor is theory monopolized by university types, whether in the United States or elsewhere. Houston A. Baker Jr. celebrates the blues as "vernacular theory" practiced by everyday people and grounded in local concerns, and Thomas McLaughlin picks up on this tradition of thinking in *Street Smarts and Critical Theory*. "Not all the sharp minds get to go to college," McLaughlin reminds us, "and not all the theorists are in [the] academy" (29).[19]

Cusset does not write about theorists outside the academy, but he does comment on how French theory's consolidation in the North American academy has played out in undergraduate education.[20] Undergraduate students, he proposes, find theory texts "better suited to the empathetic and lighthearted qualities of student conversation and its free use of tactics such as name-dropping and spontaneous association of incompatible concepts" (219). In his view, theory liberated the student from the dreariness of close reading. "For those too young to master all the implications of a text," Cusset asserts, "theory provided a great windfall." Theory deals in fragments rather than long expositions, thereby giving the excitable "twenty-two year old" "a freer hand intellectually" (219). Unfortunately, Cusset does not stop there, going on to develop a psychocultural account of theory's seduction of young users. Theoretical texts, he contends, slip "into the chinks of existential angst," becoming "living objects of both desire and disapproval—in a word, something quite different from the conceptual material that academic intellectuals skillfully integrated into their theoretical constructions" (218). Pointing to student-made theory spinoffs such as fanzines and websites, Cusset speculates that undergraduate theory-fetishizing meets developmental and social needs. "Thus, as the term *Bildungsroman* appeared in the nineteenth century in Germany," he proposes, "referring to a literature of initiation, avidly consumed by adolescents, we might venture to coin the term *Bildungstheorie* for this new theoretical presence, intimately embraced by many students for its familiar otherness, so different from other required readings" (224).

Cusset grants that students are not the only ones undergoing *Bildungstheorie*. "Looking beyond the student population," he continues, we can find this "subjective, and it might be said, atmospheric connection to the works of French theory" among other groups who are not (yet) credentialed. "These groups might typically include teachers engaged in research, assistant professors, young students feeling uncertain after graduation . . . and all the other 'dominated' members of the strict hierarchy of knowledge and publication" (226). Rather than sympathize with those members, Cusset psychologizes them, and not flatteringly. In his view, theory works as a coping strategy for those unable to produce legitimate readings and claim legitimate status.

Cusset underscores that we do not know enough about how students and others use theory, and perhaps there is some truth in his analysis of Bildungstheorie. Even so, he draws too firm a distinction between casual and serious users. I can agree that beginners' "link to theory is not grounded in the mediating institution, or in a career project"—at least not as much—but I cannot concede that their relationship to theory originates "in a fear or sense of mystery, a prerational aura that they attempt to disperse by short-circuiting the overall logic" (226). The typical undergraduate student's interest in theory may be brief, but it is not necessarily superficial or defensive. I am more persuaded by the attitude of McLaughlin and James Sosnoski, who find students and others perfectly capable of theorizing. And if speculating about Bildungstheorie, let us consider how theory meets the needs of advanced users also. I doubt that only impressionable youth and the uncredentialed mishandle theory or that advanced users always get things right. Theory surely calls to established professors for many of the reasons it calls to students as well as to all those "without a published work to their name," including (Cusset speculates) "teachers engaged in research, assistant professors . . . and all the other 'dominated' members of the strict hierarchy of knowledge" (225). Among many other things, theory helps readers at all levels of experience and career formation "carve out for themselves a bio/bibliography" (226).

If hard on students, Cusset usefully underscores how the American pedagogical tradition of summary/digest paved the way for French theory's reception in the United States. "In literature courses in the United States," he reminds us, "students most often encounter works via the impressionistic format of excerpts and overviews. Reading, moreover, is less concentrated on the literary works themselves . . . than on comparing, evaluating, and commenting on the various critical and theoretical approaches" (220). Cusset cites Gustave Lanson's astonishment in 1912 (when he came to teach at Columbia) at the "singular ability to do without the texts . . . to substitute a knowledge of what has been said about authors for that of what the authors said" (quoted in Cusset 220). In his preface to the English edition of his book, Cusset notes that French theory was transplanted in part because "the French issue of writing became the American issue of reading" (xiv), "reading" meaning the literal act of reading but also the work of summary and interpretation. Reading was at once a practical affair and an increasingly theoretical one too.[21] Moreover, visual literature has been used for teaching purposes in America since the late nineteenth century, making theory in imagetext form more palatable than not.[22]

Graphic guides to theory took off in America in large measure because of this long-standing enthusiasm for introductory materials, including visual literature. An industry of imagetext volumes for adult beginners emerged from and alongside picturebooks, comics, manga, illustrated histories, and other sorts of imagetexts for younger readers. The relays among these genres harken back at least to the early twentieth century. The guides align with American middlebrow projects such as book clubs, book reviews, and literary radio programs designed to help everyday readers or listeners better understand subjects of interest. An especially successful middlebrow form anticipating the guides was the book-length "outline." Some examples include the American edition of H. G. Wells's *The Outline of History* (1920), J. Arthur Thomson's *The Outline of Science* (1922), Hendrik Willem van Loon's *The Story of Mankind* (1921),[23] and Will Durant's *The Story of Philosophy* (1926).[24] Durant went on to produce a series called *The Story of Civilization*, which ran from 1935 to 1967. As Joan Shelley Rubin notes, the middlebrow outline depended upon "unapologetic generalists—individuals who believed in the ability of ordinary persons to grasp what they had to say" (210).

Literature for beginners remains very popular in the United States. Whereas books with the tag "for beginners" continue to target academics and intellectuals and deal with academic topics, contemporary volumes for "dummies" and "idiots" are pitched to general readers and are usually about more practical subjects. All three are in the how-to genre, but books for beginners of academic or intellectual topics, what I am calling "graphic guides" in this chapter, generally deal with knowledge that is less obviously applied. *Kierkegaard for Beginners* may or may not teach you how to use Kierkegaard, although it implies some possibility in that direction, whereas *MAC OS X Tiger for Dummies* should get you up and running. Books for dummies and idiots—and not just idiots, mind you, but "complete" idiots[25]—are more practical in aim and content. The first Dummies book was *DOS for Dummies*, published in 1991, which was followed by other titles on technological issues such as PC computing, Windows management, internet navigation, and so forth. Tens of millions of Dummies titles are in print, in multiple languages and covering topics like cooking, managing one's finances, planning a trip, and eating right. (There are also extensive online materials.) The Dummies brand now extends to online articles and podcasts.[26] From the start, the company appealed to and sought to assuage the anxiety that people feel about learning something new. The Complete Idiot's series backstory similarly begins with *The Complete Idiot's Guide to DOS* (1993), published just two years after the Dummies title. First published by Macmillan, and then by Pearson Education, the Complete Idiot's series is now handled by the conglomerate Dorling Kindersley Limited (DK). The original webpage for the Complete Idiot's series, now inaccessible, traced the philosophy of the series to John Muir's 1969 *How to Keep Your Volkswagen Alive, A Guide for the Compleat Idiot*, a humorous 1969 guide to car repair by John Muir. DK continues to publish the Complete Idiot's series—a search of the DK website in March 2020 yields 1,177 volumes—but now also offers books titled "Complete," such as *The Complete Golf Manual*.[27] Both the Dummies and the Complete Idiot's series include titles by celebrity authors such as Kristi Yamaguchi (on ice skating) and Wendy's founder, Dave Thomas (on franchising).

With these materials, practical knowledge takes priority over credentialing. The dummy and the idiot especially are descendants of the self-made American man or autodidact. At the same time, the identities of dummy, idiot, and beginner allow for strategic knowledge leveraging. Maybe it is okay to be an idiot about car repair, if you are a successful accountant, or to be a beginner of anthropology if a master of Hegel. For whatever reasons, and with whatever consequences, the dummy, the idiot, and the beginner are not just comfortable but exemplary identities.

The For Dummies and Complete Idiot's books began with practical subjects and have expanded into other areas, even fields of study—hence *Statistics for Dummies* and *The Complete Idiot's Guide to English Literature*. The books for beginners of academic topics, however, or graphic guides, began with profiles of influential thinkers and theorists from Marx forward and still focus on intellectual or cultural topics. The academic beginners books are not written by celebrities, not even by celebrity theorists. These books actually predate and may have provided inspiration for the For Dummies and Complete Idiot's series. Another important difference is that while the For Dummies and Complete Idiot's titles do include illustrations, images do not play as significant a role as they do in the graphic guides. The aforementioned *Complete Idiot's Guide to English Literature*, for example, features cartoons and graphic memes but is comparatively devoid of images.[28]

Ease of access is a major selling point even for the graphic guides. The guides work for adults not unlike the "high-interest, low readability" (hi-lo) books for younger readers, which offer high-interest themes at accessible reading levels (hi-lo theory, perhaps?).[29] Observable in the advertising language, and in the guides themselves, are both a populist rhetoric of access and a tongue-in-cheek attitude toward learning. In this sales pitch there is also a touch of antiestablishment sentiment—why should experts hoard knowledge and make it so darn intimidating? Such language appeals to the earnest desire to learn something new and perhaps challenging but also echoes the belief that intellectual work is unnecessarily difficult and insufficiently transparent. The claim in the sales pitch is that the graphic guides, however innovative, present material clearly and thus also ethically. We know, of course, that philosophy and theory cannot and perhaps should not always be easy to understand and that neither words nor pictures are transparent.[30] We can see in the guides themselves acknowledgment of the complexities and difficulties of language and thought alongside faith in their deliverability. The guides promise not total and immediate comprehension, as do the books for dummies and complete idiots, but rather provisional knowledge and a place to begin.

I Can Theorize!

The graphic guides are not just self-help books for aspiring intellectuals. They are theory for beginners. They approach and even resemble theory more properly in two respects: first, they cultivate an oppositional sensibility and encourage critique, and second, they model and encourage playful and imaginative thinking. The guides do not so much help us visualize theory as remind us that theory has visual as well as verbal dimensions. Theory comprehension involves an appreciation not only for ideas but for their presentation or dramatization.

While American middlebrow and DIY culture is not especially political, the graphic guides were openly leftist and especially critical of US policy. Rius, who launched the guides with *Cuba Para Principiantes*, began cartooning in the early 1960s, making two famous comics, *Los Supermachos* (The Supermales) and *Los Agachados* (The Crouching Ones), both of which criticize the Mexican government as well as foreign exploitation of Mexico (the first was made into a film by Alfonso Arau).[31] While many North American comics found their way south, including the imperialist Donald Duck comics of Walt Disney—hence Ariel Dorfman's and Armand Mattelart's stinging rebuttal *How to Read Donald Duck*[32]—the Mexican comic book has long been a vibrant genre with roots in satire despite some conservative impulses.[33] Stressing the artist's iconoclastic style—Rius uses multiple sorts of writing to indicate multiple voices, hand-writing almost everything because he does not like the homogenized look of computer design—Aaron Humphrey credits Rius with inspiring a genre and showing that there are "other ways of thinking, and thinking about, theoretical arguments." "Digital humanities as a discipline has shown an interest in producing scholarship which crosses and combines modalities in inventive and unexpected ways," notes Humphrey. "Many years before digital humanities, cartoonist-scholars like Rius were doing the same thing."

Dedicated to the people of Cuba, *Cuba for Beginners* offers a devastating critique of economic and cultural imperialism. Rius takes special aim at American rhetorics of democracy, as in this passage: "At the triumph of the [Castro] revolution Cuba was—like any of the countries of Latin America—a 'great little democracy' . . . part of the 'free world' and pride of 'western civilization.' . . . A representative democracy. This means: Sugar, her greatest wealth, was controlled, bought and sold by Uncle Sam. Banks? All controlled by Uncle Sam. Coffee? Fruit? Milk? Uncle Sam's too" (72). Rius questions the reputation of Castro as a dictator and concludes the volume by arguing that Cuba "is creating the possibility of a new man, of a new society based not only on money but in the common and better life" (153). As Rius acknowledges, "Cartoons from Mexican, Cuban, Canadian and American colleagues appear (mostly involuntarily) in this book. I want to say thanks to all of them." Illustrations from *Alice in Wonderland* also surface in a two-page spread (111–12). The Cuba book was translated into English, French, and German within a year of its debut. Writing on comics journalism, Santiago García cites Rocco Versaci's observation that "journalism in comics form has a sincerity superior to that of the conventional media, since the marginal position of the medium allows it to transmit truths that are silenced or manipulated by economic interests in the mainstream press" (167). Rius was among the first to use comics for political critique, pushing back against the function of some comics as conservative propaganda. Rius's popularity and his radical politics led to his abduction by the military and his presentation before a firing squad for a mock execution, staged to scare him into quiescence. It did not work (Duncan et al. 372).

The first wave of the For Beginners graphic guides appeared at least a decade before the first theory anthologies designed for university use.[34] The first theorist to be featured in the guides was Karl Marx, and indeed Marx features prominently in the next several titles as well. After *Cuba for Beginners* came *Marx for Beginners* (1976), also by Rius, followed by *Lenin for Beginners* (1977), *The Anti-Nuclear Handbook* (1978), later retitled *Nuclear Power for Beginners*, then titles in 1979 on Einstein and Freud and in 1980 on Mao and Trotsky. (*Marx for Beginners* was even made into a seven-minute film in 1978 by Cucumber Studios, though no other such projects followed.) The year 1981 brought *Capitalism for Beginners*; 1982, Marx's *Kapital for Beginners*, alongside other titles. In short, the translation of Rius's Cuba book kicked off the For Beginners series and a decidedly leftist tradition of "introductions," which were really interventions aimed at educable youth. *Lenin for Beginners*, for instance, is written against American fear of the Soviets and Communism; the book is dedicated to Rius, who "showed us the way." Its author, Richard Appignanesi—a poet, novelist, and art historian who holds a PhD in the social history of art—positions myth against facts, even bolding key terms lest we miss the lesson: "Anti-Bolshevik propaganda has always claimed that Lenin merely 'seized power,' that October [1917] was a **coup d'etat**, a conspiracy led by an undemocratic minority, etc. But the **facts** are that, throughout the summer of 1917 and after, **popular support** was shifting rapidly towards Bolshevism, and this was expressed dramatically in the urban and Soviet elections across Russia" (150). *Lenin for Beginners* is illustrated by Oscar Zarate, an Argentinean comic book artist and children's author best known in the United States as the illustrator of Alan Moore's *A Small Killing*.[35] The guides were not at first attentive to French theory, even though French theorists were beginning to find translation and circulation around the same time.

From the start, Rius identified as an academic outsider and autodidact, setting the tone of the series. In the second of his guides, *Marx for Beginners*, Rius opens with a long, handwritten preface about the challenges of the project for someone with his own modest educational background ("fifth grade elementary!") (8). Properly "academic" Marxists, he explains, would consider the book "sacrilege" (7), and the many scholarly volumes on Marx are "more difficult than Charlie himself" (8). Rius admits to remaining challenged by Marx, even after having finished *Marx for Beginners*: "Another reason for trying to take on Charlie was my wish to understand him—an ambition which I haven't satisfied" (7). In addition, the book is full of authorial warnings about Rius's ostensibly imperfect knowledge. Rius presumes that the reader, like himself, is curious but not too knowledgeable about the topic. The book is in fact a pretty masterful performance. It covers a lot of territory—religion, history, philosophy, and politics—smartly sampling and contextualizing Marx's writings. The first and best-known of the graphic guide creators, Rius has the ethos of a scholar or theorist himself, albeit a self-schooled one working for the people. "I like knowing that I have changed my readers' minds, that I have turned them into vegetarians, or that I have interested them in leftist politics," remarks Rius in an interview (Priego). Throughout the book he encourages his readers to go to the source, read Marx for themselves. This endorsement of autodidacticism continues throughout the series. No wonder, as Rius reports that he got little help from credentialed experts. Sarcastically he thanks "the illustrious Marx theoreticians who, when I asked them for a hand, replied politely that I must be out of my mind to start such a work. I really appreciate their 'spirit of co-operation'" (*Marx* 9).

There are actually two lines of graphic guides for beginners: the For Beginners series and the Introducing series. The publishing history here is a little confusing, as the original For Beginners series now appears under the Introducing title. The original For Beginners series began not with *Cuba for Beginners* but with Rius's second title, *Marx for Beginners*, or more precisely the English translation of that title. That series was published by Writers and Readers Publishing Cooperative and billed as "documentary comics books," a tag that emphasizes their realism more than their complexity or inventiveness.[36] The driving force behind the cooperative was Glenn Thompson, an activist and book publisher born in Harlem, New York. Thompson did not learn to read until age twelve, and he left school at fourteen, but he read voraciously as he traveled around the world and eventually moved to London. There he worked first as a social worker before opening up a progressive bookshop. He took inspiration from educator Paulo Freire, philosopher Ivan Illich, and novelist Arundhati Roy. In their 2001 obituary, John Berger and Margaret Busby remark that for Thompson, "literacy was more than the capacity to read, it was the capacity to lay claim to a legitimate inheritance." Thompson was a fierce advocate of self-education and his cooperative—also made up of Sian Williams, Richard Appignanesi, Lisa Appignanesi, John Berger, Arnold Wesker, and Chris Searle—oversaw the successful launch and fast expansion of the For Beginners line. The cooperative later fractured, however, and Thompson moved back to New York, where he founded a second branch called Writers and Readers Publishing, Inc. The original series stayed based in England and was later renamed the Introducing series. It is now under the direction of Richard Appignanesi and managed by Icon Books, which publishes related nonfiction titles such as the best-selling *Why Do People Hate America?* and *50 Facts That Should Change the World.* Icon is also behind the Postmodern Encounters series—short information books with color covers but no interior illustrations—as well as a children's imprint called Wizard Books, which specializes in the gamebook genre.[37] Between the For Beginners and the Introducing series, hundreds of graphic guides have appeared to date, although not all remain in print.

The leftist energies of the For Beginners series continued into the 1990s. The year 1993 saw the publication of Ron David's *Arabs and Israel for Beginners*, a critique of Zionism and probably the most polemical title since the heyday of Rius. Like Rius, David self-positions as a beginner to encourage reader identification and to prepare the reader for a difficult (re)education based on his own experiences. "Until six or seven years ago," David writes, "I was certain that the Israelis were on the side of the Angels, *period*. No questions, no conditions, no mitigating factors—just the Good Guys versus the Bad Guys." "A researcher who has his mind made up in advance," however, "is not a researcher, he's an ideologue and a justifier (He's also a liar and a fake, but we won't mention that)" (1). David even identifies as ex-dumb: "The second thing that strikes you is how dumb you've been. . . . It's like the Emperor's clothes: once you see the Emperor standing there with his little dingus hanging out, it's all you can do not to burst out laughing" (2). The beginner is here educated into a childlike awareness of reality. David pulls no punches: "I AM saying that the Palestinians, when *any version* of the *real* story is told, have a cause that conforms to EVERY PRINCIPLE in which Americans and others who pay lip-service to democracy believe. *That* is what this book is about. Read it with an open mind and decide for yourself" (3).[38] On the strength of that volume, David served for four years as series editor for the For Beginners line, producing over thirty-five titles.

Robert Lekachman's *Capitalism for Beginners*, to take another example, is as much a polemical meditation on the financial situation of 1981 as a (critical) history of capitalism. Its author, former chair of economics at Stony Brook University–SUNY, expresses concern about inflation, unemployment, and deficits and even calls for the "replacement of capitalism by democratic socialism" (173). He admonishes his readers to pay attention to the inequities of capitalism and think carefully about career choice: "Feel free to study art history, medieval Latin or classic Greek," he writes. "Just don't be astounded or resentful that your agemates who cannily opted for business administration, econometrics and computer science drive better cars, live in bigger houses, and mix their drinks with better brands of liquor—for the next forty years" (27). In these and other For Beginners titles, there is the sense that the beginner is a potentially dangerous dummy or idiot if they do not take certain lessons to heart.

Graphic guides to theory have since moved away from their leftist origins and their left-political didacticism. In Mexico, too, leftist politics were finally limited by the comic book form and the cultural nationalism that underwrote such. In many respects, Rius deviated from standard Mexican comic books, known as *historietas* ("little stories"), especially as he moved into the beginning books and other nonfiction projects. Anne Rubenstein claims that by that point he had left behind the common reader, courting instead (and to his own disappointment) "students, and certain people of the middle class with certain political worries" (quoted in Rubenstein, 158–59). Rubenstein explains that because historietas, like much of Mexican popular culture, were so allied with cultural nationalism, Rius failed to develop a left-wing alternative to the genre, despite his stature. Ironically, he wound up in the camp of the censors to some degree, arguing that comics were dangerously capitalist in outlook and thus should be regulated. In any case, he "now makes books for the university-educated art audience" (Rubenstein 160).[39] That conclusion may be a little harsh. No doubt the interplay of leftist and more custodial energies then and now is quite complex. It is true that the For Beginners books have best resonated with left-leaning and intellectual but increasingly middle-class and academic-professional types.[40] In and around these books, the beginner at least persists as an educable figure.

While expanding theory's form and texture, the guides have also gotten less Marxist-materialist, which for some also means less theoretical.[41] They were launched with hope for political awareness and consciousness-raising and have morphed into something less ideologically revolutionary and more predictable, shoring up rather than challenging the middle-class professionalism of academia. Their ideal reader these days is not the potential activist but rather the undergraduate or graduate student keen to enter the academy, or the general reader with an interest in intellectual and cultural topics. Recent titles, for instance, cover things as varied as queer theory, the American presidency, the Black Panthers, black women, and epigenetics. The guides have morphed in keeping with user expectations and practices. And granted, the guides have other influences and origins besides Rius.[42] Rius himself has meanwhile continued to publish leftist graphic works on a huge range of topics with the Grijalbo publishing conglomerate in Mexico.

If the guides encourage oppositional thinking and critique, at least at the level of theory, they also emphasize theory's imaginative dimension in their imagetext presentation. They recall not only the middlebrow materials I have already discussed but also imagetext genres for children and teenagers, specifically comics, beginning reader picturebooks pioneered for children in the 1950s, and contemporary graphic novels or book-length comic narratives.[43] Recognized as educationally valuable as early as the 1930s,[44] comics were not widely incorporated into school curricula until decades later, with the rise of the ostensibly more respectable "graphic novel," which may have also helped popularize the graphic guides.[45] The guides resemble graphic novels in a number of respects—(auto)biographical focus, self-reflexiveness, antiauthoritarian tone—and while beyond the scope of this chapter, a comparative analysis of the guides and graphic novels might be instructive. Both genres emerged around 1970 and proliferated in the next few years.[46]

The graphic guides also resemble the beginning reader picturebooks designed to help children learn to read. Responding to alarms sounded by John Hersey and Rudolf Flesch that America's children were failing on that front, and that partly to blame were the "Pallid Primers" (Hersey's phrase) used in the schools, HarperCollins and Random House each launched a series of early readers to fill the ostensible void. The HarperCollins series was titled I Can Read! and Random House's was Beginner Books. As Rebekah Fitzsimmons explains in her analysis of this genre, the early reader picturebook is a sixty-four-page text designed to facilitate reading by way of strategic word-image correspondence. The language is deliberately simple; words are usually drawn from a predetermined list of acceptable, age-appropriate (sometimes age-aspirant) selections. *The Cat in the Hat* (1957), first in the Beginner Books series, resulted from a challenge issued to Dr. Seuss: to write a "whole word" book appropriate for six- and seven-year-olds, using no more than 225 different words from an approved list. Seuss decided "that the first two words on the list that rhymed would be the basis for the book's title," hence *The Cat in the Hat* (Mintz, *Huck's Raft* 296). Meanwhile, HarperCollins introduced its I Can Read! series with another successful picturebook, *Little Bear*, written by Else Holmelund Minarik and illustrated by Maurice Sendak. The major selling point for the early reader picturebook, Fitzsimmons emphasizes, is that children can read it "by themselves"; that phrase appears in many advertisements, she points out, and might be read as a not-so-subtle dig at the public school system (23). The early reader picturebook was designed for home more than for school use and to encourage independent reading.

It is a short step from "I can read!" to "I can theorize!," especially if we understand reading as theorizing. Like the beginning reader picturebooks, the guides are designed to help readers "read," not in the more literal sense but in the sense of understanding ideas and concepts as well as tone. In so doing, they arguably play on as much as respond to anxiety about the lack of comprehension and knowledge. Like the beginning readers, they help adult beginners of theory catch up independently of school. Making and decoding meaning, understanding the relation of word to world, individuating but also joining discourse communities: these are among the pleasures of reading in the enlarged sense, the pleasures of theorizing. Like the beginning readers, the graphic guides presume a desire to learn. They capitalize upon and help draw out the sense of excitement that can attend learning and reading. Bruss remarks that the thrill of theory hinges on the promise that confusion will resolve into understanding. "There is an intoxication even in this simple passage from obscurity to sense, from helplessness to mastery—or to (increasingly) a mastery just out of reach, always promised but forever postponed" (129). And the understanding they bring hinges on the imagetext presentation, which allows simultaneous and layered meanings as well as tonalities.[47]

The guides generally narrate the development of an influential life and body of work, making various adjustments and offering historical or other contextualizations to present a clear story of origin, maturation, and influence—not unlike the case study genre, in which original material is reworked for the reader's instruction. In a sense, they are didactic, seeking to convey certain ideas and to enable comprehension. There is also a touch of fandom and superhero fetish about some (and are not these supertheorists?), but some titles are gently critical of their subjects. The guides are humorous and sometimes even satirical.[48] In this way, they come closer tonally to theory proper than do most academic textbooks on theory, which tend to be more earnest than playful. The guides seek to enliven and entertain but they are also ambitious and heady at times. In the first 20 (out of 176) pages of *Introducing Foucault*, for example, we encounter the ideas not only of Foucault but also of Hegel, Hyppolite, Kojève, Sartre, Heidegger, Husserl, Merleau-Ponty, Bachelard, Koyré, Kuhn, and Canguilhem.

The guides tend to run a hundred pages or more, some substantially so; at 379 pages long, *The History of Cinema for Beginners* seems more like a standard textbook. Recent For Beginner books have slightly larger dimensions, about 6 x 9 inches, as opposed to the 5 x 8-1/4 size of the Introducing line. Their format seems simultaneously high and low, reminiscent of comics and avant-garde art alike. The guides have glossy color covers but the inside text is always black and white, presumably to minimize costs but probably also to accentuate the documentary effect. The black and white is generally effective and occasionally surreal, as in *Introducing Mind and Brain*, reminiscent of Charles Adams and Edward Gorey. Image styles vary across the guides. By and large, the images amplify, enrich, and even complicate the expository narrative; they rarely illustrate in a narrow sense. In one of only two scholarly treatments of the guides,[49] William Nericcio remarks that Oscar Zarate's illustration of Freud sitting as a child for a family portrait in *Freud for Beginners* "is as succinct a summary of psychoanalytic suggestions regarding the dynamics of sexuality in bourgeois European families as any that one might find in a prose account" (83). Moreover, he continues, "who better than a graphic artist to render critically the contours of 'dreamwork' and 'the unconscious'?" (83). Generally, the guides are written and illustrated by different people, and occasionally an illustrator outshines the author, as with *Introducing Kafka*, drawn by Robert Crumb and considered a masterpiece of graphic art. Many make use of collage, layering different kinds of images in inventive patterns.

In *Words about Pictures*, Nodelman emphasizes that the image-text relation in picturebooks is not merely complementary but also combative, in that words and pictures convey information differently even when supposedly in sync. This combination of complementarity and combativeness is also typical of the guides, even if they are closer in form to "sequential art" like comics and graphic novels (rather than the "suspended animation" of picturebooks, as Nathalie op de Beeck puts it in *Suspended Animation*). In other words, while they do partake in the tradition of American digest and summary, which presumes the easy and transparent delivery of information through visuals, the guides also take full advantage of the complexity and ambiguity of images and of image-text coordination, not unlike the contemporary picturebooks used in P4C. There are plenty of examples in the guides of image-text tension (sometimes playful), which gets interesting since most of the books are not written and illustrated by the same people. In *Nietzsche for Beginners*, for instance, Marc Sautet's text earnestly recounts Nietzsche's breakdown and withdrawal from the world, but Patrick Boussignac's illustrations show Nietzsche telling Jesus—seemingly in a dream sequence[50]—that God is dead, then Jesus getting down off the cross and kicking the shit out of Nietzsche, such that Nietzsche softens his rhetoric, going from "God is dying!" to "God looks ill" and finally "God's in good shape . . . damn it!" (181–83; see Figure 2). These declarations are part of an illustrative bubble, so I am assuming creative license by the artist, but perhaps Sautet wrote the bubble text? Another example comes in *Introducing Anthropology*, written by Merryl Wyn Davies and illustrated by Piero, in a section about Margaret Mead's influence on the childcare expert Dr. Benjamin Spock. Instead of Dr. Spock, however, we see *Star Trek*'s Mr. Spock. Our wise Vulcan verifies that Mead "gained insight into American culture" through her studies of other cultures (153), comparative culture study being a topic about which Mr. Spock knows a thing or two. This image might approach what W. J. T. Mitchell calls a "metapicture," a picture about the art of picturing, although it is perhaps more culturally dependent than the metapicture examples Mitchell gives, most famously the rabbit-duck drawing that so preoccupied psychologist Joseph Jastrow and Wittgenstein after him (*Picture Theory*).

Nietzsche for Beginners is organized in "movements" rather than chapters, probably to play up the Wagnerian drama for which Nietzsche had a complicated regard. The book—words and images both—is comic and

FIGURE 2. Marc Sautet and Patrick Boussignac, *Nietzsche for Beginners* (1990).

theatrical. As with many of these books, it is hard to distinguish words from pictures. Freud appears at one point to make a psychological diagnosis. Key lines are in capital letters and punctuated with exclamation marks. Recounting Nietzsche's original plan to be a priest (like his father and grandfather before him), the text by then reads, "However, Satan was also very interested in young Fritz's career, judging from the company he kept at the age of 18!" (Sautet 17). This is followed by "Who was to win the battle for his soul, the Devil or God?" in bold type and on top of the page, at which point we are escorted to the Nietzsche Museum, guided in our biographical tour by a crone-like docent dressed in all black. Later we see Nietzsche posing questions to influential thinkers such as F. A. Lange and Schopenhauer—or rather, we see Nietzsche's head in the back of an armchair as our philosopher engages in imaginary dialogue with these thinkers (24–25). And so on. As information about Nietzsche's life and influences comes fast and furious, we are reassured in small type at the bottom of page 44: "Don't panic: there's a glossary at the end of this book!!!" *Nietzsche for Beginners* is over the top, but so was Nietzsche.

Foucault for Beginners (1993) is one of the more metafictional if not also metapictional guides, largely because the author, Lydia Alix Fillingham, is drawn into the text by the book's illustrator, Moshe Süsser. A likeness of Fillingham pops out of Foucault's head on the first page, accompanied by the text "First of all, who is this guy, Michel Foucault?" (2; see Figure 3). Foucault's head is styled as a coconut, probably because we are also told that his "name is pronounced like the English girl's name, Michelle. Foucault is **foo** as in fooey, plus **co** as in coco-nut, coming down harder on the coconut" (2). The image is comic but also sets up a slightly adversarial stance toward Foucault, a stance that is decidedly feminist. At several points in the volume, Fillingham (or Fillingham's image) talks back to our famous theorist. Musing on Foucault's snootiness—"He thought you needed to have a very good background in philosophy and history or his work would just be misunderstood. He wouldn't have approved of this book at all"—Fillingham (and Süsser?) follows with a sketch of Foucault saying, "A little knowledge is a dangerous thing" (which Foucault never said exactly; that is a paraphrase of Alexander Pope's famous line), followed in turn by a sketch of Fillingham wagging her finger and saying, "I don't care what he would have thought. I think a little understanding is better than none, and you have to start somewhere" (79). At another point, reviewing Foucault's declarations about "man" (as in humankind), the author or illustrator adds this full-page parenthetical comment: "(Foucault doesn't ever comment on the maleness of man)" (84). Later still, Fillingham "completes" Foucault's thoughts about prostitution, adding another parenthetical note: "(Whoa. Did Foucault say all that? Almost. Almost all of it. . . . He didn't quite get around to saying that this potential threat to gender roles is contained by an overemphasis on gender roles. But I'm sure he was just about to.)" (132). Fillingham and Süsser also give Simone de Beauvoir a cameo when discussing Foucault's debts to Jean-Paul Sartre and their shared indifference (if not hostility) to women. Understanding Foucault involves understanding his limitations, and *Foucault for Beginners* effectively conveys Foucault's ideas alongside feminist criticism of such.

Fillingham's feminist critique of Foucault (and Sartre) applies to theory more generally as well as to the graphic guides. Needless to say, the conceptualization and practice of theory has been a rather masculinist affair from the start (no matter where we say it does start). The guides reproduce more than challenge the sexism and male privilege of theory. There is still no book devoted to de Beauvoir, for instance, despite her status and influence. Or to Hannah Arendt, Julia Kristeva, Hélène Cixous, Eve Kosofsky Sedgwick, bell hooks, Judith Butler, Gayatri Spivak, J. Jack Halberstam—the list goes on. In the Introducing series, only one woman theorist gets her own book, psychoanalyst Melanie Klein. In the For Beginners series,

FIGURE 3. Lydia Alix Fillingham and Moshe Susser, *Foucault for Beginners* (1993).

none does. There is a "Women" category on the For Beginners website that features volumes on Ayn Rand, Harriet Tubman, Jane Austen, and Toni Morrison. But no women thinkers are listed in the "Philosophy and Literature" category (and only two writers, Austen and Morrison). Meanwhile, plenty of male theorists get stand-alone attention, from those I have already mentioned to Deleuze, Derrida, Descartes, Fanon, Hegel, Heidegger, Jung, Kant, Kierkegaard, McLuhan, Piaget, Plato, and Saussure (alongside literary writers). The omissions are not only a matter of gender bias; we do not see volumes on queer of color critique, or on Edward Said, or on Fred Moten. There is no *Introducing Intersectionality*.

The guides, then, have some limitations individually and taken as a whole. They do not fix the biases of theory, nor are they always improvements upon source material. They do work to complicate and sometimes improve theory dissemination. Looking at the various modalities in and through which these texts operate—in the only other scholarly article about the guides[51]—Aaron Scott Humphrey comes to a similar conclusion. He sees these texts as constructing "an argument which is larger than, and different from, our sense of a book's purely linguistic meaning." At the least, thinks Humphrey, the guides interrogate the idea that singular "authorial voice is central to academic writing" and help us "challenge and re-evaluate normative academic discourses and hegemonic textual practices." He stops short of calling the guides "theory," but the implication is there. At the least, we can say that the guides have a complex relationship to their source texts and to more academic sorts of theory dissemination. They sometimes affirm what one learns in a theory class, but they also offer and capitalize upon knowledge in other registers. They work to demystify thought and accommodate the reader. Certainly they help to manage anxiety in the face of theory. As such, they set the stage for more contemporary ventures in theory expression articulation, including web comic strips such as Hannah McCann's "Foucault Explained with Hipsters." Not to mention theory action figures and other merchandise. In *Avidly Reads Theory*, which I am tempted to describe as a graphic guide to theory without the graphics, Jordan Alexander Stein attends to how theory feels or is experienced personally and (inter)generationally. The five chapters of the book consider "silly theory," "stupid theory," "sexy theory," "seething theory," and "stuck theory." "Silly Theory" focuses on the playing of "silly games with serious ideas" in theory, very much connected to the development of new media platforms and experiences such as Twitter and Buzzfeed (3). "Many media-literature (and especially younger theory heads)," Stein writes, "are ever more inclined to see that philosophical ideas can be pithy, aphoristic, and even pertinent to the kinds of banalities that swell social media feeds. Hence the existence of Chaka Lacan" (15). Stein also emphasizes that the "ultimate context for these experiments is their form" and that their experimental or novel form not only resonates with media culture but also pushes against intellectual snobbery (16).

The affective aspects of the graphic guides, alongside their metatextual and metapictorial tendencies, arguably bring the guides closer to theory as it is understood and practiced today. Trask argues that the postwar ironic style of play and detachment lives on in contemporary criticism and theory. Belief is no longer required for analysis; quite the opposite, according to Trask. "The postwar university does not reject belief," writes Trask, "but brackets it, turns it into a pliable faculty" (22). Professors revel in a "makeshift sense of belonging" and practice an "array of ironizing strategies" (22). The playfulness—even the campiness—of the guides may well support or at least align with the skeptical or ironic style of modern academia. The guides certainly model tone and posture even as they deliver content. *Foucault for Beginners* teaches us about Foucault but also encourages a healthy skepticism toward Foucault. We are not asked to believe or disbelieve; rather, we are encouraged to think and play with the material. This playful style or investment may be liberating or it may be a feature of the contemporary academic habitus—or both.

Anecdotes of Use

I doubt that Durant could have titled *The Story of Philosophy* as instead *Philosophy for Complete Idiots*. It never would have occurred to him anyway. On the one hand, earnestness seems to mark the earlier historical scene of middlebrow uplift, while playfulness and parody seem more typical now. On the other hand, as I have noted already, there is a long-standing enthusiasm for the American autodidact, understood to be wise or profound in his ignorance/innocence. Americans are the ultimate beginners, the national mythology goes, open to experience and thirsty for knowledge. For whatever reason, judging from the success of contemporary how-to books, there is little shame now in being a dummy or idiot—or, rather, a "dummy" or "idiot," the quotation marks signaling a certain self-awareness (perhaps mock self-deprecation).

But what about the guides and their users? Situated somewhere between popular and academic culture, the guides are tricky to categorize and potentially embarrassing to use in formal learning situations. They are likely used by two groups of people: general readers interested in intellectual topics and academics who want some quick information and orientation. In the current moment, I assume the latter to be mostly graduate students either already working within or hoping to join academia, with some advanced undergraduates as well as some newish faculty members (and maybe also scholars tackling a new field). The student is a particular sort of beginner, and the graduate student is an even more particular sort. Graduate students make for an interesting group, poised between beginner and professional status, in need of pedagogical support but seeking knowledge and legitimacy. Not that established scholars are immune to such pressures.

Cusset considers how undergraduate students employ theory source texts; here I consider how graduate students and faculty use this ostensibly supplemental graphic material. I wonder, is it okay (professionally as much as psychologically) for graduate students and faculty to self-present as beginners within their disciplines? How much does the particular topic matter? Being an academic beginner is potentially risky, perhaps all the more so when it comes to theory. In his essay "The Fear of Theory," Roger Simon opines that learning theory makes graduate students anxious because it disrupts their desire to repeat past experiences of knowledge and competency. The experience can be agonizing because these people are not only accomplished students but successful adults by other measures. Reflecting on Simon's essay and the fear of theory, Deborah Britzman counters that theory is anxiety-making for everyone because it "may remind us of something we cannot remember: the passionate inexperience of having to learn before we understand while feeling the force of wishing to know without having to learn" (*Psychoanalyst* 63). Of course, this ostensible fear of theory may be contingent on the lack of theory education or encounter in undergraduate schooling. And it may be overstated. If we believe Cusset, undergraduates are delighted by theory, which might suggest that some graduate students would not find theory too unnerving. In fact, some might have been seduced by theory into the profession. I have already suggested, too, that the guides work to convey an ironic or at least playful relationship to theory, whether or not we see that as a good thing. My impression, though, is that even new graduate students conversant with theory do worry that they do not know theory well enough. That concern is rarely as pronounced when it comes to literature, as some English professors bemoan. What happens when emergent scholars feel underprepared in their encounters with theory and turn to the graphic guides for help? Do they see themselves as learning about theory or also learning to theorize?

With such issues in mind, I queried friends and colleagues by email and on social media three times—in 2011, 2012, and 2016—both in my home department at the University of Florida and within my broader academic network, asking for anecdotes about use of the graphic guides. I wanted to sound out Pierre Bourdieu's argument in *Distinction* that while scholastic popularizations such as handbooks are acceptable within academic culture, more "ordinary" popularizations tend to stigmatize the individual who tries to use them.[52] Graphic guides make for an interesting test of this claim, as they reside somewhere between scholastic and ordinary popularization. Also, I wondered, is Bourdieu right to claim that those admitted into serious culture adopt an ironic relation to that culture, one that looks nearly like disavowal, as indicated by those quotation marks around "idiot" or "beginner"? Bourdieu holds that while the autodidact approaches learning with zeal, perhaps even fanaticism, the credentialed learner wears knowledge dispassionately, as if to say, "What, this old thing, Lacan?" According to Bourdieu, those making the strongest claims to knowledge do so with strategic affect, such that this style of relation is what really distinguishes the wannabe from the presumed master.[53] When I repeated the query in 2016, I found myself curious also about how the responses by graduate students and faculty alike might complicate Cusset's distinction between amateur and serious theory user (recognizing that the use of the guides does not equal the use of theory source texts).

I did not encourage respondents to be anonymous, so it is possible that responses might have differed under conditions of anonymity, but I was not after objectivity necessarily. Some respondents reported feeling underprepared when starting graduate school but also intuiting that they should not admit to such or reveal their methods of redress. Consider these remarks from former doctoral student Rebekah Fitzsimmons:

> Everyone in class spoke so knowledgeably about essays that were "Derridean" or "Lacanian" or dropped names of philosophers or German thinkers that I had never heard of, never mind read. The typical academic inferiority complex set in—I had wasted all of that time reading Shakespeare, contemporary African American lit, Romantic poetry, modernist drama when I should have been buried in all of this THEORY! My roommates at the time, both higher level PhDs, assured me that I would pick up the lingo over time but I felt like I was sitting in on all of these conversations that I was sure were really interesting if only I could understand them!
>
> I did not, however, admit to anyone to having read these books (until now). I was embarrassed that I was so far behind even my fellow first year MA students, many of whom were younger than I was because I delayed starting grad school after graduating college.

> I essentially took a "Intro to Theory" course on my own, over the first semester of graduate school and think I would have continued to be very, very lost without it. I am willing to admit that I tend to be rather linear in my thinking sometimes—I like to read my books from the beginning through to the end, hate watching movies from the middle and want very much to know where a thinker or theory is situated in terms of a historical time line (if there is a such thing as history of course). Jumping into the middle of a theoretical discourse doesn't seem to be a problem for others, or perhaps they were reading these books in private too.

Another former doctoral student, Chris Gage, was less embarrassed to report on his use of the illustrated guides and indeed described such as transformative. Chris came first to *Introducing Evolutionary Psychology* (by way of *The Matrix*—long story) and later used similar titles on critical theory as he switched fields and sought admission to English graduate programs. On the one hand, Chris's experience suggests that the not-yet-credentialed can crash the institutional party. On the other hand, both reports underscore that use of the guides is understood in developmental terms, meaning that the guides are eventually outgrown and left behind. As for the posture of irony and disavowal discussed by Bourdieu, I saw some of that in the responses, too, both in the humor of some accounts and in more cautious reports that these books are helpful to a point.

Colleagues at Florida and elsewhere expressed much the same range of opinions and attitudes. "I used some of those (on Foucault, Derrida, and Lacan, if I remember correctly) to survive doctoral studies," reported Annette Wannamaker of Eastern Michigan University. "It was not something I shared with too many people at the time because I was embarrassed about not knowing things, but I recommend them to my grad students all the time now." "Any former or current graduate student who says they don't use them is lying," declared Tali Noimann at the Borough of Manhattan Community College. "Anything that saves people the soul-deadening experience of reading Heidegger," opines my Florida colleague Raúl Sánchez, "can only be considered a boon to the (post)human race." One respondent emphasized that she tends to use graphic guides not as an introduction to a subject but as a refresher course.

Some doctoral students offered intriguing critiques of the guides. Elliott Kuecker took issue with both their content and their narrative form:

> When you read a "For Beginners" book on a topic you know a lot about, however, you realize how subjective these books are. I read *Anarchism For Beginners* and saw that Americans were largely excluded

> and the emphasis was on political anarchism, rather than gender and sexuality. That is fine, but the book then misleads folks who view it more like a history of the topic, not a single approach to the topic. Of course, all books are like that, but the "For Beginners" title is misleading and most of them are written by a single author, meaning they are so completely subjective. His view of the history of anarchism is really limited to how he learned about it and what he has read. A more peer-reviewed or multi-author approach might live up to the "For Beginners" title better. It seems like the press company does not get editors who are experts on the topic, but instead solicits authors who know something about the topic and edits for issues other than content.
>
> Lastly, if you read the "about us" section on the press website, you get a long story about how the founder was a self-taught drop-out and how the books are inspired by his inner-city experience. It says that the founder wanted to "unlock" knowledge that was exclusively for "academia" by making illustrated guides. I think it's a bit insulting to suggest that "inner-city" people and "average" people are unable to understand "academic" language and therefore must read PICTURES and certainly would not be able to understand full paragraphs! I understand the problems with access to knowledge, but their argument suggests that non-scholarly readers are illiterate and needs things given to them in the most simple manner. Besides, some of the theories they are writing about are not simple, and providing pictures and short sentences doesn't work if the ideas are complicated enough. You do a disservice to the theory if you dumb it down enough.

Elliott felt that the attempt to democratize via an imagetext presentation too easily borders upon anti-intellectualism and condescension. He was not the only one to express ambivalence about the guides. Several responders noted a preference for nonillustrated and more officially scholastic guides, such as the Very Short Introductions series. Their lack of illustration, alongside their connections to academic institutions, may make these more comfortable.

My most recent query about these guides prompted several current and past UF doctoral students to reflect on the growing acceptance of multimodal forms as scholarship and as an aid to theorizing. "I think as more scholarship becomes public and incorporates visual media," muses Shannon Butts, "the use of open source, social networks, and illustrated guides gain credibility." Poushali Bhadury gave similar feedback, underscoring also the proliferation of theory and criticism memes such as Research Wahlberg and Feminist Ryan Gosling. I detected in 2016 a bit more willingness to see the guides as legitimate and even to understand them as academic work—even theorizing—in their own right. Gwen Athene Tarbox at Western Michigan University concurs with this general line of thinking, noting that "the graduate acceptance of comics studies as a discipline will undoubtedly impact that way that subsequent generations of scholars view the theory guides. . . . In fact, I feel that the guides, whether illustrated or not, must be very difficult to write, as one is called upon to synthesize so much information in a way that is accessible to non-experts."

The most common and least vexed response I got was that the guides can be helpful in teaching. I agree, having used *The Body for Beginners* and the more recent *Queer: A Graphic History* in undergraduate classes. Regine Rossi of St. Thomas Aquinas College writes she is happy to use anything that works with her graduate students as "I've got enough instructional battles to wage elsewhere." My Florida colleague Roger Maioli pointed to the need for clear explanation of problems and difficult ideas in a political climate hostile to thinking. Craig Dionne (now at Eastern Michigan) recalls that teaching these books in the 1990s at Carnegie Mellon led to some ribbing from colleagues. And a few respondents had mixed feelings about teaching (with) the guides. Cydney Alexis recalled teaching *Introducing Barthes* in courses at the University of Wisconsin–Madison and remarked that her students "always find the illustrations hilariously off-point and terrible." She was the only one to criticize the illustrations, although I did not ask for evaluations of such. Katherine Arens of the University of Texas at Austin worried that the guides tend to present theory more as a "secret handshake than a tool."[54]

No one drew a connection between the guides and the sort of beginner-friendly theory I discuss earlier in this chapter. Ed White of Tulane University did speculate that the appeal of the guides might "have to do with the use of visual formulas (the Greimas rectangle, Lacanian knots, Saussurian equations), mostly in French theory."[55] He reflected further that teaching theory "often involves drawing on the board and then sketching around the image, as if there's something visual about the explanatory process that works well with pictures," which suggests a theorizing dimension to the guides as much as a pedagogical aspect to theory. As he reminds us, the guides are pedagogical but can trend theoretical in interesting ways, just as theory can trend pedagogical. Lauren Berlant of the University of Chicago did not comment on the guides but instead directed me to Hannah McCann's "Judith Butler Explained with Cats," writing, "it's extremely good for theory anxiety management and as inspiration for producing new theory genres."

What can we conclude from these anecdotes? Most obviously, academics have ambivalent but increasingly positive attitudes toward theory-proximate materials. Users remain hesitant to see the guides as equivalent to theory source texts. The guides were typically presumed supplemental to the real thing. Even so, I got the sense that the guides did often replace the source texts because of time and labor pressures, suggesting that theory classics work rather like literary classics: we "know" them by general reference and professional situation without necessarily reading them closely (or at all). A classic, Mark Twain famously quipped, is a "book which people praise and don't read," and it turns out that there are many works of literature and theory that academics claim to know (even love) without having read. How to feel and think about this phenomenon? In his hilarious *How to Talk about Books You Haven't Read*, Pierre Bayard mock-praises the many strategies of "not reading" we all employ, recognizing that literary knowledge is indeed contextual, provisional, and prone to memory loss and distortion. We often can get away with not reading a text but instead skimming it, knowing about it, maybe seeing the movie. Even if we read something, we may not retain it. But through a comic web of misreadings and misunderstandings, Bayard finally pushes us toward the conclusion that reading actually does matter in our understanding. No doubt. I do not think *Foucault for Beginners* gives us the same insight into and appreciation for Foucault's ideas or style as do Foucault's own materials (even in translation). And yet, theory, like literature, is an overwhelming subject, ever shifting and expanding. We cannot read everything.

However we feel about reading the guides vis-à-vis reading source texts, it is nice to see there has been an easing of anxiety about the use of the guides and especially as imagetexts, thanks to growing interest in comics, the digital humanities, and multimodal materialities more generally. Increasingly, comics are considered not only a serious literary undertaking but also an appropriate—even superior—form for scholarship.[56] Building on the insights of Thierry Groensteen and others, Nick Sousanis argues that "comics hold sequential and simultaneous modes" of presentation "in electric tension," playing on and perhaps altering our perception as much as our cognitive understanding (63). Sousanis wrote the first dissertation in comic form, which Harvard University Press published as *Unflattening*. Sousanis may overstate the flatness of scholarship, but he is right to say that comics offer an ideal "means to capture and convey our thoughts, in

Not-Index · *Andrew Causey and C. Thresher*

PART OF THIS STORY YOU HAVE TO TELL YOURSELF

Things, cracked, *passim*
Writing the world back to form, 34, 43, 69
Duck: following like a, 7
Fixing, repairing, mending, 82, 128
Empty spaces: filling in, 84

Symptoms: just one more thing, 66, 94
Improvising in the Midst, 58, 109
Stories: pondering weak links, 72, 92

FIGURE 4. Andrew Causey and C. Thresher, "Not-Index," in *The Hundreds*, by Lauren Berlant and Kathleen Stewart (2019).

all their tangled complexity, and a vehicle well-suited for explorations to come" (67). In their experimental work *The Hundreds* (2019), Lauren Berlant and Kathleen Stewart invited four colleagues to compose indexes to the book, and Andrew Causey and C. Thresher responded with a graphic "Not-Index" very reminiscent of the guides (see Figure 4). At Florida, we host a comics studies journal called *ImageTexT*, the brainchild of my late colleague Donald Ault, and we have just launched another journal called *Sequentials*, which "solicits and publishes interpretations of various academic subjects or themes drawn and explained through the comics medium."[57] The guides likewise hold sequence and simultaneity in tension and might qualify as theory or criticism.

Reflecting on Cusset, I do not see, finally, much distinction between serious and casual users of theory. Perhaps the distinctions Cusset observes are more specific to the Ivy League institutions where French theory manifested. Perhaps I am too casual a user to judge. Or perhaps the casualization of theory is so widespread and diversified that undergraduates (especially at more elite colleges) are no longer the only ones prone to theory infatuation. I will confess to a little infatuation myself. But even as I love theory, I am not wedded to theory source texts, since ideas migrate and morph. Whatever we conclude about the guides and their cultural meaning, I encourage more investigation of theory's forms and users and, in particular, its investment in beginners, which at the very least pushes against more elitist attitudes and practices.

3 / Literature for Minors

The previous chapter considered imagetext materials about critical theory and related topics pitched to beginners. This chapter returns to children's literature more conventionally understood, tracing the construction of children's literature as theoretical and oppositional—as, in short, a literature for minors, and perhaps approaching what Gilles Deleuze and Félix Guattari called a minor literature. The term *minor* is a legal as well as broadly conceptual one, variously reflecting, shoring up, and contesting the adult-child hierarchy. As an adjective it means lesser in significance or scale (as in a minor chord or key); as a verb, *minor* means to study something in a secondary way. As a noun, *minor* designates a person not yet accorded full legal status. Children's literature might also be described as a literature for minors, or for people with certain needs and even rights but not yet accorded adult standing. Adults can also be minors, of course, when not fully enfranchised in a society.[1] Much progressive children's literature in fact deals with how some adults as well as children are discriminated against, dispossessed, impoverished, and otherwise made minor socially if not also legally. In that sense, it is a literature for as well as about minors.

Literature for minors also approaches the category of minor literature as outlined by Gilles Deleuze and Félix Guattari in *Kafka: Toward a Minor Literature*. Minor literature is nonnormative but typically written in the language of the oppressor and "affected with a high coefficient of deterritorialization" (16). In their reading, Kafka "marks the impasse that bars access to writing for the Jews of Prague and turns their literature into something impossible—the impossibility of not writing, the impossibility of writing in German, the impossibility of writing otherwise" (16).[2] I hear echoes of Rose's claim that children's literature is an impossibility because children do not write their own literature or what they produce is not usually understood as literature.[3] True, children's literature might better fit the category were it written by kids in the "language" of adults. Fanfiction written by young people might be a better example of minor literature in these terms. But even as an adult endeavor, conventionally published children's literature resembles minor literature to the extent that its practitioners contradict normative attitudes about what children should or can do.[4]

The idea that children's literature is a literature for minors if not also a minor literature underwrites P4C's interest in children's materials from the early 1970s forward, and especially so for contemporary PwC with its emphasis on child agency and children's rights (if also posthumanism). Matthews believed that the best children's literature challenges conventional perception and models philosophical thinking; even Lipman saw it had the potential for such. Murris sees metafictional picturebooks as crucial for PwC pedagogy. This broad understanding has emerged from the literature itself but also from commentary by philosophers, theorists, and scholars. In *Freud in Oz*, I underscore the significance of psychoanalysis along these lines. Here I spotlight some additional contexts and figures in the theorization of literature for minors. After that, I will focus on queer theory more specifically, arguing that some children's literature functions like queer theory for kids, even as queer theory has moved closer to narrative forms we associate with younger readers.

Lest anyone doubt the pervasiveness of this belief in children's literature as theoretical and oppositional, consider recent scholarship in children's literature studies. In her 2008 *The Outside Child, in and out of the Book*, for instance, Christine Wilkie-Stibbs notes that "children's literature has long been a forum for championing the cause of the underdog" but sees an intensification of that function with the late twentieth-century "wave of new realism" marked by "innovative writers" writing on taboo topics and bringing into the field various "outsider" subjectivities (ix–x). In support of this claim she cites scholarship by Roberta Seelinger Trites, Hamida Bosmajian, Clare Bradford, John Stephens, and Robyn McCallum on the critical/ideological work of recent writing for children and young adults. In joined and separate works, Mickenberg and Nel document the progressive and even radical history of Anglophone children's literature. They focus on American material, as does Gary D. Schmidt, who demonstrates how children's literature from 1930 to 1960 was self-consciously engaged with the democratic experiment called America. If not consistently progressive, he suggests, books from this period were mindful of cultural diversity and committed to a pluralist, even international vision. That commitment intensified into the 1970s, responding to and further spurring the growth of the children's book market and the expansion of alternative niche markets and presses (L. Marcus 273). Sara L. Schwebel explains in turn how American works of historical fiction came in the 1980s to serve as textbooks in middle school classrooms especially, further cementing the association of children's literature with progressive social energies. Reynolds, meanwhile, tracks early twentieth-century radical British children's literature in *Left Out*, providing a companion volume to Mickenberg. With Jane and Michael Rosen, Reynolds has also published an anthology of radical British children's literature published between 1900 and 1960.

That is not to say, of course, that everyone claims children's literature is more progressive than not. Michelle Ann Abate provides a useful counterpoint in *Raising Your Kids Right*, her study of American right-wing literature for children, and Nel's *Was the Cat in the Hat Black?* highlights the structural racism in children's books, the publishing industry, and the broader culture. Other scholars have weighed in on these matters, taking Marxist, feminist, and postcolonial perspectives, such that there is a substantial literature of scholarship on the more unfortunate ideologies of children's literature.[5] But Reynolds speaks for much of the field in calling children's literature "a curious and paradoxical space" but a space also "in which writers, illustrators, printers, and publishers have piloted ideas, experimented with voices, formats, and media, played with conventions, and contested thinking about cultural norms" (*Radical Children's Literature* 3). Here Reynolds expands upon Juliet Dusinberre's *Alice to the Lighthouse: Children's Books and Radical Experiments in Art* (1987), showing how children's literature did not abandon modernism and the avant-garde but rather maintained their innovations and subversiveness.[6]

The notion that children's literature might be critical-theoretical is now ascendant but not new. It is true that theory has generally paid little attention to children's literature and that the work of commentary has rested on children's literature scholars, as well as the writers and illustrators of children's books. But some early commentators did propose that childhood, children's forms, and even children's books are good to think with and have transformative potential. They were in the minority themselves, but they have been influential in the long term. They did not tend to weigh in on children's literature as a category, much less as an academic field (since it did not yet exist), but they did anticipate and help shape theory's investment in childhood as a state of productive alterity. This chapter opens with a review of Walter Benjamin's engagement with children's materials, followed by a case study of *Alice* as a theoretical work, then a discussion of children's literature as queer theory for kids, and finally a treatment of Alison Bechdel's graphic memoir *Are You My Mother?* In the material I consider, queer theory and queer narrative merge the minor-child with the minor-queer as well as return the desiring child of psychoanalysis to the scene of philosophical investigation.

Walter Benjamin and Children's Forms

The work of cultural critic Walter Benjamin provides an early and important intersection of theory and children's literature, one with ongoing impact. Benjamin believed in the rejuvenating power of childhood and children's forms and even in the possibility of something like a children's public sphere, as Jack Zipes emphasizes in his 1988 assessment of Benjamin's legacy. Benjamin's faith in childhood and rejuvenation had many causes and vectors, including the more general cult of the child operative in the early twentieth century and visible across a wide domain of contexts, including art movements, youth movements, social science research (anthropology especially), psychological and medical initiatives, and social advocacy for child welfare. Though enthusiasm for youth and the powers of youthfulness was sometimes bound up with fascist politics, it also inspired anticolonial movements and social justice activism. In any case, Zipes points out that Benjamin helped to stimulate new forms of children's culture in both West and East Germany in the 1960s (Zipes 2). Benjamin did write about children's books, but those pieces have not been as influential as his work on proletarian children's theater or childhood experience more generally. Benjamin is bracingly skeptical about the uses of children's literature, associating it with bourgeois indoctrination. Thus, in his 1929 radio address "Children's Literature," he makes this cheerful declaration: "If there is any field in the whole world where specialization is bound to fail, it must be in creating things for children. And the beginning of the decline in children's literature can be seen at the moment it fell into the hands of the specialists. I mean the decline of *children's literature*, not of *children's books*" (252). This remark is all the more striking given Benjamin's passion for children's books and his interest in children's forms more generally. Benjamin was an avid collector of children's books, assembling an impressive library of nineteenth-century German, French, and Dutch texts, out of which he composed essays and addresses including the one cited above and many others: "A Child's View of Color" (1914/1915), "Notes for a Study of the Beauty of Colored Illustrations in

Children's Books" (1918–1921), "Old Forgotten Children's Books" (1924), "A Glimpse into the World of Children's Books" (1926), "On the Mimetic Faculty" (1933), and "Doctrine of the Similar" (1933). The mere act of collecting children's books, of course, helped to support the emergence of a research tradition on children's literature, as Hans-Heino Ewers underscores. Meanwhile, "One-Way Street" (1928) offers scenes of child reading, pilfering, and hiding, and *Berlin Childhood around 1900* (published posthumously in 1950) expands this project. Benjamin scholars emphasize that these are not autobiographies but rather exercises in "involuntary memory" and strategic rejuvenation.[7]

Benjamin relished children's books but saw "children's literature" as a pedagogically custodial program. In "Old Forgotten Children's Books," he writes that children "want adults to give them clear, comprehensible but not childlike books. Least of all do they want what adults think of as childlike" (407). Old forgotten children's books were the best sort for children, Benjamin felt, mostly because of their colorful, often dramatic illustrations but also because they lack a pedagogical apparatus and can thus be appropriated for new forms of thinking and imagining.[8] Benjamin, too, endorses the uses of enchantment, believing that adults cannot predict, much less control, what children will do or become. "When children think up stories, they are like theater-producers who refuse to be bound by 'sense,'" he writes in "A Glimpse into the World of Children's Books" (435). Another well-known essay, "Program for a Proletarian Children's Theater" (1929), celebrates the anarchic improvisations of children against the scripts of adults. "When grownups act for children," Benjamin declares therein, "the result is archness" (205). Benjamin anticipates the critique later made by Rose. He, too, saw children's literature as an adult plot, in Rose's oft-quoted words "something of a soliciting, a chase, or even a seduction" (2). For Benjamin, adult projects for children cannot furnish the stimulation children manage for themselves. Benjamin saw children as little scavengers and flaneurs, making and remaking what they need. A more authentic children's literature for Benjamin might thus include anything that children build, manipulate, or simply like (including those old forgotten books). Only in that sense can a "children's literature" be legitimate. What Benjamin really imagined was a literature for minors, or a literature in which the minor status of children was respected and preserved. Benjamin "not only anticipated the productive possibilities for new forms of children's literature and theater," writes Zipes, "but he continues to be provocative and stimulating in the struggles to bring about a children's public sphere" (5). And implicit in Benjamin's work is "a notion about the adult critic as mediator or 'co-worker'" of that sphere (Zipes 3), which recalls P4C's approach to adults as coinquirers with children.

Benjamin also wrote plays for children and hoped to compile a book of fairy tales and legends. His only published work "for children," however, were the "radio stories" and "radio plays" he composed and delivered to young listeners in Frankfurt and Berlin, styled after the work of classical German storyteller Johann Peter Hebel (Doderer 172). "Children's Literature," cited above, was originally a radio show, and therein we can see, notes Klaus Doderer, "the rudiments of a realistic, critical and emancipatory theory of children's literature. . . . The notion of childhood, so extraordinarily significant to Benjamin, is paraphrased here and seen as a sort of philosophical place in which knowledge is absorbed and assimilated" (174). Doderer emphasizes that Benjamin tried "within the medium of broadcasting—a new medium at the time—to use the narrative form to provide explanations which would be equally understandable, entertaining, and interesting to young and old audiences alike" (169).

These shows were part of a larger body of eighty to ninety broadcasts delivered between 1927 and 1933. Left behind in Paris, the typescripts for the broadcasts were confiscated by the Gestapo but (through various twists and turns) found their way to the Soviet Union and then the German Democratic Republic. Only in 2014 did English-speaking readers and listeners gain access to the typescripts, when Lecia Rosenthal produced her edited volume *Radio Benjamin*. In her introduction to the book, Rosenthal emphasizes that we do not know exactly how many broadcasts there were since not all typescripts have survived. We do know that he delivered around thirty radio shows for children as well as two radio plays, *Much Ado about Kaspar* and *The Cold Heart* (Lecia Rosenthal xi). The radio programs are fascinating for many reasons, among them Benjamin's preoccupation with the acousmatic voice and the challenge of radio's ephemerality, aligned with his general interest in "typologies of vanished life" (xxiii). Rosenthal warns against making too much of these programs, as Benjamin generated them for money and was sometimes self-disparaging about the work. But she also underscores the significance of the "for children" programming, noting how it encouraged a critique of commodity fetishism (as in "Berlin Toy Tour I") (Rosenthal xxvi). Daniela Caselli takes the argument further, proposing that Benjamin's radio broadcasts for children "enter child and adult into an interminable mutual interpellation in which each element constitutes the other" (462). In effect, she proposes, the plays "explain the problem of the child to dialectical materialists by performing a pedagogy that does not see the child as the object of educational methods but as a collective ideology at play" (473). In her view, they "explain" through strategies of address and reference particular to the radio; "they do not so much discuss childhood as philosophical problem as perform the problematic of the child" (460).

Benjamin's scripts are remarkable in their complexity and their ambition for listeners. Benjamin spoke to children about subjects such as environmental and man-made catastrophe, bootlegging and swindling, suicide, and the persecution of "witches," inviting his listeners to think with him. In "The Rental Barracks," for example, he gives his young listeners an alternative history of architecture, while another show on the Bastille emphasizes the prison's function as a "tool of power" more than a "means of justice" (Benjamin 110). Some of the broadcasts raise the question of audience and audience-appropriateness, as in "The Bootleggers," in which Benjamin asks, "should children even hear these kinds of stories? . . . It's a legitimate question" (Benjamin 139). He plunges forward anyway and points out that Prohibition was introduced in large measure because alcohol consumption slowed down the efficiency of factory workers. And at the end of "The Mississippi Flood of 1927," he remarks, "stay tuned for the Ku Klux Klan and Judge Lynch and the unsavory characters that have populated the human wilderness of Mississippi, and still populate it today" (180).

It is no accident that these shows promote critical-theoretical engagement for minors in terms of both topic and address. Caselli suggests they have lessons to teach dialectical materialists, and in *Walter Benjamin for Children*, his own commentary on the shows, Jeffrey Mehlman calls them "at first blush, as implausible as an anthology of fairy tales by Hegel, a child's garden of deconstruction by Derrida" (2). He continues:

> And yet it is precisely that latter case, a hybrid of the French philosopher with Robert Louis Stevenson, which gives an indication of some of the stakes entailed in our own reading of these deceptively simple pieces. For Benjamin, I shall attempt to demonstrate, in texts that are at times as analytically forceful as anything in what one hesitates to call his "adult" writings, comes close to offering us just such a child's garden: one whose blooms, transplanted, much of an entire critical generation, my own, might be construed, after the fact, as having passed its maturity cultivating. (2)

Benjamin was "an entertainer of children with words we never heard, but which, after the fact, may be read, such is my intent, as an unsuspected matrix out of which much of what is forceful in contemporary criticism may be derived" (7). Mehlman understands Benjamin's radio addresses not as practice runs on the way toward mature work for adult listeners but rather as a critique of the ideals of maturity and progress, precisely through their address to "children," including some adults as well as children who grew up to be theorists.[9] Mehlman ascribes to Benjamin a strong if diffuse pedagogical program different from that of the "specialists." Benjamin appeals to the classical tradition of address to youth, collapsing the child-adult hierarchy and including adults as potential children as much as the reverse. For Benjamin, childhood is the key to dialectical thinking more generally. Stopping short of articulating a philosophy of childhood, observes Tyson Lewis, Benjamin presents childhood as "a potent resource for philosophical practice" ("Constellation" 179). "In the phenomenology of childhood," continues Lewis, "the very idea of the world is to once again be rekindled for the adult" (179).

Benjamin's resistance to children's literature might thus be recast as a more expansive vision for such. On the one hand, anything a child makes or touches is worthy of attention; on the other hand, adults can and should write for children, he believed, so long as we respect their abilities and reach them through compelling formats. Benjamin's radio addresses assume that young people can think about and even act in response to difficult topics. It is that assumption that qualifies the addresses as children's literature in this reconstructed sense. We are catching up with this vision. Doderer and Zipes paved the way, the latter emphasizing that Benjamin's work "could have a great impact on contemporary research in the field of children's literature and culture" (2). More recently, Anastasia Ulanowicz draws inventively on Benjamin in her *Second-Generation Memory and Contemporary Children's Literature: Ghost Images*, as does Eric L. Tribunella in two provocative essays, the most recent an exploration of the parallels between Benjamin's conception of the child and that of contemporaneous writer E. F. Benson.[10] For Tribunella, Benjamin provides "a useful heuristic for understanding the figure of the child in children's literature since he uses the child as a model for a particular way of looking" ("Benjamin" 505–6).

Meanwhile, Mehlman's commentary, alongside other work, suggests that theory more generally owes something to Benjamin's perspective on childhood as a state or experience pushing against as much as affirming "the human."[11] Henry Sussman emphasizes that debt in his comments on Benjamin in *Around the Book*,[12] as do Bignell, Lewis, and Carlo Salzani. Benjamin modeled and encouraged the idea that childhood and its forms are resources for critical thinking and cultural refashioning. That idea continues to thicken.

Alice in Theory

Freud in Oz includes a chapter on literary-critical case writing on and around three Anglo-American ("Golden Age") children's classics: Lewis Carroll's *Alice*, J. M. Barrie's *Peter Pan*, and L. Frank Baum's *The Wizard of Oz*. Such case writing trends psychological and psychotherapeutic, but there is also a tradition of philosophical and theoretical engagement with these and other texts, most especially *Alice*. Rose, of course, made her case against children's fiction through an extended treatment of *Peter Pan*, just a year after Dan Kiley's popular self-help book *The Peter Pan Syndrome: Men Who Have Never Grown Up*. As if in rebuttal to Kiley, *Peter Pan* pseudo-manifests in Judith Butler's queer theoretical work *The Psychic Life of Power* (1997), in her description of same-sex love as a kind of "never-never" land within the melancholic structure of heterosexuality.[13] Kiley cites *Peter Pan* rather homophobically as proof that men (especially gay men) rarely grow up, while Butler channels it to frame growing up as a straight plot foreclosing queer possibility. Rose, meanwhile, pits theory (Freud, Lacan, Marx) against children's fiction, but in so doing she situates *Peter Pan* as approximate to theory if not also a kind of theory, emphasizing its multiplicity, performativity, metafictionality. *Peter Pan* never quite approaches the status of *Alice*, however, as a candidate for theory itself.

Other children's classics have been linked with philosophical and theoretical culture. Beauvais situates Antoine de Saint-Exupéry's *The Little Prince* (1943) in the context of French existentialism, noting that Martin Heidegger identified it as a major existentialist book (although that attribution may be apocryphal, she reports) (*Mighty Child* 21). The Italian philosopher Giorgio Agamben gives considerable space to Carlo Collodi's *The Adventures of Pinocchio: Story of a Puppet* (1881), in part because every major Italian writer and critic seems to have engaged with the ubiquitous book, "Pinocchiology"—the collective discourse about *Pinocchio*—being something of a pastime for Italian writers.[14] Drawing also on anthropology, Agamben uses Playland in *Infancy and History* (1978) to discuss how the opposition of play and ritual serve opposite but balanced functions for time and culture. Ritual maintains the calendar, he suggests, and play tears it apart. While Playland is a dangerous place for our feckless puppet in Collodi's version—he turns into a donkey as a consequence for idleness—Agamben reads it as necessary to any sustainable society, as well as any understanding of history. Elsewhere in the book, Agamben draws on "The Princess and the Frog" in "The Question of Method in Adorno and Benjamin." Agamben picks up on Benjamin's faith in the oppositional potential of both children and play, and scholars debate whether or not Agamben "romanticizes" the child and violates the terms of his own analysis. I dodge that question and note merely that Agamben's Pinocchiology stops short of framing *Pinocchio* as a work of theory. Indeed, that is a hard case to make, as Collodi's novel is overtly didactic and not particularly whimsical or speculative.

The children's literature canon within theory is narrow and (with the exception of Collodi) very Anglophone, composed of these familiar classics. P4C, especially its contemporary iterations, offers a sharp contrast here, drawing as it does from a much more diverse set of children's materials, including many contemporary picturebooks and chapter books. If theory knows only a few classics, the classic it knows best is *Alice*, understood from the start as a kind of cultural critique, one spoofing the assumptions of normative philosophical and literary discourse, playing with language—divorcing sign and signified—and turning English social customs upside down. *Alice* is so provocative, Frida Beckman suggests, because it poses questions that have no answers ("Why is a raven like a writing-desk?") and thereby "opens up space for what we truly cannot expect—space that cannot be predicted based on what has come before" (2). Time has only intensified its reputation as a rebel or troublemaker. *Alice* also looms so large because it is now built into the collective apparatus of Victorian literature, children's literature, modernism, psychoanalysis, and popular culture. *Alice* is often characterized as a literary breath of fresh air in the Victorian period, even as a radical break with what came before. Such is not the case, as literary historians have shown. What Carroll did manage to do was innovate within the existing literary polysystem, notes Zohar Shavit. Carroll wrote in the immediate wake of translated European fairy tales and published fantasy texts (Paget, Ruskin, Thackeray, Kingsley, among others) that made possible Carroll's innovations (Shavit 75–77). "It was Carroll's manipulation of the existing model of the fantasy story," writes Shavit, "as well as other prevailing models in English literature at the time, that created a new model; making the text a classic and a subject for imitation" (79).[15] *Alice* functions as an "ambivalent text" in Shavit's terminology, one forged from three different "models" within children's literature: adventure story, fantasy tale, and nonsense story. Moreover, "Carroll blurred relations between fantasy and reality" (Shavit 83). *Alice* is also (famously) a satire of moralistic writing. And, of course, *Alice* is shorthand for multiple texts, not only the two ostensible source texts, *Alice's Adventures in Wonderland* (1865) and *Through the Looking Glass and What Alice Found There* (1871), but also other accounts by Carroll, including the first written version presented to Alice Liddell

(*Alice's Adventures Underground*) and the version intended for children more exclusively (*Nursery Alice*). The publication history of *Alice* is not as messy as that of *Peter Pan*, but it likewise confounds any easy sense of origin and takes on a folkloric quality. That Carroll was experimenting with genre heightens the perception of *Alice* as a meta text from the start; now, of course, the many reboots and aftertexts of *Alice* encourage us toward something like a "meta-*Alice*, a work that of necessity creates intertextual relations amongst many" (Jaques and Giddens 6). "That such a wide body of work can be reduced to a single-word title," note Jaques and Giddens in their excellent publication history, "is indicative of the ways that Carroll's works are both infinitely inflatable and infinitely collapsible" (2).

For Dusinberre, Carroll pioneered a poetics of childhood that influenced the English modernists within but also beyond literary circles. She sees traces of Carroll in the experiments of Virginia Woolf and other modernist greats. Carroll's masterpiece meanwhile captured the interest of early psychoanalysts as well as philosophers, critics, artists, and creative writers. G. K. Chesterton opined in 1901 that while *Alice* may look like a children's book, "it is rather sages and grey-haired philosophers who ought to sit up all night reading *Alice in Wonderland* in order to study the darkest problems of metaphysics, the borderland between reason and unreason, and the nature of the most erratic of spiritual forces, humor, which eternally dances between the two" (26). The persistence of *Alice* in theory derives not only from *Alice*'s hypercanonicity but also from the ongoing sense that *Alice* is a work of philosophy and (more recently) theory. Theoretical reflections on and extensions of *Alice* converge with novelistic and film adaptations, such that there is no firm line between literary and critical reboots.

Anglo-European fairy tales served as a common currency for Freud and the early analysts, a sort of populist version of the Greek dramas and classical European literature that Freud invoked. The so-called Golden Age Anglo-American fantasies from *Alice* forward have since also been absorbed into psychoanalytic discourse in the wake of, and sometimes also in the manner of, fairy tales. Psychoanalysis was the first theoretical system to invest in *Alice* and in children's literature more broadly. Analysts and psychoanalytically inclined critics took up *Alice* in part because the text was both popular and sufficiently literary. *Alice* also presented as an excellent case study in authorial creativity, with its dream logic, language play, and thematics of depth. It helped psychoanalysts test their ideas, and it helped them professionalize.[16] By the time Virginia Woolf wrote her 1939 "appreciation" of Carroll,[17] psychoanalysts had published case studies of Carroll and *Alice*. Freudian engagement with *Alice* may have begun in jest, with A. M. E. Goldschmidt's "*Alice in Wonderland* Psychoanalyzed" (1933), which some scholars consider a parody. Likening *Alice*'s fall down the rabbit hole to the act of coitus, Goldschmidt claims that Carroll's fantasy is an unconscious distortion of the author's desire for little girls. Parody or not, that reading quickly took root. At the same time, an idealized portrait of Carroll persisted, and the interplay between the "Saint Lewis" strain and the Carroll-as-pervert strain is ongoing (Brooker 1). In any case, psychoanalysts recognized *Alice* as a convenient illustration of Freud's theories early on. Writing in 1935, William Empson claimed that "to make the dream-story from which *Wonderland* was elaborated seem Freudian one only has to tell it" (414). While Empson seems nearly to frame *Alice* as a companion project to psychoanalysis, the early psychoanalytic literature was largely psychobiographical.

Jacques Lacan further encouraged the theoretical canonization of *Alice*. Lacan referred to *Alice* a number of time across his corpus, as Shuli Barzilai emphasizes in her study *Lacan and the Matter of Origins*.[18] Most famously, there is the reference to Humpty Dumpty in his so-called Rome discourse of 1953.[19] Lacan's first presentations on the mirror-stage were originally titled in English "The Looking Glass Phase," though there is no proof he had Carroll in mind. More recently, Christopher Lane points out that in 1966 Lacan gave a short tribute to Carroll on French national radio explaining his interest in Carroll (and that of the surrealists before him). Lacan saw in Carroll "an approach to subjectivity that has much in common with psychoanalysis," according to Lane (1030). In his address, Lacan emphasized the unease of Wonderland, seeing in Carroll's story a critique of the absurdity of cultural rules and human symbolization. Lacan stops short of treating Carroll as a theorist, largely because he gives interpretive priority to psychoanalysis. Lane edges closer to such an acknowledgment about Lacan and Carroll, writing that "Carroll's fiction most often focuses on the play and limits of meaning across semantic and ontological registers" (1035). Lane later adds that by making Alice too small and then too big for the world, Carroll "deftly anticipates the radical argument that Lacan would popularize from Freud's (1920) *Beyond the Pleasure Principle*: because of our capacity for reflection and consciousness, we miss the 'right moment' of biology and arrive too quickly into a symbolic order that we can grasp and comprehend only quizzically and belatedly" (1041).[20] Lacan did at least understand Carroll as an intellectual predecessor.[21]

Meanwhile, philosophy had been taking select note of *Alice*, rethinking its earlier skepticism toward imaginative literature. Wittgenstein admired Carroll—*Alice* was reportedly Wittgenstein's favorite English-language work—and shared his perspective on philosophy and/as nonsense (May; Pitcher). Some see in Wittgenstein's *Philosophical Investigations* a Carrollian sensibility. Carroll, of course, was a logician himself. He wrote two books on logic for a general audience—*Symbolic Logic* and *The Game of Logic*. In 1959, Roger W. Holmes wrote an article called "The Philosopher's *Alice in Wonderland*" in which he enumerates the attractions of Carroll for continental and analytic philosophers both:

> Wonderland and the Looking-Glass country belong to the logician and the philosopher as much as to parents and children. These regions are crowded with the problems and paraphernalia of logic and metaphysics and theory of knowledge and ethics. Here are superbly imaginative treatments of logical principles, the uses and meanings of words, the functions of names, the perplexities connected with time and space, the problem of personal identity, the status of substance in relation to its qualities, the mind-body problem. (199–200)

Carroll can be a pathway into philosophy, as Holmes notes in his closing lines: "If this essay has any 'porpoise' it is to send you, the reader, to the pleasure of philosophy and logic by way of the unique fascination with Lewis Carroll. . . . Do not promise yourself the delights of philosophy tomorrow. Enjoy them now: take Lewis Carroll down from the shelf tonight" (216). Holmes anticipates by several decades both the P4C movement and the "philosophy for all" publishing trend of today, in which philosophy is introduced through children's literature and popular culture. *Alice* features prominently in both, which play up the big questions in life over logic and language games. Books such as *Alice in Wonderland and Philosophy* (edited by Richard Brian Davis) are primers in practical rather than theoretical philosophy.[22]

Deleuze offers the most vivid portrait of Carroll as theorist. Published in French in 1969, his *The Logic of Sense* takes inspiration from Carroll and also from the Stoic philosophers. *The Logic of Sense* is a challenging work, part of his developing critique of psychoanalysis and representational philosophy. Deleuze scholars see it as a transitional text in Deleuze's thinking. Focused on the structure and genesis of "sense," the book also introduces Deleuze's theory of the event and of becoming. Deleuze opens both his preface and his first chapter with extended reflections on Carroll and engages extensively with *Alice* and *Sylvie and Bruno* in the body of the text. "The privileged place assigned to Lewis Carroll," notes Deleuze in his preface, "is due to his having provided the first great account, the first great *mise en scene* of the paradoxes of sense—sometimes collecting, sometimes renewing, sometimes inventing, and sometimes preparing them. The privileged place assigned to the Stoics is due to their having been the initiators of a new image of the philosopher which broke away from the pre-Socratics, Socratic philosophy, and Platonism" (xiii–xiv). Deleuze is drawn to Carroll for a number of reasons. In the first of thirty-four chapters, all explicating a "series of paradoxes," Deleuze explains that the *Alice* books "involve a category of very special things: events, pure events" (1). He understands Carroll as a master of the paradox, affirming more than one sense or direction at the same time. Deleuze admires Alice as a naive narrator because she allows Carroll to reflect playfully on the slippery dance of words and things. Deleuze acknowledges but resists the symptomatic reading of Carroll as suffering from Oedipal frustration (flight from the father, renunciation of the mother, projection onto the little girl), saying that authors, "if they are great, more like doctors than patients," are themselves "astonishing diagnosticians or symptomatologists" (237). Deleuze wants to read *Alice* as a study in surface meaning and play. He proposes that despite the depth thematics that mark the first section of the book (falling down the rabbit hole especially), *Alice* is mostly a work of horizontality (22). Recounting Antonin Artaud's critique of Carroll—as (Deleuze's gloss) "a little pervert, who holds onto the establishment of a surface language, and who has not felt the real problem of a language in depth—namely, the schizophrenic problem of suffering, of death, and of life" (84)—Deleuze does not disagree, and even says he "would not give a page for Artaud for all of Carroll," but Carroll "remains the master and surveyor of surfaces—surfaces which were taken to be so well-known that nobody was exploring them anymore. On the surfaces, nonetheless, the entire logic of sense is located" (93).

Deleuze claims also that the "loss of the proper name is the adventure which is repeated throughout all Alice's adventures" (*Logic* 3) and that nonsense undermines not sense but common sense (3). For Deleuze, Carroll's fantasy works to expose the paradoxes of signification and the particular fault lines of propositional logic. As Eugene B. Young summarizes, "Carroll's fantastic works make use of logic, but only to invert or distort it according to the expression of non-sense which occurs in domains where logical propositions encounter their own outside" (58). This is what interests Deleuze most. Deleuze even claims that Carroll has invented "a serial method in literature" (*Logic* 43), on display in *Alice* but especially in *Sylvie and Bruno*. The latter work, often panned, is for Deleuze a "masterpiece" of "entirely new techniques" (41).[23] Deleuze's book is telling not only in what it says about Carroll but also how it emulates Carroll's style or sensibility. *The Logic of Sense* is a work of theory rather than fantasy, of course. But it has fantastic elements, and its episodic structure (the "series") recalls the episodic structure of Carroll's work, *Sylvie and Bruno* most especially. Plus, Deleuze shares with Carroll a fondness for language games. Commentators on Deleuze stress not only his respect for literature but his tendency to engage with and even emulate it. Deleuze wrote monographs on Proust, Kafka, and Sacher-Masoch and admired Anglo-American literature. He believed that philosophy poses problems and that art and literature work them out much better than philosophy.[24] Deleuze does not use *Alice* to do philosophy; rather, for him *Alice* = philosophy or theory.[25]

Other theorists have been intrigued by Carroll but found him wanting. Artaud translated a chapter from *Through the Looking-Glass* in 1945 but found Carroll superficial (exactly! says Deleuze). Artaud hoped to see more sustained disruption of language and meaning, something closer to the schizoanalysis that Deleuze eventually identified as a practice (Lecercle, *Philosophy through the Looking Glass* 31–36). Hélène Cixous likewise plays up Carroll's conservatism: "Carroll wasn't an avant-garde theoretician but a scholar, worried by the fact that, in spite of himself, his knowledge was undermining institutions" (234). As if responding to Deleuze, she sees no "author's intention" to develop a "literary machine."

Jacques Derrida gives Carroll a little more credit in "The Animal that Therefore I Am (More to Follow)," seeing in *Alice* the exploration of the animal's point of view and a potential challenge to human exceptionalism. But after indulging Carroll's cats and hedgehogs at some length, and reflecting more generally on the "bestiary at the origin of philosophy" (including his own), Derrida decides that Carroll backs down from such a challenge.[26] Possibly so.[27] It is intriguing all the same that Derrida seems nearly to treat Carroll as a theorist, even if he does not see Carroll's work as a model for a new theoretical practice, as does Deleuze. Like Carroll, Derrida is playful, fond of puns and language games. If *Alice* fails as an indictment of human exceptionalism, perhaps it succeeds as a model of philosophical-creative writing. Derrida teases us, after all, that he "would of course have liked to inscribe my whole talk within a reading of Lewis Carroll. In fact, you can't be certain that I am not doing that, for better or for worse, silently, unconsciously, or without your knowing" (*Animal* 6). How indeed? If Derrida emphasizes the limit of Carroll's radicality, he seems to appreciate and even imitate Carroll's style. And of course, Derrida spends time with Carroll because Woolf, Joyce, André Breton, Lacan, and Deleuze did so before him—because *Alice* is part of the Anglo-European intellectual repertoire, even part of French theory.[28]

Alice has long intrigued scholars working on questions of desire, sexuality, and identity, with or without psychoanalysis. Coats, for instance, reads the character Alice as Carroll's (Lacanian) *objet petit a* and as emblematic in turn of the reader's desire "to know, to understand, and most of all, the desire to know oneself, to *be* oneself" (79). A doomed project, if we believe James Kincaid in *Child-Loving*, published just as queer theory was emergent. Kincaid treats Alice and Peter Pan together as the "two most persistent and stimulating images of the erotic child," seductive precisely in their radical alterity. "No figures are most insistently Other," he writes, "more adept at resisting satisfaction, blocking fulfillment, keeping the chase and desire alive" (276).[29] Some of this scholarship picks up on earlier feminist commentary, notably Nina Auerbach's 1973 essay on Alice as a "curious child." *Alice* is "Exhibit A" in Steven Bruhm and Natasha Hurley's introduction to the 2004 volume *Curiouser: On the Queerness of Children*.[30] Pointing to *Alice* and other "exhibits," editors Bruhm and Hurley draw attention to how "the very effort to flatten the narrative of the child into a story of innocence has some queer effects" (iv). More recently, Hurley uses *Alice* to theorize queer book history, exploring how aftertexts such as the Alan Moore and Melinda Gebbie graphic trilogy *Lost Girls* encode and amplify the queer energies of its sources. Such works, she proposes in this provocative piece (titled "Alice Lost and Found"), "offer up queer children as figures for queer literary history itself" (102), against more normative sorts of textual reproductions and circulations. We might see Alice not only as a fictional queer child but as a queer theorist. Beyond the level of character, notes Hurley, just as we benefit from thinking of queer productivity outside biological reproduction, "one may also gain something in tracking queer literary history through its noncanonical texts, the inferior versions of canonical texts, and the nonstandard readings of texts that nonetheless propel the texts . . . through the world in unexpected ways" (107).

Meanwhile, *Alice* is not merely linked with but understood as a version of both postmodernism and posthumanism. In the *Cambridge Introduction to Postmodernism*, Brian McHale dates "Postmodern *Alice*" to 1966, in his view a pivotal year for both postmodernism and *Alice* recycling. *Alice* is claimed by postmodern culture as a "precursor text, postmodern before the fact—always already postmodern—and thus a source of multiple rewritings, partial and complete, overt and covert, throughout the postmodern decades." (51). (He notes that Salvador Dali's illustrated edition of *Alice* appeared the same year as *The Logic of Sense*.) "So ubiquitous are allusions to *Alice* in postmodern novels," McHale writes, "that the presence of *Alice* might almost be considered a *marker* of literary postmodernism" (53). As for posthumanism, Zoe Jaques notes that for all its humanist commitments, children's literature also exhibits its strong posthumanist tendencies, devoting considerable space in her study to *Alice*.

In 2017, Lisa Sainsbury published her terrific article on thought experiments in children's literature, which I mentioned in this book's introduction. She begins and ends with Carroll, positing Alice as a foundational "child of wonder" (155) and remarking that Alice's questions (beginning with the famous "what is the use of a book . . . without pictures or conversations"?) underscore "the importance of the conversational mode, not only in Carroll's novels, but in the wider field of children's literature" (167). Contemporary authors, proposes Sainsbury, take cue from Carroll and develop "various thought experiments to be executed by the child of wonder" (167). Sainsbury's discussion of language games and the formal properties of thought experiments—"conversational mode, double engagement and modal positioning"—adds a rich dimension to the history of *Alice* reception and circulation (154). Scholars are both catching up and contributing to the critical dimension of *Alice*.

Two more observations. First, while *Alice* is an expository narrative, it is also a story in pictures, not just illustrated but an imagetext that foregrounds the tension between words and pictures, as in the verbal-visual pun of tale and tail (a tale is told while a tail is shown). Things are often not what they seem, or look like, in the *Alice* books. While books without pictures have plenty of uses, books with pictures do too, one of which apparently is to play with the instabilities of language. Even the character of Alice is as much picture as name. Alice is a verbal-visual figure, something like a composite snapshot or type but evolving and dynamic. ("Character" itself carries visual meaning.) *Alice* is so layered and multimodal that it is hard not only to identify authoritative versions but to separate word from picture or image.

Second, if *Alice* circulates in theory, theory in turn is part of *Alice*'s circulation. And in using *Alice*, theorists and scholars like myself are maintaining and reinventing *Alice* no less than novelists and filmmakers. Granted, Benjamin aside, theory is much more inclined to play with *Alice* than to entertain the question of children's literature as a category or enterprise. In fact, across the broader tradition of commentary and recycling *Alice* ostensibly stands for something *other and/or more than* children's literature or children's books.[31] In any case, theory is attracted to canonical children's works and especially to *Alice* not only because they are famous but also because they are so overdetermined, so formally and intellectually provocative. Theory may not often use children's literature categorically, but it certainly mobilizes select titles and, in turn, becomes a part of their cultural life.

Queer Theory for Kids

If theory sometimes courts the child, accentuating her position as a minor and working with children's forms, queer theory focuses on the sexual and cultural minor, most often but not exclusively the adult. Queer theory works both inside and against existing philosophical and theoretical systems and is perhaps a minor literature in this sense, although that might be overstating its positionality. Whatever its own status in the academy or beyond, queer theory seeks out and celebrates minor energies and minor moments, sometimes in connection with the child. And unlike P4C, whose child subject seems all mind and no body (no sexuality, in other words), queer theory for kids gives priority to matters of identification and desire.

Children's and YA literature offer an embarrassment of riches for those working in queer studies. LGBT-specific material for children and young adults has proliferated and diversified, and there is an even larger body of work we might call queer. Queerish characters abound even in more mainstream texts, among them Peter Pan, Mary Poppins, Pippi Longstocking, Anne of Green Gables, the Moomintrolls, Stuart Little, Jackeen J. O'Malley, Harriet the Spy, Albus Dumbledore, Flat Stanley, and Miss Peregrine and her peculiar children. Plus everyone in Oz. In this section of the chapter, though, I propose that children's literature is not just enticing source material but also a form of queer theory for kids, in that it accomplishes some of the same tasks that queer theory accomplishes for adults. Not all children's literature works this way, of course, but there is a case to be made. In her entry for "queer" in *Keywords for Children's Literature*, Kerry Mallan stresses the shared function of queer theory and queer fiction for young readers. "From a queer perspective," she writes, "the most successful fiction for children makes visible the processes that seek to enforce heteronormative categories and binaries, and that foreground subjectivity as multifaceted and shifting. The most successful queer stories 'queer' their readers by provoking them to query the assumptions that underpin notions of normal and abnormal identity, especially sexual identity" (189). And those stories often feature "curious" child characters as reader companions and role models, as already noted with respect to Alice.

Maria Nikolajeva made this point in 2006, treating Astrid Lindgren's beloved heroine Pippi Longstocking not merely as a queer character but as a "true queer theorist" who "does not wish to supplant one norm by another, but on the contrary shows that all the ways and attitudes are equally normal" ("Misunderstood Tragedy" 69).[32] Ann Weinstone got there even earlier, in her 1999 piece "Science Fiction as a Young Person's First Queer Theory," a review of Sedgwick's edited volume *Novel Gazing* but also a meditation on queer child reading practices. Sedgwick herself invites that focus in her introduction to the book, the first version of her paranoid/reparative reading essay, wherein she notes that a "very palpable presiding image here—a kind of *genius loci* for queer reading—is the interpretive absorption of the child or adolescent whose sense of personal queerness may or may not (yet?) have resolved into a sexual specificity," a child who is "reading for important news about herself, without knowing what form that news will take" ("Paranoid Reading" 2–3). Thus prompted, Weinstone recalls her ten-year-old queer self reading science fiction and longing for aliens to arrive and bring her some joy or "at least relief" (41). She identifies William Pène du Bois's children's book *The Twenty-One Balloons* (which won the Newbery Medal in 1948) as the first science fiction work she read, appealing for its "queer flaunting of the excessive gesture and bravura recycling of the materials of the mundane world" (46). The novel, also one of my childhood favorites, revolves around a group of San Franciscans who secede from the real world to live on the volcanic island of Krakatoa, where they develop a "restaurant government," dress in finery, and experiment with fantastic home devices like electrified living room furniture. It is a fun and ridiculous novel, queer enough on its own terms and certainly encouraging to a queer child reader. Weinstone ends the review reflecting on the possibilities for expanding upon the "queer, delinquent, immersive scene of sf [science fiction] reading" (47) and asking, "Is it time now for queer sf theory?" (48).

That children's literature and science fiction can look like queer theory might come from queer theory's capaciousness; that is, queer theory encourages us to look anew at everything, even as it lends itself to and sometimes seems commensurate with other cultural projects. The fungibility of queer theory (and queer more generally) is both a strength and a weakness. Theory at large is pretty elastic, so pairing it with queer would only enhance the elasticity. Queer theory does imply some commitment to queer visibility, analysis, or politics, if not necessarily queer affirmation. Queer theory often seeks to challenge hetero- and other normativities. Thinking about queer theory with children's literature, we can make different sorts of observations. We can say, for instance, that the conceit of children's literature is itself a queer theory, and not necessarily a happy one. Hence Rose's critique of children's literature, a queer theory of adult seduction and manipulation and one exploiting the man-boy erotics in and around *Peter Pan* (there is a whiff of homophobia in her critique).[33] A "negative" queer theory of children's literature put forward in a queer-affirmative way is Tison Pugh's proposition that children are systematically presumed both innocent and heterosexual, such that children's literature must grapple with this paradox. Most children's literature falls in line, he concludes. Ruminating on *Alice* by way of Sedgwick, and thinking about the various open secrets that swirl in and around children's texts, Perry Nodelman offers this mostly positive and queer-affirmative theory: "children's literature might be viewed as a way in which adult writers, pretending to be childlike, gain access to their own inherent queerness" (*Hidden Adult* 42). If so, he qualifies, "it's instructive that the 'happy endings' of children's literature tend, at least theoretically, to deny that queerness—to empty purple from the jar" (42–43).

Meanwhile, queer theory is fashioned out of varied materials, including but not limited to philosophy and scholarship as well as imaginative writing.[34] Queer theory often experiments with form and citationality, using fragments, for instance, or dialogue. Some recent works incorporate memoir, as with Ann Cvetkovich's *Depression: A Public Feeling* (2012) and Maggie Nelson's *The Argonauts* (2015), billed as "autotheory." The literary archive of queer theory was initially more canonical than not, perhaps for strategic reasons, but has since expanded, if not quite to children's literature (aside from the children's literature critics I have been citing). Jack Halberstam turns to Pixar animated children's film as an example of a "silly archive" and also "low theory," "a kind of theoretical mode that flies below the radar, that is assembled from eccentric texts and examples and that refuses to confirm the hierarchies of knowing that maintain the *high* in high theory" (16). "Animated films nowadays succeed," he writes, "to the extent to which they are able to address the disorderly child, the child who sees his or her family and parents as the problem, the child who knows there is a bigger world out there" (27). "I would be bold enough to argue that it is only in the realm of animation that we actually find" that message (23). Halberstam seems to be describing minor theory in more ways than one. Halberstam finds animation chock-full of anarchic energy.[35] He entertains but rejects the possibility that children's literature is another silly archive of low theory. "While much children's literature simply offers a new world too closely matched to the old one it left behind," he concludes, "recent animated films actually revel in innovation and make ample use of the wonderfully childish territory of revolt" (28). Halberstam concedes the revolting power of fairy tales but does not associate them with children's literature. I find this strange, since children's literature has close ties to animation, but the crucial lesson is that a silly archive might also be a kind of (queer) theory.

Queer theory for children is no less diverse in materials and methods than queer theory the academic formation. It is perhaps more so, since queer theory for adults, for all its variations, is imagined for and pitched to readers of the same general sophistication or experience. Genre is a more varied factor for queer theory for children, since different genres are presumed more effective with or appealing to different age groups. Queer theory for children might thus take the form of a picturebook, or a middle-grade novel, or a young adult memoir. Queer theory can work for the child no less than theory for beginners or P4C or children's literature conventionally construed. It stands up for the child in all her varieties and temporalities.

From the start, queer theory has aligned itself with the child and even seen itself as a venture in child-saving. We recall Sedgwick's comments in *Novel Gazing* and her similar remark in *Tendencies* (1993) that everyone working in queer studies seeks "to keep faith with vividly remembered promises made to ourselves in childhood: promises to make invisible possibilities and desires visible; to make the tacit things explicit; to smuggle queer representation in where it must be smuggled and, with the relative freedom of adulthood, to challenge queer-eradicating impulses" (3). Sedgwick gave us powerful work on the queer/proto-gay child, some of it collaborative with Michael Moon,[36] while Natasha Hurley, Steven Bruhm, and especially Kathryn Bond Stockton have expanded upon such. There is even a small body of work we might call queer childhood studies, pursued by scholars such as Erica Rand, Nicholas Sammond, Carol Mavor, Moon (again), Sarah Chinn, and Susan Honeyman.[37] But we may have forgotten that Judith Butler opens *Gender Trouble* (1990) with a portrait of the queer theorist as a young girl, describing how she learned at an early age that trouble was something not that one made but that one was always already in. In fact, the more trouble she tried not to make, the more hopeless the cause. Trying to avoid trouble meant being-in-trouble. This realization gives rise to her first "critical insight into the subtle ruse of power. . . . Hence, I concluded that trouble is inevitable and the task, how best to make it, what best way to be in it" (ix). Butler writes back to the gender trouble first encountered in childhood.

The best way to test the idea of children's literature as queer theory for kids is to consider some examples. After looking at a number of texts, some of which I discuss below, I offer these propositions about queer theory for kids.

Like queer theory for adults (academic queer theory), queer theory for kids:

1. Questions the status quo and encourages and models alternative worldviews. It is both critical and creative.
2. Pushes against the normal and normative, especially but not exclusively the homonormative or gay-affirmative.
3. Approaches topics from surprising angles, takes unpredictable twists and turns in content and form. It surprises and delights, if sometimes vexes.
4. Functions as self-help or DIY literature.

Unlike queer theory for adults, queer theory for kids:

5. Tends away from explicit engagement with questions of sexuality and sexual identity, especially in genres targeting younger readers. YA literature engages more with sexuality and social norms.
6. Tends away from explicit social critique.
7. Trends fictional rather than nonfictional in presentation.
8. Takes imagetext as well as expository form.

As to materials, we do not have to create a new canon. As Mallan implies, texts that are provocatively queer tend to be queer-theoretical. Both Hurley, in "The Perversions of Children's Literature," and Melynda Huskey, in "Queering the Picture Book," emphasize the importance of queer or perverse reading strategies over stable queer content, echoing Weinstone. We can never say definitively whether a text is queer or might be used queerly. Therefore, I focus on texts that encourage queer reading practices by way of queer narrative strategies.

Picturebooks tend to work by indirection, symbolization, and allegory when it comes to adult topics especially. Sexuality is a difficult topic to negotiate because of anxieties about childhood, and that fact seems to extend to theorizing about sexuality. It is interesting that we can tolerate certain kinds of topics only in mock or imaginary picturebooks like *A Child's Guide to Freud*. To my knowledge, no one ever tried to create an earnest informational picturebook for kids on the topic of Freud or psychoanalysis or any other theoretical account of sexuality or gender or both. Probably it would be hard to do and would not feel much like queer theory in tone or intent. Maybe we can imagine *A Child's Guide to Queer Theory*, with illustrated scenes stylized after those in *A Child's Guide to Freud*—one page could explain, "When mommy stays over at her friend Eliza's house, this is called THE LESBIAN CONTINUUM. When Daddy calls her home the next day, this is called COMPULSORY HETEROSEXUALITY." But that is not queer theory for kids but rather a satire or funny coffee table book for adults. There are, of course, informational picturebooks about sexuality—quite a few. But they do not address concepts or paradigms, nor do they model critique. Rarely do they challenge heteronormativity or delink sexuality and reproduction. And they are rarely if ever playful, since play and sex do not mix well when it comes to picturebooks. The picturebook's evasions of sexuality would seem to support Pugh's thesis that children are presumed both innocent and straight.

At the same time, the pressures that shape the picturebook in particular ways also make it capacious and elastic. The seeming lack of an explicitly queer-theoretical discourse can make picturebooks all the queerer. Picturebook creators devise oblique and sometimes surreal narrative and visual strategies for figuring sexuality and identity and for encouraging awareness. These strategies evidence success, not failure, in the face of a heteronormative society and publishing industry. As Huskey writes, "the picture book has never been without a queer presence. There's no shortage of queer picture books if you're looking in the right places, or with the right eyes" (68). And once we put aside desires for gay affirmation, she notes, "we enter the connotative realm, the elusive, impossible-to-deny because impossible-to-prove world of implication" (69).

Recently, I asked friends on social media to name the queerest picturebook they knew, and I got an interesting assortment of replies. Based on this and my own reading and research, I would identify at least four categories of queer picturebooks (there are surely more):

1. Books in which gay and lesbian families (not children) are affirmed and normalized. In the United States, this genre began in the late 1980s and early 1990s with titles such *Heather Has Two Mommies* (1989), *Asha's Mums* (1990), and *Daddy's Roommate* (1990). The tone in such books is straightforward. An earlier and, by American standards, more provocative example is the 1981 Danish photobook *Jenny Lives with Eric and Martin*. Such books are usually produced by small presses to reach niche audiences, and this trend continues as writers and publishers take advantage of social media and devise new publishing structures.

2. Queer-affirmative picturebooks that shift focus to the gender-nonconforming child, most often a boy who identifies as a girl or who prefers girl stuff.[38] The general message is the importance of being true to oneself. Early titles include *William's Doll* (1972) and *Oliver Button Is a Sissy* (1979). A contemporary example in this tradition is Myles E. Johnson's *Large Fears*, about a black boy named Jeremiah Nebula who loves pink and longs to go to Mars, where he hopes he will find acceptance.[39] Another

is Jessica Love's *Julián Is a Mermaid* (2018), which won the Mike Morgan & Larry Romans Children's & Young Adult Literature Award (one of the Stonewall Book Awards). Riding the subway with his abuela, young Julián sees three people fabulously dressed up as mermaids and is inspired to do the same. At home he makes his own glamorous outfit, including a yellow curtain for a tail and a potted fern as a headdress. Instead of chastising him, his abuela delights in Julián and takes him to the Coney Island Mermaid Parade. It is key that Julián does not want to be a merman but a mermaid. While the mermaid tale has been heterosexualized, it is fundamentally about otherness or species (if not also gender) trouble. Love's book is also remarkable in depicting people of many colors, sizes, and genders, not only at the parade but also in the subway and even at home.

3. Stories of same-sex romance, some featuring human protagonists and some animal lovers. In the earlier titles, same-sex love is impossible because the lovers are separated by time, the elements (*Hello, Sailor*), or species difference—or all three, as in Eric Jon Nones's *Caleb's Friend* (1993), about a human boy and a merboy. More recent titles show same-sex love, most powerfully in *Jerome by Heart* (2018), written by Thomas Scotto and illustrated by Olivier Tallac, translated from *Jérôme par coeur* (2009). Raphael and Jerome do everything together at school, after school, and on the weekends. They share jokes and snacks and they buddy up on field trips. "It doesn't bother me at all," explains Raphael, who narrates the book. "Raphael loves Jerome. / I can say it. / It's easy." Encountering fatherly disapproval of their closeness, Raphael refuses to back down, dreaming of a future with Jerome. "I forget my mom and dad," reads the text on the final page. "I think only about Jerome, / who I know by heart. And I say—yes. / Raphael loves Jerome. I can say it. / It's easy." *Jerome by Heart* is both the sweetest and the most defiant gay love story I have seen in picturebook form. It is one of the few featuring (without naming them as) gay or proto-gay kids.

4. Queer-theoretical titles predating or just uninvested in gay identity affirmation. I will give some examples now to make the case that something like a queer-theoretical tradition of picturebooks emerged before and alongside queer theory.

A number of classic picturebooks showcase the imaginative child at work/play. Crockett Johnson's 1955 *Harold and the Purple Crayon* is one of the most famous and features the trope of the drawing child (Harold literally draws his world into existence). In 1956, Ruth Krauss, Johnson's wife and also a talented author-illustrator, published a decidedly queer version of this type of story, *I Want to Paint My Bathroom Blue*, illustrated by none other than Sendak, who was gay (Krauss and Sendak were frequent collaborators). Marah Gubar alerted me to this lovely book, one of her favorites and a candidate for the queerest picturebook. A theatrical (okay, flamboyant) child longs to paint their bathroom blue, their kitchen yellow, their sitting room white "with turtles," and so forth. I use the gender-neutral pronoun because the text is first-person voiced and the illustrations show an androgynous child who could be a boy but also a girl with short hair and a preference for pants. "I'll make a big white door / with a little pink doorknob," the text continues, "and a song about the doorknob goes / a doorknob a doorknob / a dear little doorknob / a dearknob a dearknob / a door little dearknob." The accompanying illustration shows the child leaping into the air and gesturing to the moon, their body nearly in ballet pose (see Figure 5). A few pages later appears a left-page illustration of a house filled with diverse people, their faces all different colors; the right-page text reads: "I'll make a house the kind I dream about / not the kind I see. It's a house like a rainbow. / And my friends all live with me there." The following page reads: "And someday will be grass and trees," with the text below a two-page spread that looks awfully like the "wild rumpus" center pages in *Where the Wild Things Are*, except here it is kids playing and hugging trees and sniffing flowers. The final page reads: "and I'd make an ocean," the text below another two-page illustration, this one of the rainbow house filled with their friends and tucked safely away on a verdant island in the ocean. It is telling that these are things the child

FIGURE 5. *I Want to Paint My Bathroom Blue* by Ruth Krauss. Illustrated By: Maurice Sendak. Text copyright © 1956, Ruth Krauss, copyright renewed 1984 by Ruth Krauss. Pictures copyright © 1956, Maurice Sendak, copyright renewed 1984 by Maurice Sendak. Used by permission of HarperCollins Publishers.

wants to do rather than is already doing. Unlike Harold, this child cannot yet draw their house and life into existence. This book is about the future, imagining it, planning for it, in the queer utopian mode articulated so beautifully by José Esteban Muñoz. The child dreams of another world that will improve upon and replace the current one. *I Want to Paint My Bathroom Blue* anticipates queer theory by several decades. Possibilities open up when we emphasize queer reading practices and the "connotative realm" (to quote Huskey again).[40]

Consider also Arthur Yorinks's *Louis the Fish* (1980), illustrated by Richard Egielski. Popular with adults and children alike, *Louis the Fish* was a *School Library Journal* Best Book of the Year and also a Reading Rainbow Featured Selection. The book tells the story of a man named Louis, a butcher by family trade. His father was a butcher, as was his grandfather. Problem is, Louis hates meat. Also, since he was young, Louis has longed to be a fish. You know, the usual. So after an unhappy time in human form, after feeling like a fish out of water, he actually becomes a fish. A salmon, more specifically. "Louis soon forgot everything about being a butcher . . . or even being a human being at all. After a hard life"—this is the final page—"Louis was a happy fish."[41] Through inventive words and pictures, *Louis the Fish* invites young readers to imagine a state of existence different from their own and to imagine such as desirable. The impact of the pictures is undeniable; this is queer theory in imagetext. So is David Small's *Imogene's Antlers* (1985), another story of becoming animal. "On Thursday," the book begins, "when Imogene woke up, she found she had grown a pair of antlers" (see Figure 6). Her family is decidedly upset. A queer problem, one would think, but no big deal for Imogene. She is taken to the doctor, but the doctor finds nothing wrong. The school principal glares at her and offers no help. In contrast, the kitchen maid and the cook admire the antlers and look forward to decorating them. Life goes on. At the book's end, Imogene wakes up antlerless and "the family was overjoyed to see her back to normal" until she returns, on the last page, sporting peacock feathers. Perhaps a more satisfying ending than what we get in *Louis the Fish*, since Louis ends up living in a friend's aquarium. Then again, living as a free salmon has its risks.

We might agree that these are queer picturebooks. But are they queer theory? A better question might be, why not? Neither *Louis the Fish* nor *Imogene's Antlers* deals directly with gender or sexuality. But both engage with questions of desire and identity and go beyond mere affirmation in their becoming-animality. One could read Louis's story as another tale of wrong-body living set right. But aspiring to salmonhood seems a queer ambition for an adult man, one not resolved by the transformation. If

FIGURE 6. David Small, *Imogene's Antlers* (1985).

anything, Louis seems queerer than ever in his salmonhood, and the book holds the reader uncomfortably in our collective human exceptionalism, ahead of queer theory's critique of such. As for *Imogene's Antlers*, the only female deer who grow antlers are reindeer, apparently, and there is something suggestively sexual about those antlers. They certainly freak out her family. Despite the book's seeming radicalism, the book remains very popular with both children and adults, since it humorously encourages the acceptance of difference. Both books encourage questions and work to destabilize reader expectations. They lead us to an unexpected conclusion or future. What they do not do is explicitly theorize; they do not introduce and apply terminology in the manner of academic queer theory. Along with a metaphorical approach to questions to embodiment and identity, their lack of theorizing may be the main thing disqualifying them as queer theory for adults. How significant is this lack? Is it not possible that queer theory necessarily takes more fictional than explanatory form in such materials? The pictures, moreover, are vital to the queer plots. One reason why these two books are so arresting is that they are not postmodern or metafictional. Unlike, say, David Macaulay's *Black and White* (1990), or Jon Scieszka and Lane Smith's *The Stinky Cheese Man and Other Fairly Stupid Tales* (1992), they do not experiment with layout, break the fourth wall, talk to the reader. Rather, they are traditionally expository and even realistic. That means we must absorb these strange transformations of title character, accept without assimilating them.

There are other examples of queer picturebooks that approach the theoretical, such as *Otter and Odder* (2012), written by James Howe and illustrated by Chris Raschka.[42] In this book, an otter falls in love with a fish while looking for dinner. As you might imagine, this presents a bare life sort of conundrum. The fish in question is terrified that Otter will eat her. The story proceeds in a very postmodern fashion, illustrating a seriously weird love story with surreal crayon drawings. The book deconstructs love not only by showing cross-species relation but by emphasizing that love is hard to differentiate from a desperate clinging to life: "All she wanted was a loosening of his grip / a slippery escape / But then . . . her own tremulous / fish-not-wanting-to-be-dinner / heart— / awakened to something / new and surprising: / not only love but a future / she could never have imagined." Howe toys with the conventions of happy tale and tragic tale before eventually setting on something like the former. Confronted with species prejudice from his brethren, Otter comes to realize, with the help of a sage, apple-eating Beaver, that the "way of the otter" is a thing of the mind only and will yield to the "way of the heart." Here again is something beyond affirmation, something closer to a philosophy of life, the queer proposition that you can love and not merely consume someone despite even biological pressure. Otter gets odder and does not care; he is happy.

None of these picturebooks is *Gender Trouble*. But all explore their protagonist's desires and qualities against normative human expectation and culture (even human nature). They conceive of sexuality not in narrow identarian terms but as part of the broader social fabric. They do so with humor and style, appealing to parents as much as children. They do not affirm gay identity exactly, but that is not necessarily the task or responsibility of queer theory for adults either. Picturebook queer theory for kids sometimes turns to animals to create alternative identities and trajectories for its protagonists, hence the preponderance of becoming-animal (and staying-animal) stories. That strategy is less noticeable in books for older readers. Granted, the recent upsurge of picturebooks with eccentric characters and plots could be read more skeptically, as evidence that queerness is now comfortably commodifiable.

There is also a queer-theoretical category in the middle-grade novel form, which may or may not align with the gay-affirmative. Some middle-grade novels are queer-theoretical in their design as models for queer living and survival. Some are realist in presentation; some have metafictional tendencies. On the more realistic end of the spectrum are Louise Fitzhugh's famous *Harriet the Spy* (1964) and her less well-known *Nobody's Family Is Going to Change* (1974). These are conventionally realist middle-grade novels in which eccentric child characters go their own way in the world and push against adult power as well as peer expectation. Here again sexuality tends to be implicit rather than explicit. The case for *Harriet* as queer-theoretical work hinges on the circulations of the text as well as its contents. Robin Bernstein notes that "queer and proto-queer children saw themselves mirrored in and inspired by the brash, blunt girl who wears boys' clothes, spies on adults, and records all she sees in her notebook" ("Queerness" 111). Bechdel is one in a long line of lesbian creatives who identify Harriet as a queer role model. In the novel, Harriet's governess, Ole Golly, advises Harriet to lie in order to preserve her friendships and to convert her unflattering spy observations into fiction, which we might read as Fitzhugh's advice to her young queer readers.[43] In *Nobody's Family Is Going to Change*—the title less a queer theory than a brutal truth—Emma dreams of being a lawyer, while her younger brother Willie longs to be a dancer and even dreams of a male lover. Their parents are no help. Emma's mother advises her to marry a lawyer, not become one. Instead, the kids get involved with a child activist group called the Children's Army. Like *Harriet the Spy, Nobody's Family Is Going to Change* interrogates the normativities of age, as well as that of gender and race. It seems to say: follow your heart, find your people, take action.

Staying with realism, and straddling the middle-grade and young adult novel genres, Virginia Hamilton's *The Planet of Junior Brown* (1971) features the odd couple of Junior Brown, an overweight musical prodigy, and Buddy, a streetwise homeless kid who looks after Junior (they are both eighth-graders). These are kids queered by race, to borrow from Stockton, or rather racism, as well as by age, time, and poverty. Their unlikely but powerful friendship makes survival possible for both, even when Junior has a nervous breakdown. Before this crisis, the two hide out with the school janitor, Mr. Pool, in a secret room inside the school, where they help him assemble a model of the solar system, one altered to include an enormous brown planet—the planet of Junior Brown. The language of "planets," however, also applies to secret groups of homeless boys over which Buddy watches, hidden away in various recesses of New York City. Mr. Pool takes care of Junior and Buddy while Buddy takes care of these various planets or communities. When Junior begins to hallucinate, Buddy and Mr. Pool take him not to his mother or to a hospital but to one of the planets, where he can be properly nursed. Home and school are both suspect. The novel's not perfect. The few women characters, while drawn sympathetically, cannot be relied upon; rather, this book is about the bonds between men and boys, and among boys. The only trustworthy adult is Mr. Pool. Once again, the message seems to be that survival requires self-reliance alongside a supportive queer (and here, secret) community. Hamilton's attention to racism, homelessness, and poverty may even position the book as analogous to queer of color critique.

The years 2014 and 2015 saw the publication of two realistic chapter books for upper elementary school readers that deal with gender identity rather than sexuality through inventive plots about a school play. In Ami Polonsky's *Gracefully Grayson*, which appeared first, the title character has been holding onto secret knowledge that she is not a boy as everyone assumes. Encouraged by a supportive and probably gay male teacher named Finn, Grayson tries out for the part of Persephone in the school's production of the Demeter and Persephone myth and wins the role (cast by Finn), despite opposition from just about everyone, especially Grayson's aunt (Grayson is being raised by her aunt and uncle following the death of her parents). Grayson goes on stage as planned and is triumphant in the role, which feels much more natural than the daily drag of boyhood. Finn, meanwhile, is driven from the school, taking the fall for casting Grayson and raising the specter of gay teacher-student recruitment. Alex Gino's *George* tells the story of another girl misrecognized by her family and classmates as a boy. George lives with her mom and older brother Scott. George tries several times to tell her mother that she is a girl, but this news is unwelcome. George's best friend Kelly is a much better advocate, agreeing energetically that George is a girl. "'So,'" Kelly asks about midway through the book, "'you're, like, transgender or something? . . . I was reading on the Internet, and there are lots of people like you. Did you know you can take hormones so that your body, you know, doesn't go all manlike?'" (104). "'Yeah, I know,'" answers George. For George "had been reading websites about transitions since Scott had taught her how to clear the web browser history on Mom's computer" (105). Here the school play is an adaptation of E. B. White's classic children's book *Charlotte's Web*. George auditions for Charlotte, the spider who saves the pig Wilbur from death through some clever spinning of human language, but her anxious teacher refuses to cast her in that starring role. Kelly is cast instead. They rehearse together anyway, and Kelly secretly switches George into her Charlotte costume. George performs brilliantly, and George's mother gradually comes around. The novel emphasizes not only the relief George feels at finally getting her news across but her transformative experience through the play: "Charlotte was dead, but George was alive in a way she had never imagined" (157). "The play passed quickly, and yet it seemed to George as though she had been onstage since the beginning of time, as if she were born there and had only now found herself where she had always been" (156).

When George's mom expresses concern that being different in the world is hard, George responds, "'Trying to be a boy is really hard'" (170). After the play, and as George's mom takes the first step toward acceptance, Kelly concocts a plan to take George with her on a visit to the Bronx Zoo with her uncle. She helps George dress as a girl, and even though George can be an androgynous name, they rename George "Melissa." Here again, the message of the book is not only about communicating an identity to the outside world, although that is important, but feeling like oneself finally. Melissa is wearing boys' underwear underneath her skirt and pink tank top. "No one would be able to see them, but she would know all day that they were there" (187). Kelly shouts, "'Ew! Yuck! Pull them off!,'" and hands Melissa a pair of her own underwear. At the Zoo, she uses the girls' restroom, leaving her awestruck. The book concludes with the zoo expedition and with the symbolic death of George. In an afterword, Gino answers questions about the book, explains terms like *transgender*, *genderqueer*, and *binary/nonbinary*. They (Gino's pronoun) remark that while it is okay if readers slip and call Melissa "George," they should try to use "Melissa," as that is her name. I love that Gino makes this demand of readers so late in the game, respecting Melissa's experience and challenging all of us to reboot our perceptions. *Gracefully Grayson*, in contrast, does not get into the question of names; indeed, the book refers to Grayson using the masculine pronoun even after her appearance as Persephone.

In any case, both books effectively translate ideas about gender and/as performance into narratives for younger readers. In both, the opportunity not just to perform but to live one's real gender in public paves the way for identity acceptance. To be sure, there are tensions in the books, most obviously one between the "wrong body" trans narrative and a more fluid conception of gender. That tension marks queer theory itself, especially in conversation with trans theory. Both novels are written for younger people whose gender identity conflicts with their assigned gender and who may or may not come to identify as trans. Melissa and Grayson are certain of their gender identities even as they learn to question assumptions about gender and sexuality. Both books—one written by a trans author (Gino), the other by a cisgender heterosexual woman (Polonsky)—prioritize the child's perspective and voice over the authority of adults. Anger and outrage are not only allowed on the part of the characters but encouraged for the reader. These books are probably already serving as survival manuals for queer kids.

On the more fanciful side of these books for upper elementary and middle-school readers is John Boyne's *The Terrible Thing That Happened to Barnaby Brocket* (2012), in which eight-year-old Barnaby literally floats if not firmly tethered to the ground. The terrible thing that happens to Barnaby is that his horrible parents let him float away because they are embarrassed by him. After seeing the world, making queer friends, and returning home, Barnaby is confronted with an option: undergo a simple surgery to become normal or escape with his queerness intact. He opts for the latter and floats away again, this time deliberately. He turns something terrible into liberation and pride. From the cover: "This whimsical novel will delight middle graders, and make readers of all ages question the meaning of normal."

Or consider the immensely beloved chapter book series of Lemony Snicket, a.k.a. Daniel Handler, *A Series of Unfortunate Events*, located somewhere between realism and fantasy. This series of thirteen novels ran from 1999 through 2006 and led to several film adaptations. If children's book authors tend not to editorialize these days, Handler takes the opposite tack in his persona of Snicket, hilariously so, recalling the overly involved and often mournful narrators of some historical children's literature. You surely know the overarching storyline: after a series of unfortunate events, most principally the death of their parents, the children must live with their relative Count Olaf until Violet comes of age and can inherit the family fortune. They discover that Olaf is evil—okay, they know this from the start, unlike the adults—and must continually escape his clutches in installment after installment.

The inaugural volume of the series, *The Bad Beginning* (1999), opens with this representative address to the reader: "If you are interested in stories with happy endings, you would be better off reading some other book. In this book, not only is there no happy ending, there is no happy beginning and very few happy things in the middle." The paragraph concludes: "I'm sorry to tell you this, but that is how the story goes." This is the playful stuff of metafiction, of course, but it is also queer advice literature.[44] It continues throughout the series.[45] The Snicket books ask the young reader to think about what she wants to read and what she *really* wants to read. They introduce her to the idea that while we are supposed to crave happy stories, we might crave something else. *A Series of Unfortunate Events* queers the contemporary children's book by recalling (if also ironizing) its bad beginnings in cautionary tales and Puritan primers and gothic melodramas. It teaches us that we are always already perverse readers. And like queer theory, it acknowledges loss, sadness, frustration, and the interplay of paranoia and reparation.

Snicket's protagonists, the Baudelaire children, are resourceful and capable minors: an inventor (Violet), a bookworm (Klaus), an inveterate biter (baby Sunny). The theme of the series is survival or, more particularly, the endurance of adults, principally Olaf but also the clueless and indifferent adults who exacerbate an already bad situation. In *The Bad Beginning*, Count Olaf tries to marry the very underage Violet in a ploy to seize control of the Baudelaire estate. Violet outwits him by signing the contract with her left hand. The narrator chimes in on the queerness of law and legality:

> Unless you are a lawyer, it will probably strike you as odd that Count Olaf's plan was defeated by Violet signing with her left hand instead of her right. But the law is an odd thing. For instance, one country in Europe has a law that requires all its bakers to sell bread at the exact same price. A certain island has a law that forbids anyone from removing its fruit. And a town not too far from where you live has a law that bars me from coming within five miles of its borders. (153)

The peculiarity of Violet's solution, he seems to say, is no more peculiar than the law itself or is the kind of peculiarity for which the law calls. Such editorializing approaches that of queer theory for grown-ups, which has a thing or two to say about jurisprudence.

While there is much to praise about the "It Gets Better" testimonial project launched by Dan Savage and Terry Miller in 2011, that project has received a lot of criticism, especially for its white male privilege. As many people have replied, things do not get better for a lot of queer kids out there, especially those who might be poor, brown, or black. Handler makes it pretty clear in his series that before things better—if ever they do—they get worse. Sometimes far worse. Life can be a series of unfortunate events. You may, however, survive anyway: that is the good news. *A Series of Unfortunate Events* offers lessons in affect management, and in irony and double meaning, typical of metafiction but also of queer discourse and theoretical writing. The children speak in code—in a minor language—in order to have private conversations. The narrator recruits the young reader into a sympathetic relation with these characters and their plight with formulations such as "Unless you have been very, very lucky, you have undoubtedly experienced events in your life that have made you cry" (*Bad* 57) or "I don't know if you've ever noticed this, but first impressions are often entirely wrong" (27). These little lessons do not often yield happy results, but they do point to the potential for happiness of a sort, a strategic, attitudinal one. The narrator implies that *eventually* things *might* get better, and in the meantime, we can mitigate the awfulness.[46] One strategy for survival is reading. Our narrator again:

> It is very useful, when one is young, to learn the difference between "literally" and "figuratively." If something happens literally, it actually happens; if something happens figuratively, it *feels like* it's happening. If you are literally jumping for joy, for instance, it means you are leaping in the air because you are very happy. If you are figuratively jumping for joy, it means you are so happy that you *could* jump for joy, but are saving your energy for other matters. . . . Figuratively, they escaped from Count Olaf and their miserable existence. They did not *literally* escape, because they were still in his house and vulnerable to Olaf's evil in loco parentis ways. But by immersing themselves in their favorite reading topics, they felt far away from their predicament, as if they had escaped. (68–69)

Is this not advice literature for child readers living in challenging situations? And is this not queer theory, long invested in the survival of queer children and sometimes functioning as a kind of self-help literature?[47] Queer theory may be axiomatically antidefinitional, as many insist, but it nonetheless affirms queer lives and presence. In this light, I see Snicket/Handler as queer theorist, glossing terms and concepts, making promises, smuggling in queer thoughts. Often his advice is tongue in cheek. His fictional kids show a fiercely queer optimism and resilience, asserting in *The Miserable Mill*, for instance, that "you never know" what might come next (maybe something good!), even as Snicket mournfully editorializes to the contrary.[48] The kids press on, sometimes bolstered by a queer sense of community, as in this passage from *The Grim Grotto*: "In wearing the uniform of the *Queequeg*, the siblings felt a part of something—not a family, exactly, but a gathering of people who had all volunteered for the same mission" (65). Whatever we make of all this, there is surely some pleasure for the reader who walks a tightrope between hope and anxiety, enduring the unfortunate events but hoping for a more fortunate future. Probably most readers have faith that the children will come to no harm, despite the ongoing awfulness. At the least, kids engaging with this material can indulge a taste for self-reflexive storytelling and learn about language, irony, self-knowledge, and adult failing. *A Series of Unfortunate Events* is queer theory for kids, involving the constructing, testing, and playing out of scenarios and hypotheses, some unpleasant. It is also a literature about and for minors, dwelling on the dependent status of the Baudelaires and the trouble it brings them.

Speaking of adult failing, Handler set in motion his own rather unfortunate event that casts a shadow over his work and the queer radicality I have been granting it. Emceeing the National Book Awards in 2014, Handler made a watermelon joke at the expense of his fellow author and ostensible friend Jacqueline Woodson, winner of the National Book Award for Young People for her terrific verse memoir *Brown Girl Dreaming*. Handler apologized and has attempted reparation in the form of charitable contributions, but the damage was done. As Woodson notes in an op-ed, with "a few short words, the audience and I were asked to take a step back from everything I've ever written, a step back from the power and meaning of the National Book Award, lest we forget, lest I forget, where I came from." Handler's remark "came from a place of ignorance," writes Woodson, and "showed that he believed we were at a point where we could laugh about it all." We are not at that point, as she makes clear. Racism is not an occasional annoyance but a structural problem in children's and young adult literature, as in the broader culture, and Handler's remark is a painful reminder that even progressive voices can be reactionary and that queer theory (of whatever iteration) must check its privilege.

Are You My Mother?

The closer we move to writing for adults, the more some literary material looks like queer theory as conventionally understood. YA literature has included queer content at least since 1969, the year of the Stonewall Riots and also the publication of John Donovan's YA novel *I'll Get There. It Better Be Worth the Trip.*[49] Many YA narratives have queer-theoretical tendencies as well as queer themes or plots. There is a growing body of literature for and about queer teens, some of it pushing beyond the gay-affirmative and taking up questions of identity and desire. Characters mull over "labels" (gay, queer, trans) and refashion their understanding of how gender and sexuality play out in life and culture. Other scholars such as Roberta Seelinger Trites, Lydia Kokkola, and Derritt Mason elaborate on the intensity of YA literature with respect to themes of sexuality and power. Mason proposes that we think of YA literature more in terms of what it does than what it ostensibly "is"; putting aside traditional ideas about genre, theme, and audience, he sees YA literature as comprising particular affects and effects, anxiety especially. He situates his analysis of queer YA literature in the context of the explosion of that literature in recent years, from some 10 titles in the 1970s to a remarkable 513 titles in 2010–2016 (Jenkins and Cart). And those numbers reflect only explicitly gay or queer content, only a subset of what might be regarded as queer YA material.

A good example of this literature, although not fiction, is Katie Rain Hill's 2014 trans memoir for teens, *Rethinking Normal*, which elaborates upon key terms of queer and gender theory while telling Hill's personal story. Hill emphasizes the power of language, discussing her own self-creation from fiction as well as ostensible nonfiction. As a child, Hill wrote a fantasy series about a protagonist named Rainfall, and when she later transitions she takes "Rain" as her new middle name. *Rethinking Normal* is at once memoir and DIY queer theory manual. Works for younger readers like this one share much with recent titles for adults that are child-affiliated as well as experimental in form, such as David Pratt's novel *Bob the Book* (2010) and Alison Bechdel's graphic memoirs *Fun Home* (2006) and *Are You My Mother?* (2012), which enjoy a wide audience including young adults.

Bob the Book is a comic gay novel with theoretical tendencies that also feels rather like a children's book, from its simple title and cover design to its short chapters, alliterative prose, and generally upbeat plot with a happy enough ending. Moreover, Pratt's novel exploits the classic literary device of the sentient object that tells its life story. The object can be, say, an umbrella or a doll; often it is currency such as a penny or guinea, underscoring the thematic of circulation. Not a few narratives for children employ this device, from classics like *Hitty, Her First Hundred Years* to contemporary films like *Brave Little Toaster*, *Cars*, *Sausage Party*, and the *Toy Story* franchise. Here that object is not a toaster or a toy but a book—more specifically, a copy of a book named Bob. Or rather, the copy is named Bob; the book's title is *Private Pleasures: Myth and Representation in Male Photo Sets and Pornography from the Pre-Stonewall Era to 1979*. This scenario recalls the "Haddocks' Eyes" portion of Carroll's *Through the Looking Glass*, in which poor Alice confuses the song with what the song is called, the name of the song, and what the name of the song is called. Anyway, Bob the Book (copy and character) is gay, being made that way, and the novel recounts his adventures being bought, sold, and exchanged. Along the way he meets other copies of books, two of whom he learns to love.

Bob the Book brilliantly dramatizes how "gay" books circulate in and around gay male culture in particular and even engage in their own form of queer world-building, as the books strike up unusual alliances and make the most of accidental proximity (literally who is closest on the shelf). In the process, readers get a glimpse into the lives of gay men, including at least one who is HIV+. Pratt's novel confirms Natasha Hurley's thesis in *Circulating Queerness* that the gay and lesbian novel is the product of queer circulation(s). Most accounts of the gay and lesbian novel start with the "first" examples and move forward in time, but also we should be looking backward too, she argues, attending to how the movements of authors and their texts created certain alignments and densities of identity. We see some of those dynamics in Pratt's novel. If Bob was born gay, he also becomes gay in the novel by falling in love, evaluating his feelings, and building a community. Pratt tells a coming of age story, in that Bob begins to understand the world, his interactions with others, and his experiences on the shelf. *Bob the Book*'s gayness derives not only from Pratt's identity but also from the book's circulations. Pratt knows this and has great fun with human practices of book use and abuse. We learn, for instance, that while books long to be read by their owners—the worst thing for a book being neglect—it is also stressful to be owned by scholars, as scholars read books too intensely. We crack their spines and mark up their pages (especially those poor teaching copies).

Bechdel's work has long been crucial to the queer comics scene, which dates at least to Stonewall-era gay strips and runs through today's queer web comics.[50] Prior to *Fun Home*, Bechdel was best known for *Dykes to Watch Out For*, a cartoon strip that ran from 1983 to 2008 in alternative newspapers connected to local queer communities. The success of *Fun Home* as a book and Tony-award-winning musical has brought Bechdel financial security and mainstream success if not also some celebrity (she is the recipient of a MacArthur "genius grant" as well). *Fun Home* deals with the suicide of Bechdel's closeted gay father, Bruce, and is narrated with a certain emotional detachment, even irony. Full of references to modernist and other writers, *Fun Home* seems on the surface to aspire to literary legitimacy, disavowing its origins in comics. And critics, notes Pizzino, have obliged this presumptive aspiration by suggesting that the book "is not just a comic, or is somehow *more* than a comic" (107)—recalling similar arguments about children's books such as *Alice* that ostensibly rise above their genre. In his chapter devoted to *Fun Home*, Pizzino contends that Bechdel is in fact ironizing literary aspiration and the general desire for cultural capital. Her own father was motivated by just that desire, preferring highbrow literature to other materials, and *Fun Home* is "less a serious exploration of high literary tradition than a droll exercise in feeling well read" (111). Bechdel loved and was influenced by *MAD* magazine and comics culture, he shows, and to insist that *Fun Home* is literary or modernist only or mostly is to miss that crucial context and the whole point of the book. Pizzino is hardly alone in emphasizing the diversity of Bechdel's archive or in underscoring Bechdel's challenges to received wisdom about good or great books. Kashtan, for instance, sees *Fun Home* as a highly self-reflexive meditation on the materiality of books, attending to the interplay of handwriting and typewriting as well as to *Fun Home*'s iterations as hardcover, paperback, and digital book. Noting that its many sources are hand-drawn by Bechdel rather than reproduced photographically, Chute similarly observes that *Fun Home* "is invested in offering up the archival documents on which it meditates to its readers" (183) as part of Bechdel's story of coming into artistry. *Fun Home* may be "a deeply crafted, intensely structured object" (Chute 178) but Cvetkovich emphasizes how Bechdel's archive features "insurgent genres of queer culture, such as memoir, solo performance, women's music, and autoethnographic documentary film and video" ("Drawing" 112). Margaret Galvan makes a similar case, looking at Bechdel's involvement with queer communities and "queer-adjacent and queer grassroots archives" (409).

Cvetkovich, Galvan, and Pizzino all suggest that *Fun Home*, and Bechdel's work more generally, functions as queer critique. For Pizzino, *Fun Home* offers a "larger critique not only of heteronormative culture, but also of prescriptive notions of literary and cultural respectability" (113). For Cvetkovich, the book furnishes a "welcome alternative to public discourses about LGBTQ politics that are increasingly homonormative and dedicated to family values" ("Drawing" 111), meaning that the book queers even gay affirmation. Galvan sees queer comics as "establish[ing] particular techniques in expressing queer experience," likening them to the work of feminist cinema as accounted for by Teresa de Lauretis (414). Bechdel and de Lauretis "theorize each other," she proposes, leading her in turn to theorize the queer archive as something like queer theory itself (Galvan 414).

Are You My Mother? also claims proximity to academic queer theory and queer critique. It has not, however, received the acclaim that has greeted *Fun Home*. Reviewers complain that *Are You My Mother?* is not as compelling or balanced as its predecessor, and in some ways that is true.[51] But if *Fun Home* is more aesthetically satisfying, *Are You My Mother?*

might be the more interesting of the two memoirs as an exercise in thinking and writing, one continuing the queer-theoretical project of *Fun Home* and taking it in some new directions. *Are You My Mother?* focuses on Bechdel's ongoing relationship with her very much alive mother, Helen, and with Bechdel's attempts to create in the wake of *Fun Home*'s success. For Pizzino, the second memoir draws its energy "from the intense self-thwarting Bechdel experienced while creating it, which she turns inward on the page in layer after layer of self-referentiality," such that it feels almost "like a meditation on the luxury of writer's block" (132).

Drawn in black and white, generally realist but occasionally surreal in presentation, the book received mixed reviews, although it did win the Judy Grahn Award for Lesbian Nonfiction and was shortlisted for a Lambda Literary Award. It is obsessively engaged with imaginative and especially psychoanalytic literature. There are so many intertexts that it is tough to keep track of them. A partial list of just the literary ones includes *To the Lighthouse*, Dr. Seuss's *The Sleep Book*, *Winnie-the-Pooh*, and *The Lion, the Witch, and the Wardrobe*. Virginia Woolf is a key figure, chiefly because in *To the Lighthouse* Woolf was able to work through a long obsession with her own mother, who died when Woolf was young. Psychoanalytic writing looms particularly large, beginning with Freud's *The Interpretation of Dreams*—each of the seven chapters of *Are You My Mother?* opens with a dream and Bechdel's dream analysis—and continuing through the revisionist work of Alice Miller and especially Donald Winnicott. Winnicott's ideas about transitional objects, good enough mothering, and the safe holding environment inform every page of the memoir, to the point that we could nearly retitle it *Winnicott for Beginners*. Bechdel interweaves Winnicott's biography with passages from his work, applying his insights to her own life. At one point, she reveals that the memoir actually began as a book about Winnicott and only gradually became a book about her mother. Or *also* about her mother, for Winnicott remains a key presence and plays the role of mother-therapist. (Bechdel even named her cat Donald, a choice she may now regret.)

While Bechdel acknowledges just about every other text important to her story, she makes no mention of the book from which she takes her title, P. D. Eastman's illustrated early reader for children *Are You My Mother?*, published in 1960 as part of Random House's Beginner Books series. Eastman's book tells the story of a hatchling bird who leaves the nest and goes in search of his mother. He asks a series of animals "Are you my mother?" and they each say no. He moves on to a car, a boat, a plane, and finally a power shovel, whose terrifying "SNORT" prompts him to declare, "You are not my mother! You are a Snort! I want my mother!"

(I suppose a more radical storyline would show him becoming a shovel.) Mother and baby bird finally reunite. Bechdel likewise "finds" her mother in time, although the moral of her story is more complicated, something like: "you are—and *are not*—my mother" or "you are not always the mother for whom I hoped, but you are my good enough mother." Bechdel comes to accept the limitations of her relationship with her mother and to recognize what her mother provides as good enough. Bechdel seems to present her memoir as a version of Eastman's classic, although I have seen no acknowledgment of the book's influence. If, as Pizzino holds, *Fun Home* embraces its identity as a comic, then perhaps the allusion to Eastman's book in this sequel acknowledges the significance of children's books for Bechdel. The references to Pooh and Narnia and Dr. Seuss suggest more than a passing familiarity with these materials, and we know from *Fun Home* that Bechdel's love for maps was inspired partially by Kenneth Grahame's *The Wind in the Willows*. At the least, children's books join with comics and those "insurgent genres" mentioned by Cvetkovich as part of Bechdel's working archive. It is notable, too, that while Eastman's *Are You My Mother?* is much beloved and still in print, it is not generally considered a picturebook classic. Eastman's story is unsettling, besides, as the poor hatchling wanders about in a frightening landscape. It is an odd but appropriate choice.

Like academic queer theory, and like *Fun Home*, *Are You My Mother?* confronts compulsory heterosexuality and gives voice to queer experience. As such, it too can be described as literature for minors if not children's literature exactly. Perhaps even more than *Fun Home*, it is fashioned out of discourses of feminism and psychoanalysis that have been vital to queer theory. It takes up matters of identity, desire, memory, and time from a queer-identified perspective. The question of the mother is a queer question in lesbian literature, which thinks about the role and influence of literal and symbolic mothers. As I noted already, Woolf is hugely important in the book, as is Adrienne Rich. There is also mention of the early American poet Anne Bradstreet. Bechdel's story is written with the cumulative lessons of these women in mind. They, too, are her mothers. The memoir's engagement with psychoanalysis more generally, and with Winnicott in particular, further aligns it with queer theory, as queer theory often works off the scripts of psychoanalysis. And Winnicott is lately in vogue within queer theory.[52]

Bechdel queers Winnicott by adapting his insights to her own situation. At the same time, she figuratively and literally draws out the queer in Winnicott, without questioning his heterosexuality. She notes that Winnicott was of slight build and on the fey side. A pediatrician and also a child analyst trained by Klein, he played with children a lot, and Bechdel sketches him on the floor and eye-to-eye with his young patients. Meanwhile, Bechdel underscores that Winnicott's insights ran counter to polite culture as well as normative analysis. For instance, he believed that "juvenile delinquents" are more likely to be psychologically healthy than compliant children. In various ways, Winnicott was a minor or oppositional analyst.

Winnicott's most fundamental insight was perhaps also his most counterintuitive—namely, that there is "no such thing as a baby"; rather, babies are always babies *and* someone else (usually the mother).[53] In his account, the space between baby and caretaker is one of mutual make-believe and co-constitution. Bechdel takes this lesson to heart, composing a memoir of herself with and through her mother. Her mother is Bechdel's best reader and editor, and she is also a creative collaborator if not coauthor. Bechdel comes to accept the limitations of her relationship with her mother while also emphasizing its many rewards. While her mother fails to meet some of Bechdel's needs, she encourages her daughter's capacity for storytelling and creative work, thereby providing for her by failing her. Drawing on Winnicott, Bechdel decides that her mother is good enough, having offered herself up as an object to be used and having survived her daughter's anger and disappointment. Only then can the subject move beyond narcissistic projection and into genuine interpersonal relationships, thought Winnicott. "The Use of an Object" is the last chapter of Bechdel's memoir, just as it was the title of Winnicott's last major paper. Winnicott, too, is the good enough mother, who allows himself to be used, just as Bechdel's mother is also the good enough therapist. Bechdel also takes to heart Winnicott's belief that the maturation process is benign and even enjoyable under good-enough mothering. Bechdel seems to be working through trauma and shame and toward something like queer optimism. Like other queer theorists, she tells the story of queer child survival without suppressing any of the difficulties involved. The format of *Are You My Mother?* nicely renders the interdependence of identity, with Bechdel drawing her mother and Winnicott repeatedly and even appearing with them in some panels, thereby emphasizing their proximity and impact more dramatically than might be possible in a conventional narrative. Graphic texts have an ongoing association with theoretical discourse and with nonfiction more broadly, from which Bechdel draws and to which she contributes. Moreover, she coins new genres for both memoirs, calling *Fun Home* a "tragicomic" and the more upbeat *Are You My Mother?* a "comic drama." Bechdel self-presents as a (queer) theorist-practitioner of imagetext form.

Winnicott invites others to use his work assertively, even "ruthlessly," as Margaret Boyle Spelman notes (39). Bechdel accepts and issues the same invitation. *Are You My Mother?* can be a self-help project for the reader as well as the author, showing us how and why to apply theory to our own lives, or how to theorize *from* our own lives: queer theory for the autodidact. Bechdel confronts the urgency of such theorizing, musing that "if it weren't for the unconventionality of my desires, my mind might never have been forced to reckon with my body" (156). "It was only my lesbianism, and my determination not to hide it," she acknowledges, "that saved me from being compliant to the core" (188). Bechdel sketches a moving portrait of the artist as a queer theorist, who fashions from the traumas and resources of childhood a good enough queer life. This is what queer theory can look like outside the academy proper. The reflexivity and self-interrogation we associate with queer theory are on abundant display. And whatever the book's quality, I appreciate that Bechdel attempts something different with it, a more domestic, everyday, and overtly analytical story about mother-daughter relation and the creative life. Good enough mothering makes for good enough queer theory.[54]

We cannot know in advance what, if any, differences exist between what we call children's literature and what we call queer theory, especially as the latter moves toward memoir, experimental writing, and collaborative work. It is not any more outlandish to call children's literature queer theory for kids than to talk about philosophy for children. If nothing else, and even if it "fails," imagining queer theory for kids can be a generative thought experiment.

A Very Short Conclusion

I have argued throughout this book that children's literature thrives inside as much as alongside those ostensibly adult projects we call philosophy and theory. As it turns out, philosophy and theory both invest in the child and in children's literary and cultural forms. That is especially true of P4C, which engages children's literature first as a curriculum and then as a companion enterprise and even as a role model. Theory, meanwhile, sporadically draws on children's books and helps to create a literature for beginners that runs parallel to and sometimes intersects with imagetext forms like the picturebook and the graphic novel. And in turn, as this chapter has proposed, children's literature itself has theoretical as well as philosophical coordinates and energies. Judith Butler may not be writing children's books (yet!), but children's books have been tackling gender trouble, the psychic life of power, and bodies that matter (along with cruel optimism, the promise of happiness, and the queer art of failure). That does not seem such a radical proposition, given our more general expectation that children's books educate and enlighten, support as well as challenge children emotionally, intellectually, and socially. Children's literature in this way is a literature of and for potential "majors" as well as a literature of and for minors, helping to transform young people from imaginary to actual citizens, as Courtney Weikle-Mills persuasively argues.

If philosophy and theory are subjects that help constitute rather than stand outside of children's literature, that is in part because we make philosophy and theory as much as observe them. Philosophy and theory are activities and commitments. Philosophy is for children because people have insisted on such and helped make it so. I want philosophy and theory to be child-friendly as well as beginner-friendly. I observe the philosophical turn in my primary field of children's literature studies but also support it and try to build on the efforts of my colleagues. I hope this book, despite its flaws, will also interest those in theory studies, especially in its argument that theory production and dissemination can work in surprising if not mysterious ways.

Acknowledgments

I appreciate everyone who gave feedback on pieces of this project in talks at the University of Hawaii, Hollins University, Simmons College, and Homerton College, Cambridge, as well as scholarly meetings of ACLAR, ChLA, IRSCL, and PAMLA. Thanks to Kristine Alexander for the opportunity to participate in the "Forever Young?" symposium at the German Historical Institute. The late Patricia Smith Yaeger invited me to write on queer theory and children's literature, which helped me imagine their connections. I had stimulating conversations with Robert B. Ray about philosophy with children, Wittgenstein, and the idea of wonder. Kristen Gregory brought me up to speed on the gifted child. Rebekah Fitzsimmons, Carl F. Miller, and Marah Gubar have been especially helpful as friends and scholars working on overlapping topics, and I thank them for collegiality and conversation. Leslie A. Paris generously shared her work in progress about childhood and children's rights in the 1960s and 1970s. Margaret Galvan educated me about queer comics and provided helpful feedback. Anastasia Ulanowicz responded in her usual smart and generous way to chunks of this material. John P. Leavey suffered through and commented on the full manuscript, and I thank him for his incisive comments and ongoing friendship. I also thank my reviewers for Fordham University Press, whose reports were helpful and encouraging. The Fordham team has been terrific, and I thank especially Richard Morrison for his encouragement and patience.

I've benefitted from the work and presence of many others at Florida and elsewhere, among them Michelle Ann Abate, Suzan Alteri, Kathryn

Baker, Poushali Bhadury, Marsha Bryant, Steven Bruhm, Ramona Caponegro, Kate Capshaw, John Cech, the much-missed June Cummins, Sid Dobrin, Gabriel L. Duckels, Kim Emery, Rebekah Fitzsimmons, Richard Flynn, Joseba Gabilondo, Eugene Giddens, Pamela K. Gilbert, Paige Glotzer, Jerry Griswold, Naomi Hamer, Terry Harpold, Tace Hedrick, Susan Hegeman, Emily Hind, Susan Honeyman, Natasha Hurley, Zoe Jaques, Marilisa Jimenéz-Garcia, Vanessa Joosen, Anuja Madan, Roger Maioli, Derritt Mason, Elizabeth Marshall, Michelle Martin, Farah Mendlesohn, Barbara Mennel, Julia Mickenberg, Emily Murphy, Anne Morey, Phil Nel, Claudia Nelson, Maria Nikolajeva, Megan Norcia, Judith Page, Lissa Paul, Lucy Pearson, Kimberley Reynolds, Leah Rosenberg, Teya Rosenberg, Raúl Sánchez, Joe Sutliff Sanders, Jodi Schorb, John Schueller, Malini Johar Schueller, Sara L. Schwebel, Victoria Ford Smith, Delia Steverson, Jan Susina, Gwen Athene Tarbox, Laurie Taylor, Joseph T. Thomas Jr., Roberta Seelinger Trites, Eric L. Tribunella, Maureen Turim, Lynne Vallone, Phil Wegner, Lance Weldy, Karin Westman, and Rae Yan.

My thanks also to colleagues who shared their thoughts about the graphic guides: Katherine Arens, the late Don Ault, Lauren Berlant, Poushali Bhadury, Akilah Brown, Dan Brown, Richard Burt, Shannon Butts, Jim Dillon, Craig Dionne, Rebekah Fitzsimmons, Chris Gage, Chris Garland, Mindy Garza, Peter Gitto, Sam Hamilton, Dylan Horrocks, Elliott Kuecker, David Leavitt, Roger Maioli, Patrick McHenry, JoAnn Pavletich, Regine Rossi, Joseph Michael Sommers, Michelle Superle, Craig Svonkin, Meghan Sweeney, Gwen Athene Tarbox, Maureen Turim, Annette Wannamaker, Phil Wegner, John Wiehl, and Andrea Wood.

Portions of this book were drafted during a sabbatical leave, for which I thank my chair, Sid Dobrin, and my dean, David Richardson.

Thanks, as ever, to Martin, Carolyn, Doris, and Kathryn. And to Amy Deem and Lisa Redwine for all the adventures.

Notes

Introduction: Children's Literature Otherwise

1. In this book I use "children's literature" as shorthand for both children's and young adult literature.

2. Reading specialists distinguish between functional or transactional reading, associated with basic literacy, and interpretive or deep reading, associated with cultural literacy.

3. Reader response theorists "come closest to recognizing the formative influence of childhood reading" but nonetheless shy away from children's texts, Thacker notes (4). She also points out that with feminist theory "we come closest to a dialogue, yet there is very little evidence that, even here, children's literature is considered" (6). Four years prior, Caroline Hunt suggested that YA literature in particular had "evaded" the theorists, for a host of reasons. Jones amplified these concerns in 2006, while in 2011 I made a similar complaint about queer theory's neglect of children's literature ("Queer Theory's Child"). There are exceptions to this pattern of neglect. Michael Payne proposes that the researches of little Roo in *Winnie-the-Pooh* resemble the sexual researches of young children as commented upon by Freud, while Sara Ahmed considers the child's "happiness" duty in and around the educational discourse launched by Rousseau's treatise *Émile*, hugely influential on children's literature. Ahmed also writes on Nancy Garden's YA novel *Annie on My Mind* and Toni Morrison's *The Bluest Eye*, not a children's book but concerned with childhood.

4. Saint-Amour notes that "paradigms of weak thought" have "emerged largely in fields that address difference, stigma, and inequity. This has been especially true of queer theory, whose dissident relationship to strong ideologies of sex and gender prepared it to play a central role in developing models of weak thought" (438).

5. In "On Not Defining Children's Literature," Marah Gubar writes that "we simply have to accept that the concept under consideration is complex and capacious; it may also be unstable (its meaning shifts over time and across different cultures) and fuzzy at the edges (its boundaries are not fixed and exact)" (212).

6. On other sorts of vernacular theory, see T. McLaughlin. On the "monarchialization" of theory as "high theory," see Potts and Stout.

7. In the otherwise excellent *The Palgrave Handbook of Childhood Studies* (2009), edited by Jens Qvortrup, William A. Corsaro, and Michael-Sebastian Honig, for instance, only one contributor out of twenty-eight works in literature and media studies. An important milestone in humanities-centered work is Anna Mae Duane's edited collection *The Children's Table: Childhood Studies and the Humanities.*

8. Beauvais elaborates upon Nikolajeva's concept of aetonormativity, noting the potential for literary criticism itself to lean aetonormative, or adult-favoring. Aetonormativity "gently makes the point that critics have a responsibility to recognize that the poetics of the children's book is inextricable . . . from the problematic contemplation of the child by the adult" ("Problem" 75). In *The Mighty Child*, Beauvais develops a distinction between authority and might, with "might" meaning "power" of children as potential.

9. The category of adulthood is now getting some overdue critical attention. See Mintz, *Prime of Life*; and Edelstein.

10. Nelson points to Lynne Rosenthal's term for the latter: the "children's book for adults."

11. See Clark's superb *Kiddie Lit.*

12. On the aesthetic blurring of literature for children and for adults, see Nikolajeva's *Children's Literature* and "Exit."

13. Teller's characters seek to combat the nihilism of one of their peers, Wannamaker notes, "not through philosophical discussions but by amassing a collection of things, by assembling a 'heap of meaning'" (83). They fail to find or create anything meaningful and in the process become increasingly destructive. Wannamaker optimistically argues that the novel invites us to involve the child as a partner in conversations about meaning and value.

14. Sainsbury calls Alexis Deacon's picturebook *Slow Loris* "philosophy by stealth" and likens Alan Gibbons's YA novel *The Edge* to Althusser's theory of ideological state apparatuses (*Ethics* 108, 94).

15. See Ogata on the emergence of the "creative child" at the American midcentury. In some ways, the creative child was a reboot of the nineteenth-century "imaginative child," as discussed by Sally Shuttleworth.

16. The concept of critical literacy derives from philosophy (logic especially) and educational theory, a kind of composite term for the systematic and self-reflexive examination of concepts and situations. Definitions abound, but most commentators cite as foundational Edward Glaser's 1941 *An Experiment in the Development of Critical Thinking*, concerned with critical thinking as an educational objective and practice. Glaser worried that K-12 schools promote "ready-made generalizations" (9) rather than teach students how to think for themselves. Critical thinking is usually linked to the promotion of a more civil and just society. Drawing on some of these sources, Sanders understands critical literacy as allowing "for a form of dialogue in which readers can see the process of generating knowledge, vulnerabilities in that knowledge and the people who created it, venues for resisting or redirecting conclusions drawn from that knowledge, and avenues for performing new inquiry" (*Literature*, 13–14). For Louise Joy, it is John Dewey who provides the most significant and useful articulation of critical thinking, especially in his *How We Think* (1910). In her reading, Dewey's version of critical thinking is deliberative, experimental, playful, skeptical, and self-reflexive (Joy

18–32). Joy argues that some writers for children (poets especially) anticipated Dewey by a century or more.

17. The essays of Miller and Lewis appear in Peter R. Costello's *Philosophy in Children's Literature*. In his foreword to that volume, Thomas E. Wartenberg urges us to "revise our understanding of both philosophy and children's literature" in order to recognize not only their similarities but their equivalence (ix). Wartenberg and Costello are both philosophers, Miller is a literary critic, and Lewis an educational philosopher. Contributors to the volume mostly identify as philosophers. It is no coincidence that Lewis teaches educational philosophy at Montclair State University, epicenter of the P4C movement.

18. See "Plato & Co.," Diaphanes, https://www.diaphanes.com/reihe/plato-co-40.

19. Tournier was also knowledgeable about and indebted to anthropology and especially Claude Lévi-Strauss, as Beckett explains.

20. In the same volume, Helene Høyrup proposes that Cecil Bødker's *Silas and the Black Mare* functions something like Danish modernism for children, offering as it does a vision of "cultural alterity and a highly oppositional stance to established patterns of thinking" (129). She notes the post-1968 association of children's literature study with ideological critique and compares Bødker's novel explicitly to critical theory.

21. Writing about Paul de Man's response to the MLA's request to write an accessible account of theory, Deborah Britzman remarks, "It is almost as if de Man argued for the right to be impractical and to encounter things not known" (*Psychoanalyst* 53). "Since the audacity of theory contains a kernel of aggression," she adds, "and seeks either to destroy old views or protect them from changing, theory is not benign" (51).

22. Elizabeth Bruss describes the allure of reading theory in similar terms: "At one level, the thrill of reading theory is rather like being confronted with an exotic language or a blueprint drawn to an unknown scale—an overwhelming and undifferentiated confusion that will gradually (for the patient inquirer) resolve itself into perceptible lines and a usable order. There is an intoxication even in this simple passage from obscurity to sense, from helplessness to mastery—or to (increasingly) a mastery just out of reach, always promised but forever postponed" (129).

23. Citing Brandt, Jacobs writes on comics as "sponsors" of multimodal literacy. In *Writing Youth* Jonathan Alexander identifies YA literature as another such sponsor.

24. Phillip E. Wegner argues that these graphic articulations of theory are not exercises in ahistorical abstraction (as some assume) but quite the opposite: an attempt to practice and encourage dialectical critique.

25. Jeffrey Williams remarks that for a time, theory became "the name of elite work in literary studies" ("Packaging" 283), while Mitchell calls it a "glamour" field (Introduction 1).

26. A more complicated topic is the standing of philosophy as literature, taking all sorts of forms, including autobiography, confessions, dialogues, fables, and fragments. Anthony J. Cascardi reminds us that Voltaire shunned grand philosophical argument and wrote instead in the "minor" genre of the fable-like story (*conte*) (68). "Reading Plato, we may think we are reading a kind of literature, and in fact we are" (8). See also Flaxman on the "fabulation" of philosophy.

27. An alternative chronology begins with Hegel, as Andrew Cole illustrates in *The Birth of Theory*. See also Erickson; D. Held; and Rosmarin. Rosmarin especially emphasizes the continuities of philosophy and theory.

28. On the history of literary theory, see Birns.

29. As Vincent B. Leitch observes in *Theory Matters*, the word *theory* "functions nowadays frequently as a banner of convenience, as well as a symbolic marker of professional identity and also a bogeyman" (4). Leitch identifies some half-dozen meanings for theory, among them "the broad field" of criticism, "professional common sense," "high or grand theory, with low (or vernacular) theory or posttheory arriving after structuralism and poststructuralism," and also "a historical new, postmodern mode of discourse that breaches longstanding borders, fusing literary criticism, philosophy, history, sociology, psychoanalysis and politics" (11).

30. Cusset calls the whole scene a "creative misunderstanding between French texts and American readers, a properly structural misunderstanding—in the sense that it does not refer simply to a misinterpretation, but to differences of internal organization between the French and American intellectual spheres" (5). McHale makes the same point, emphasizing that "reception" is something of a misnomer as the assimilation of thinking "was a vigorously active process, involving reframing and appropriation, even (from certain points of view) *mis*appropriation and *mis*comprehension (or 'misprision,' to use a term of act favored by Harold Bloom" (69). On the Americanness of theory, see also Culler's *Framing*; Graff; and Redfield.

31. "Even when a certain coyness leads some authorities to pretend that they do not know what philosophy is," writes Le Doeuff in her brilliant analysis, worth quoting at length, "no agnosticism remains about what philosophy is not. Philosophy is not a story, not a pictorial description, not a work of pure literature. Philosophical discourse is inscribed and declares its status as philosophy through a break with myth, fable, the poetic, the domain of the image. . . . If, however, one goes looking for this philosophy in the texts which are meant to embody it, the least that can be said is that it is not to be found there in a pure state. We shall *also* find statues that breathe the scent of roses, comedies, tragedies, architects, foundations, dwellings, doors and windows, sand, navigators, various musical instruments, islands, clocks, horses, donkeys and even a lion, representatives of every craft and trade, scenes of sea and storm, forests and trees: in short, a whole pictorial world sufficient to decorate even the dryest 'History of Philosophy'" (1).

32. For a particularly good account of Wittgenstein, see Reé 469–614.

33. In an earlier study, P4C advocate Joanna Haynes cites S. Ball on the notion of theory as also "a vehicle for thinking otherwise" (33).

34. See especially Markus P. J. Bohlmann's *Misfit Children*, including the excellent introduction.

35. In addition to the sources discussed here, see also Faulkner, "Innocents"; the 2010 special issue of *Feminist Theory* on the child and childhood in feminist theory; Shuttleworth; and Steedman. Diana Gittens suggests three interrelated (sometimes overlapping) kinds of "child": the real/actual/embodied young person; the rhetorical-theoretical-literary child; and the recollected or autobiographical child (12).

36. See Wyness 42–43.

37. There is also the influence of trauma literature and trauma studies. Writing in 2010, Kate Douglas notes the publication over the previous fifteen years of some thousand plus autobiographies of often-traumatic childhoods, which she sees as symptomatic of heightened concern about children's welfare and children's rights globally.

38. See Lesnik-Oberstein's *Children's Literature: Criticism and the Fictional Child*, which applies Rose to children's literature criticism, and also her *On Having One's Own*

Child, which argues "that the child and the desire for the child constitute in particular and specific ways 'a value, a theme of expression, an occasion of emotion'" (xxiii). In 2002, Lesnik-Oberstein and Thomson published "What Is Queer Theory Doing with the Child?," examining Eve Sedgwick and Michael Moon on the "proto-gay" child. They find Sedgwick and Moon insufficiently alert to the lessons of poststructuralism, such that the proto-gay child becomes an "antitheoretical moment" and an exercise in essentializing. In my view, Lesnik-Oberstein and Thomson go too far in recasting queer theory as an adult imposition and also fail to appreciate the utopian and performative dimension of queer theory. Their main accusation is that all this talk for the child is really something done to the child—that queer theory fails the child by loving it too much or too uncritically (either way, inappropriately). That is the implication of their title, "What Is Queer Theory Doing with the Child?" Queer theory can only be a scandal when thus presented. In fact, no child has been harmed in the making of queer theory, which makes theoretical space for the queer child and for the queerness of all children. I do agree that adults fetishize the child and even eroticize the child's ostensible innocence or emptiness, as James Kincaid proposes in two landmark books. Applying these insights to education, Jen Gilbert warns that the child is all too often imagined as an origin point for the adult rather than a creature in her own right.

39. In such mobilizations, Castañeda claims, the child represents "pure form," evacuated of materiality. She traces this pattern of appropriation into feminist theory, neoclassical psychoanalysis, and queer theory. To "inhabit the child," she theorizes, "is to inhabit the condition, once again, of possibility itself; and to inhabit the condition of possibility is to become a child" (146). In her view, psychoanalysis has been a particularly effective technology for childhood's colonization. Oddly, Castañeda seeks relief from theory's child in "the agency of nature," existing "beyond the domain of the human and human knowledge" and thus outside "either the adult or the child" (165).

40. See especially Sánchez-Eppler's *Dependent States*.

41. Jenks points out that Merleau-Ponty understood the child's linguistic abilities as evolving through personal experiences rather than formal education (49).

42. Lesnik-Oberstein and Thomson remark that the child "is made to wander around the discourse of many disciplines, accruing and fulfilling many and varied functions" (35). But the child is not some Dickensian waif adrift in the streets; rather, the child is theory, at least in part. Even so, Lee Edelman rejects the child as potential resource for queer theory. Rebekah Sheldon also has her doubts, proposing that we obsessively turn to the child in the face of both "unprecedented technoscientific control and equally unprecedented ecological disaster" (2–3) not only because the child represents a hopeful futurity but also because the child binds "a restive and agential nonhuman surround" back to the human. Like Edelman, Sheldon wants to resist "the imperative to rescue the future through the child" (4). Meanwhile, Gittens warns that not "everything is 'discursively constructed'" (17).

43. Speaking of wishful thinking, Robert Pogue Harrison goes so far as to theorize that human culture, like the human biological animal, tends to retain youthful features that enable survival and progress. Human neoteny, he explains, "is neither regression nor arrestation but a modified type of development that brings juvenile traits to new levels of maturity, where they are preserved in their youthful form" (20). So too with human culture's "juvenescence," he thinks. Stressing that his account is more theory than history, he offers case studies of three "neotenic revolutions" in Western society: the birth of Socratic philosophy, the birth of Christianity, and the birth of the

American republic. In each case, he proposes, "older legacies assume new or younger forms, thanks to a synergy between the synthetic forces of wisdom and the insurgent forces of genius" (72). Socratic philosophy privileges youthful curiosity over settled knowledge; Christianity repurposes Judaism with the child front and center; the American republic makes a faith out of reason, that upstart child of the Enlightenment. It is a provocative if troubling theory, one helpful in explaining the ongoing centrality of the child to theory and philosophy—especially to P4C as a modernization of Socratic philosophy.

44. H. M. Evans stresses the importance of cultivating an attitude of wonder in medical practice, defining *wonder* as "a very particular kind of special attentiveness" that can combat routine and produce insight into seemingly ordinary situations (127). Robert Ray links Evans's remarks to similar comments on wonder cultivation by Henry David Thoreau, Ludwig Wittgenstein, and Stanley Cavell. "Evans' wonder," writes Ray, "results in what Wittgenstein called 'the dawning of an aspect,' the sudden appearance of something previously missed—the duck in the gestalt images which had previously seemed only to offer a rabbit" (30).

45. No one makes this point more forcefully than Sedgwick in the opening pages of *Tendencies*: "I think many adults (and I am among them) are trying, in our work, to keep faith with vividly remembered promises made to ourselves in childhood . . . to make invisible possibilities and desires visible; to make the tacit things explicit; to smuggle queer representation in where it must be smuggled and, with the relative freedom of adulthood, to challenge queer eradicating impulses where they are so to be challenged" (3).

1. Philosophy for Children

1. By 1976, the IAPC had conducted two studies measuring the effect of P4C methods on the intellectual development of fifth and sixth graders. The first, conducted by Lipman and his associate Milton L. Bierman, measured an increase in reading and reasoning skills via the California Test of Mental Maturity and the Iowa Test of Basic Skills. The second study, involving four hundred fifth and sixth graders in Newark, New Jersey, likewise showed improvement in analytical reading ability (Bynum 5). These studies led to others, all showing demonstrable gains through P4C. The IAPC website maintains a bibliography of research on P4C.

2. A key tenet of P4C from the first wave forward is that almost anyone can practice it. Lipman felt that teachers needed training to become good facilitators of philosophical dialogues, but he also insisted that P4C was more a method than a subject per se.

3. Terrell Ward Bynum reports these and other developments in his introduction to a 1976 special issue of the academic journal *Metaphilosophy*, featuring articles on P4C by Lipman, Matthews, Clyde Evans, Hope J. Haas, and David Cwi. While Lipman's books were the official curriculum of the IAPC, "scientifically tested and supported by a teacher-training program," other philosophers "have experimented with materials which were not originally intended for philosophical uses" (Bynum 3). Bynum points to Clyde Evans, who used film strips designed originally for values-clarification exercises in school.

4. "It was 1963 when I first connected philosophy with childhood," Matthews explains in *The Philosophy of Childhood*. Puzzling on how the family cat got fleas, his young daughter hypothesizes that one flea must have started all the fuss, since

"the only thing that goes on and on . . . is numbers." "I can remember thinking," he continues, "'Here I am teaching my university students the argument for a First Cause and my four-year-old daughter comes up, on her own, with an argument for the First Flea!'" (1–2). "I don't want to come right out and say that children are philosophers, or that philosophers are children," he clarifies elsewhere; rather, "what philosophers do (in rather disciplined and sustained ways) is much closer than is usually appreciated to what at least some children rather naturally do (albeit fitfully, and without the benefit of sophisticated techniques)" ("Philosophy" 15).

5. In *Philosophy Goes to School*, Lipman identifies both a narrow and a broader case for P4C: the narrow case is that it contributes usefully to the curriculum; the broader justification is that it guides lifelong growth and aspires to transform society (17).

6. On philosophy's slow and grudging engagement with childhood, see Turner and Matthews.

7. If some philosophers resist the idea that literature might be philosophical and vice versa, others have embraced it—though admittedly my examples are all French.

8. Elizabeth Massa Hoiem observes that the Robinsonade genre was originally linked not only with continental philosophy but also philosophical and pedagogical radicalism, in the wake of the French revolution. English writers, however, moved away from the philosophical content "in favor of a nationalist adventure story" (1).

9. The Robinsonade generally involves a confident and robust sense of self; the challenge is more to survive and even best the environment than to interrogate identity. On the Robinsonade in children's literature, see also O'Malley; Phillips; and Sundmark.

10. For information on titles and publication dates in French, see Beckett (157–58). There were earlier adaptations of Defoe's novel for children, of course. In a feature for *Yale Alumni Magazine* about *Robinson Crusoe* and its adaptations for children, Jill Campbell speculates that when Karl Marx cites Defoe's novel to illustrate a point in *Capital*, "he mistakenly refers to Crusoe's taming of llamas rather than goats—suggesting that his ideas about political economy were first stirred by his childhood reading of the Robinsonades illustrated here."

11. The source here for Beckett is an article by Gilles Lapouge entitled "Michel Tournier's s'explique."

12. *Robinson Crusoe* has inspired not a little critical as well as literary engagement, commented on by Rousseau, Kant, Marx, Heidegger, Lacan, Deleuze, and especially Derrida, in the second volume of *The Beast and the Sovereign*. Expanding upon Marx's remarks on Defoe's novel, Derrida there develops a critique of sovereignty as a kind of fetish asserted against the messy realities of social life. Derrida credits Marx with reframing the Robinsonade as a social fantasy/ideology: "You'll find the most visible and even spectacular expression of Marx's audacity, the interesting temerity that pushes him to recognize in this an epochal structure, a great socio-economico-ideological phase that he calls, precisely, a 'Robinsonade,' and that he describes, naming in passing Rousseau's *Social Contract*—you'll find the most visible and even spectacular expression of this at the beginning of the Introduction to the *Critique of Political Economy* (1857)" (24).

13. Characteristically, Derrida teases us with the program he might have followed but decided against, in this case treating only with Defoe's novel: "In doing so, we would have followed Rousseau's advice, the advice given in *Emile*. The first book, 'the first that my Emile will read,' the 'only one' that 'for a long time will compose his entire library,' will be *Robinson Crusoe*" (*Beast* 18). There lies the fantasy of sovereignty in

miniature, notes Derrida, also a fantasy of tabula rasa, "the island as desert, the phenomenological deconstruction of all prejudices and socio-cultural stratifications, and a naïve, native, natural originary return to the things themselves before all the historical perversions of taste" (18). Maybe writers are drawn to the Robinsonade not only for its themes but also for the potential transfer in authority the genre promises by way of Rousseau (this book is the *first* and *only* book you need!). Given the genre's links with colonialism and capitalist economy, it is unclear as to how successfully the Robinsonade can be subverted.

14. For elaboration on the Platonic tradition, see Bollert. For a more comprehensive treatment of wonder as a philosophical keyword, see Deckard and Losonczi.

15. In *Libidinal Economy*, Jean-François Lyotard claims that desire always escapes the processes of rational thought. Wonder might be another name for desire.

16. On wonder and mysticism, see also R. Smith.

17. Margolin notes the "peculiar capacity" of gifted child discourse "to join the themes of Christianity with the themes of social class dominance" (136).

18. There are some striking parallels between gifted education and P4C, among them an injunction against memorization and rote learning, a call for a wide range of learning materials, and emphasis on the training of smart and flexible teachers.

19. Another P4C advocate, Michael S. Pritchard, clarifies that "childish wonder is not to be confused with childishness. The philosophical questions of children are deep and serious" (149).

20. Tony W. Johnson writes that teachers who want to engage in P4C "must have retained some of their childlike wonder" (25).

21. Matthews's *Socratic Perplexity* is situated in the context of Plato studies and classical philosophy studies more generally and speaks to other scholars of Plato and philosophy, as well as to more general readers. Matthews focuses on how Plato's representation of perplexity evolves across the three general periods of the dialogues. Matthews shows how Plato represents Socrates using three metaphors or conceits: as gadfly, as self-stinging stingray, and as midwife.

22. Both "gifted" and "wonder" designate many sorts of exceptional children, including the traumatized and the physically divergent.

23. *The Philosophical Baby* is a crossover academic monograph aimed at a more general audience. Gopnik has been interviewed by the likes of Stephen Colbert and Charlie Rose. The association of babies with world geniuses pervades popular culture, as with the musical videos *Baby Mozart*, *Baby Einstein*, and *Baby Galileo*, which promise intellectual enrichment through early exposure to classical music. One follow-up study found instead that babies who watched such videos show delayed language development (see Park). In an earlier, coauthored book, *The Scientist in the Crib: What Early Learning Tells Us about the Mind* (2000), Gopnik et al. write that "the most interesting thing about babies is that they are so enormously interested; the most wonderful thing about them is their infinite capacity for wonder" (211).

24. See, for instance, Haas.

25. The latter, notes Alan Rauch, were "less obviously instructional" than other forms and "had something of the tone of the epistolary novels of the eighteenth century" and "a veneer of narrative" (52–53). "Children were reading stories about science that included characters with whom they could identify, suggesting not only that they, too, could participate in the pursuit of science, but that knowledge was an integral part of the domestic scene" (53). There were also catechistic books on natural philosophy

or natural history published for children in the nineteenth century, such as Mary A. Swift's *First Lessons on Natural Philosophy, for Children*, which employs "remarkable simplicity of style, clearness of statement, and aptness for illustration" to make it child-friendly. First appearing in 1833, the book went through multiple editions and was energetically reviewed.

26. Nancy Vansieleghem is less sold on the dialogue idea because it assumes transparency in communication and leads potentially to monologization—and ultimately to repetition of the sort of closed system it sought to replace.

27. *Harry Stottlemeier's Discovery* is short, whereas *Philosophical Inquiry: An Instructional Manual to Accompany* Harry Stottlemeier's Discovery runs 474 pages. *Philosophical Inquiry* is a chapter-by-chapter user's manual for Lipman's novel, emphasizing "the process of inquiry" and beginning with "the structure of logical statements" and "reversing subjects and predicates." Many suggestions for related enrichment activities are offered. The manual also poses such questions as: What is a culture? What makes you *you*? The manual is heavy on teacher *don'ts*, most of which are variations on "don't be too invested in your own knowledge or authority." "Always let the discussion follow the sequence of the class's suggestions rather than the sequence of 'leading ideas' in this manual," instruct the authors. "*Your aim is to work with what the students themselves find interesting*, rather than to set the agenda yourself. Be on your guard not to confuse what you think is interesting with what the children are eager to discuss" (ii). There is not a little irony here, of course, given the size and scope of the manual and the deliberateness of the P4C program. Teachers are not encouraged to adapt *Harry Stottlemeier's Discovery* or other IAPC materials loosely or flexibly. Lipman's P4C program is very prescriptive, and dialogue among teachers is not the goal. In any case, *Philosophical Inquiry* ends with reflection on the manual itself. The question that Lipman's character Lisa poses to her class in *Harry Stottlemeier's Discovery* is also posed to the manual's readers: what are we learning here?

28. P4C offers some progressive lessons. In *Wondering at the World*, Lipman and Sharp, discussing a blind character in *Kio and Gus*, write "those who have the privilege of sight do not therefore possess an exclusively correct understanding of the ways in which the world can be said to work" (8).

29. Remarks Tony W. Johnson: "What is philosophy, stripped of its technical jargon and academic erudition, but an uncommonly stubborn attempt to think clearly?" (13).

30. Building on Nikolajeva's thoughts about chronotopes in children's literature, Beauvais points out that the Pooh stories belong to an older chronotope than Antoine de Saint-Exupéry's *The Little Prince* (1943), one in which "a sense of harmony, autonomy, nostalgia and innocence holds together the time-space" (*Mighty Child* 25). Time does not pass in the Hundred Acre Wood, and things do not really change. For Beauvais, *The Little Prince* registers the transition from *puer aeternus* (eternal child) to *puer existens* (existing/existential child).

31. As I discuss in *Freud in Oz*, the Pooh stories have proven especially popular as frames for pop philosophical as well as pop psychological discussion.

32. Matthews also suspects that resistance to philosophy derives from the unsettling questions that philosophy encourages.

33. Lacan makes a similar point in *My Teaching*: "If you ask a child questions based on a logical apparatus, especially if you yourself are a logician—and Piaget was a good one—then it is scarcely surprising that you find this logical apparatus in the child you are questioning. . . . You ask the child questions in the register of logic, and the child

answers you in the register of logic. But don't imagine children enter the field of language that way at every level. They need time, that's for sure" (34).

34. Matthews says much the same about Bettelheim: "How can anyone who has spent so much of this working life with children suppose them as limited in intellectual capacity as Bettelheim does?" (*Philosophy and the Young Child* 72).

35. "The idea of developmental psychology," notes Matthews, "has had a greater influence on the way that adults think about children than have any specific findings of developmental psychologists" (*Dialogues* 31).

36. In his 1976 *Metaphilosophy* piece, reprinted in *Philosophy and the Young Child*, Matthews excoriates Bettelheim for failing to understand both children and children's literature. He shows that Bettelheim thinks of children as "primitives," driven by unconscious emotions and virtually incapable of thinking. "How can anyone who has spent so much of his working life with children suppose them as limited in intellectual capacity as Bettelheim does?" he asks (72). As for children's literature, he remarks that while he shares some of Bettelheim's disdain for "the literary, psychological, and existential poverty of many so-called realistic stories, I am appalled . . . that anyone writing on children's literature could suppose that that domain is neatly divided into fairy stories crammed with psychological insights and goals to self-discovery and realistic stories that have no real meaning for a child's life. What about adventure stories? Detective stories? Ghost stories? Biographies? Poems? Tall tales? Histories?" (74).

37. Following Matthews's example, Thomas Wartenberg, for instance, opens and closes *Big Ideas for Little Kids* with anecdotes about the inquiries of his young son Jake, to whom the book is dedicated.

38. Matthews, Lipman, and Tony W. Johnson agree that adults must avoid strong-arming the child. "To impose a teacher's position on a child," writes Johnson, "no matter how confident the adult is in the correction of the position, is indoctrination and antithetical to philosophical inquiry" (15). But the presence of adults does not undermine child philosophy any more than it undermines children's literature.

39. Gopnik is adamant that babies have a thing or two to teach philosophy. Calling consciousness not a stream but a "turbulent, muddy mess," she concludes: "Philosophers may have to resign themselves to just playing in the mud for a while yet. At least children can tell us it might be fun" (163). Like Bettelheim, she holds that it is unnecessary to teach psychology to young children because they practice it everyday intuitively.

40. Postmodern picturebooks arguably approach the "writing machine"/minor literature that Gilles Deleuze cultivates, whereas the philosophical novel "risks the very presuppositions and methods against which Deleuze's work is waged," prone to "predictable didacticism of characters made into mouthpieces for ideas" and "the reductive semblance that submits events to correspondence," among other sins (Flaxman 1).

41. My thanks to Masako Nagai for introducing me to this text in her presentation at the 2017 IRSCL Congress. Yoshitake has since written other conceptual picturebooks such as *What Happens Next?* and *Boring, Boring.*

42. Since 1953, UNESCO has reported periodically on the teaching of philosophy worldwide, and the 2007 (most recent) edition adds an extensive and quite helpful chapter on P4C, based on survey work conducted in English, French, and Spanish.

43. Per Jespersen builds on the storytelling tradition in Denmark, and Catherine McCall draws on Scottish Enlightenment philosophy to practice what she calls "Philosophical Inquiry."

44. In the United States, the decline of enthusiasm for P4C in the 1980s can probably be attributed to an increasingly conservative political climate and to rising anti-intellectualism. But P4C may have also been a victim of its own vision. Lipman and other architects insisted it was not another subject to be added to the curriculum but rather an overarching methodology, essentially a metadiscipline—"the discipline that best prepares us to think in terms of other disciplines," as Lipman puts it (*Philosophy Goes to School* 18). But that vision made P4C hard to implement and maintain over the long run.

45. See Institute for the Advancement of Philosophy for Children Montclair State University, https://www.montclair.edu/cehs/academics/centers-and-institutes/iapc/.

46. https://www.sapere.org.uk/. SAPERE is a registered charity based near Oxford, employing staff members and a network of registered professional trainers across the United Kingdom. It too provides teaching training courses and various P4C resources (also for a fee). In email correspondence, Lewis mentions that SAPERE was founded following the popularity of the BBC documentary *Socrates for 6-Year Olds*, which focused on P4C efforts in the United States. Lewis also reports that in 2016 some two hundred schools and roughly ninety thousand pupils were introduced to P4C. She estimates that at least five hundred schools across the United Kingdom are actively practicing P4C in some way, roughly one fifth at the "Bronze, Silver, or Gold" award levels (i.e., more intensive involvement).

47. Farson holds that young people should be free to work, vote, and be sexually active. Paris points out that it is unclear how much the child liberation movement was embraced by children themselves and how much it was an adult project.

48. Like Wartenberg, Lone is a philosophy professor at a research-intensive institution while also being a leader in the contemporary movement, as founder-director of the Northwest Center for Philosophy for Children. Like Wartenberg, Haynes, and Murris, she is an advocate of collaborative learning and describes children as "co-inquirers" whose capacities for reflection are routinely underestimated (3). Pitched toward parents rather than teachers, her book is organized in seven chapters dealing with major topics of philosophy (ethics, epistemology, metaphysics, and so forth) and incorporating analysis of children's titles. She is less concerned with method, perhaps because she is not writing for teachers, although she offers many tips and techniques along the way. For instance, on the topic of epistemology, she recommends follow-up activities such as reading *The Lion, the Witch, and the Wardrobe* and watching the film *Inception* (for older kids). Her own experiments in school-based P4C were focused on eighth-grade students.

49. Writes Lone: "Picture books can be particularly important for inspiring inquiry with your child about aesthetics. They are a unique mixture of literature and visual art and generate the discovery of meaning through a combined visual and verbal experience. The whole of a picture book . . . provides fertile ground for thinking about aesthetic qualities and questions about art, beauty, ugliness, and elegance" (105).

50. Wartenberg is now emeritus professor of philosophy at Mount Holyoke and a member of the graduate faculty at the University of Massachusetts Amherst, where Matthews was long appointed. His Philosophy for Children course, in which college undergraduates teach philosophy to second graders, was featured in an Emmy award-winning PBS documentary made in 2014 (also called *Big Ideas for Little Kids*). Wartenberg observes that when he first began exploring P4C, he did not think kids were really

doing philosophy but rather were learning critical thinking. "But I nonetheless used the label of teaching philosophy because that was my academic specialty, and it had a sort of cachet that made teachers intrigued and interested in working with me" (9). As he developed his practice, however, he began to realize how puzzled children are by philosophical issues and how invested they are in having philosophical discussions. Their deep, relentless curiosity qualifies them as philosophers for him. "I no longer think of myself as someone who only helps children acquire critical thinking skills. I view myself as an advocate of sorts, who wants to enable children to do something that comes naturally to them and at which they are astoundingly good: engage in philosophical discussions of important issues" (14).

51. Wartenberg recommends six rules for discussion:

State your position on an issue—that is, answer a question that has been asked—in a clear manner after taking time to think.

Figure out if you agree or disagree with what has been said.

Present a real example of the abstract issue being discussed.

Present a counterexample to a claim that has been proposed.

Put forward a revised version of a claim in light of criticism.

Support your position with reasons.

52. The texts were chosen not only because they work so well with the topics but also because they can be read in their entirety and discussed in forty-five-minute sessions. Slightly more than half of the titles are more classic than contemporary: Margaret Wise Brown's *The Important Book*, first published in 1949; Bernard Wiseman's *Morris the Moose* (1959); Shel Silverstein's *The Giving Tree* (1964); Leo Lionni's *Frederick* (1967); "Dragons and Giants" from Arnold Lobel's *Frog and Toad Together* (1972); and—the only chapter book—L. Frank Baum's original Oz tale, *The Wonderful Wizard of Oz* (1900). More contemporary (but still older) are Peter Catalanotto's *Emily's Art* (2001), and Mo Willems's *Knuffle Bunny* (2004).

53. Haynes and Murris seek to "challenge developmentality, because it marginalises children and limits education" (4). They also challenge the idea, now commonplace, that teachers do not need any background or even training in philosophy. They also criticize Lipman for his didacticism.

54. On comics and graphic novels as philosophy, see Jeff McLaughlin's two edited volumes; on the philosophy of comics, see Meskin, and Meskin and Cook.

55. See http://www.wonderponderonline.com/home.

56. While Wall waxes too spiritual for me, I appreciate his emphasis on phenomenology, children's rights, and ethics of care.

57. In *Civil Rights Childhood*, for instance, Katharine Capshaw reminds us that African American photobooks "use the form's metatextual status in order to permit the child to recognize that meaning is constructed" (xiv) and to document child activism (ix).

58. Woodhouse retells the stories of Frederick Douglass, Helen Keller, Anne Frank, and Maya Angelou, among others, in order to show that the "basic human rights principles" of the 1989 United Nations Convention on the Rights of the Child are "already deeply embedded in American history and tradition" (11) and to insist on narrative as "a more contextually rich terrain for exploration of children's rights than philosophical reasoning or legal doctrine standing alone" (11).

59. Todres was told to wait until after tenure to take up this project.

60. "When a child's right to participation is framed through a small turtle named Mack who finds himself at the bottom of a stack of turtles," they write, "Dr. Seuss becomes the human rights educator fostering a culture of civic responsibility" (7).

2. Theory for Beginners

1. As Michelle Ann Abate and Gwen Athene Tarbox observe, recent years have seen a dramatic upsurge of interest in and production of comics for children.

2. Echoing concern by conservative pundits about the disappearance of childhood, Kapur sees such disappearance as evidence of capital's colonization of the social sphere. However, Christopher Parkes tracks the evolution through the nineteenth century of a child-figure "defined by an innate curiosity and invention, the kind that leads to capitalist innovation" (1). Fiction such as E. Nesbit's *The Treasure Seekers* and Frances Hodgson Burnett's *A Little Princess* produced "the imaginative child . . . as a figure who could dissolve the boundary between the child's playroom and the nation's industrial landscapes such that they became a part of the same imaginative project" (Parkes 188). According to Parkes, these children, because they purportedly naturally possessed the creativity required to succeed in England's capitalist systems, assuaged adults' guilt regarding industrialism's costs for young people and maintained a fiction of social mobility.

3. Benjamin and Lyotard, notes Jonathan Bignell, are "interested in the child as a figure for the political subject in modernity, and also as the object of a political discourse. Each of them positions childhood in relation to notions of process, the constitution of the subject, and the relation between a subject and an object, event, or experience" (116).

4. Granted, the *infans* is not necessarily the "child" we want to celebrate or promote (whereas natality is a good thing for Arendt). Psychoanalyst Serge Leclaire argues we must kill the infans (the phantasmatic projection of our parents) if we are to survive and thrive. Maurice Blanchot picks up on the theme in *The Writing of the Disaster*, shifting focus to the question of language and calling the infans "that in us which has not yet begun to speak and never will speak; but, more importantly, the marvelous (terrifying) child which we have been in the dreams and the desires of those who were present at our birth (parents, society in general)" (67). Blanchot and Fynsk after him theorize that the death of the infans is necessary for (to) language. Agamben, meanwhile, treats "infancy" as an experience of potentiality rather than exposure or loss, beginning in *Infancy and History* (1978) and continuing through *Remnants of Auschwitz* (1998). As Sarah Hansen observes, Agamben's "recurrent figure of infantile potentiality is the *axolotl*, or 'Mexican walking fish,' an amphibian that retains juvenile characteristics (gills) even after the development of adult traits (lungs and reproductive organs). With this figure of an 'eternal child,' Agamben suggests that a new relation between human and non-human animals might emerge via a new childlike experience of language" (167). See also Faulkner's excellent analysis of Agamben in "Innocence, Evil, and Human Frailty." Faulkner there suggests that "the child signifies potentiality for Agamben as a purely creative, experimental, and speculative way of being, without which nothing could come to pass into actuality" (210).

5. Jakob Norberg reads *Minima Moralia* as an ironized conduct manual, "a paralyzing book of advice" designed to "stimulate not readers' self-confidence but rather their lucid understanding of their utter helplessness" (407) in the face of modernity.

6. That is not to say that Adorno or Barthes make the best academic role models, given their high-culture affinities; quite the contrary, as Litvak shows in chapter 5 of *Strange Gourmets.*

7. "'I am body and soul'—so speaks the child. And why should one not speak like children?" Nietzsche declares (61). "Zarathustra has become—a child, an awakened-one: what do you want now with these sleepers?" (40).

8. John Guillory proposes that we come to love theory by loving the teachers or masters of theory in a sort of vexed and vexing "transference of transference" (*Cultural Capital* 191–207). Even if we keep loving the teacher, writes Guillory, "the transference onto theory always misses its object, the positive content of theory, by cathecting in and behind that object the image of the master. Theory is desired because it is the theory of the master, a circumstance which always renders its truth merely axiomatic, and therefore secondary" (201).

9. *My Teaching* is an assemblage of three lectures Lacan gave about psychoanalysis to "provincial" or nonacademic, nonspecialist audiences, although one was actually for psychiatric workers. Lacan is clear, succinct, and also funny. For instance, he observes that "it is very unusual for anything that happens in the university to have repercussions because the university is designed to ensure that thought never has any repercussions" (26). Still, Lacan resists making things too easy, saying, "I do not think I will give you my teaching in the form of a pill; I think that would be difficult" (3). Difficult for him, he probably means, not so much for his listener-patients. But he also starts with the end: "Perhaps that will come later. That is always how it ends. When you have been dead long enough, you find yourself being summed up in three lines of a textbook—though where I am concerned, I'm not too sure which textbook it will be. I cannot foresee which textbooks I will figure in because I cannot foresee anything to do with the future of my teaching, or in other words psychoanalysis. We don't know what will become of this psychoanalysis" (3). Lacan was often invited to speak after the publication of *Écrits*, and Lacan says many times in *My Teaching* that *Écrits* is a book for specialists, not general readers.

10. The conceit of "theory kindergarten" was introduced playfully by Eve Kosofsky Sedgwick and Adam Frank and expanded upon by Britzman. A psychoanalyst and professor of education, Britzman emphasizes the difficulties of education by way of Anna Freud and Melanie Klein. Contrary to the idea that we breeze through theory kindergarten, Britzman thinks we never graduate. Britzman's account of theory kindergarten pivots around the figure of the "question-child," which she adapts from J. B. Pontalis. As with Jean-Michel Rabaté, Britzman's account of theory is psychoanalytic, hinging not on the Hysteric but rather the question-child, residual within the theorist. The theorist never leaves theory kindergarten but rather suffers/benefits from the lifelong psychodramas of learning and desire. Theory, underscores Britzman in "Theory Kindergarten," "has the capacity to work as an ego defense, warding off uncertainty and surprise, splitting good and bad objects, and managing to put its anxiety into knowledge while protecting its illusion of omnipotence" (126). Here she sums up the basic psychoanalytic discourse on learning. One of the difficult questions Britzman asks is, if theory kindergarten keeps us grounded in early psychic realities, in a time before literacy and the convenient fiction of self, "can our sense of knowledge and our capacity to think from that which resists knowledge . . . ever escape this first terrible task of having to make something from nothing?" (133). We make mincemeat

of knowledge so it cannot make mincemeat of us, she holds. "Shall we admit our adeptness at dismissing theories that run contrary not only just to prevailing conventions but more significantly, to who we think and wish we and others might be in and for theory?" (132). Theory, in any case, is not only defensive, deforming, or dangerous. Theory also sets us "free to play and to think. . . . Kindergarten, after all, also is a fun fair of experiments, thrilling surprises, misrecognitions, near-missed encounters, spectacular mishearings, and phantasies that lead, in the strangest directions, our games of 'let's pretend'" (127).

11. In her contribution to the MLA volume *Teaching Contemporary Theory to Undergraduates*, Fuss suggests that while resistance to theory is real, we need to think about other issues besides resistance. "If I have a new theory of theory," she writes, "it is far less resistance and much more persistence" ("Teaching" 165). In an earlier essay, Fuss imagines theory as "a practice of accountability" and "a mode of responsibility, especially in the pedagogical encounter in which one party is always answerable to the Other" ("Accounting" 111).

12. The Vulgate made the Bible accessible in Latin, for example, and later the Bible was adapted for "children" and adult beginners. The nineteenth century saw a proliferation of texts designed to explain religious tradition to children, and there is no shortage of informational texts on secular topics for beginners or children.

13. While an ideal(ized) subject, the beginner simultaneously approaches what Irving Goh calls the reject, or that which comes after the subject—the articulation of which, Goh remarks, may be the "unfinished business of contemporary French thought" (4). For Goh, the reject is visible in the longer arc of philosophy, especially in the work of Derrida, Deleuze, and Cixous, which seeks alternatives to the subject and dwells on that classic reject of Western thought, the nonhuman animal (15).

14. For a classic account of theory "as a performance validated by its control of the audience and carried out within the context of the university" according to "a joyfully oedipal politics," see Kavanagh (12).

15. Theory, Bruss points out, satisfies our need for rational explanation alongside aesthetic stimulation. And if theory has some elitist tendencies, it also promises a common language. It has this potential, she thinks, precisely because it is "an extraordinary and invented language," one that belongs to no one and thus everyone (21).

16. Culler and Graff, among others, had already emphasized the importance of the research university to theory's institutionalization, and Redfield rounds out the history by focusing on deconstruction at Yale.

17. On the ongoing tension between Anglo-American philosophy of language and particular "French theory," see Lyotard, "Bizarre Partner."

18. There is no before or after theory, one might argue. Rather, theory is endlessly remodeled. See Docherty; Kavanagh; McQuillan et al.; and Payne and Schad.

19. Thomas McLaughlin offers case studies of conservative antiporn crusaders, fan writers, advocates of the whole language movement, and advertisers. Such people were "motivated into theory less by a politicized identity than by a particular institutional placement, and their theoretical insights are likely to be limited to particular cultural practices" (21). McLaughlin points also to Paulo Freire's faith in the "astuteness" of oppressed people, to Terry Eagleton's claim in *The Significance of Theory* that "children make the best theorists" (34), and to James Sosnoski's work on students as theorists. Jonathan P. Eburne likewise underscores that theory or "speculative inquiry extends

beyond the work of professional intellectuals . . . to include the work of nonprofessionals, whether amateurs, unfashionable observers, the clinically insane, or populations not commonly perceived as intellectuals" (1).

20. The student is an important beginner, and it would be interesting to undertake an analysis of how and why students are positioned as beginners. Consider, for instance, Robert Dale Parker's handbook for undergraduate students, *How to Interpret Literature: Critical Theory for Literary and Cultural Studies* (now in a fourth edition). In his introduction, Parker positions "many English professors" as gatekeepers, working "by the unspoken principle that this thing at the center of what we do had better be kept a privileged secret. The idea was, go ahead and learn all the critical and literary theory that we can, and let it drive everything we do as professors of literature, but don't tell the students" (1). Parker frames students as everyday/vernacular theorists with "their own specialized vocabulary" and argues that "many of them theorized with their own specialized languages" (2).

21. The so-called theory wars are also reading wars, as de Man shows. Theory can emerge from close reading, even as not a little scholarship evades reading and the discomforts it can bring. For de Man, reading means struggling with the difficulties and failures of language. "It turns out the resistance to theory is in fact a resistance to reading," most notable "in the methodologies that call themselves theories of reading but nevertheless avoid the function they claim as their object" (15).

22. Discussing the development of pedagogical aids in response to college entrance requirements for literature, Arthur N. Applebee notes that such aids "took two forms, one concentrating on oral presentation, the other on 'visualization.'" He traces the concern with visualization to Sir Francis Galton's argument in *Inquiries into Human Faculty and Its Development* (1883) "that the untrained mind thinks largely in terms of pictures" (61). As Gregory M. Pfitzer explains, antipictorialism dates back to the eighteenth century at least and grew from the fear that images corrupt the mind. He connects such to iconophobia, which derived from anxiety about the influence of the church. Americans, Pfitzer notes, had to be sold on the value of visual literacy. Children were perhaps the most important market for visual or imagetext genres "in a growing nation where concerns for literacy and universal education encouraged publishers to find innovative ways to advance the learning process" (13). Nick Sousanis dates the fear of the visual to Plato and Descartes but also notes that "while mounting an attack on the senses, Descartes was simultaneously investigating optic phenomena" (56).

23. *The Story of Mankind* is especially significant as both a middlebrow outline and an award-winning illustrated history text for young readers (indeed, the first winner of the Newbery Medal). *The Story of Mankind* aims to reach "ordinary persons" (young and older) through a mixture of pictures and words. A Dutch immigrant who worked in the United States as a journalist and university lecturer, van Loon was committed to popular education and sought to draw in young and adult readers alike through pictures and lively prose. As Joan Shelley Rubin observes in her history of middlebrow culture, van Loon's drawings, along with his first-person narration, helped give the book a profoundly personal feeling.

24. Against the perils of specialization, Durant recalls philosophy to the task of synthesis and the "humanization of modern knowledge." He traces the outline form back to Plato himself, remarking that the first "outlines" were Plato's dialogues, designed for

a broader audience than the more technical materials he used with his students at the academy (vi).

25. What makes an idiot "complete"? It is not the same as what completes the idiot, I am guessing. The complete idiot knows next to nothing but maybe has nothing to lose in the learning or even the exposure of ignorance. If anything, the complete idiot stands proud. Incomplete idiots need not apply (themselves)!

26. See https://www.dummies.com/.

27. See https://www.dk.com/us/.

28. Indeed, a study should be made of the broader contemporary landscape of illustrated and multimedia self-help. Consider the Animate videos of the United Kingdom's Royal Society for the Encouragement of the Arts, Manufactures, and Commerce (RSA). These are RSA lectures retroactively illustrated—cartooned by hand (https://www.thersa.org/discover/videos/rsa-animate/). For another such line, see Taunton Press's Complete Illustrated series.

29. On hi-lo readers, see Saddleback Educational Publishing's website, https://www.sdlback.com/.

30. For a defense of "bad writing" and/as academic style, see *Just Being Difficult?: Academic Writing in the Public Arena*, edited by Culler and Lamb. In their introduction, Culler and Lamb point out that bad writing rarely if ever has to be proven, only alleged, not unlike pornography. Good philosophy, counters Culler in his contribution, may necessitate "bad" writing. In the same volume, see also Palumbo-Liu on "bad writing" critique in relation to pedagogy and student identity and also Warner on competing "public of intellectual style."

31. Rius was selected Best Editorial Cartoonist in Mexico in 1959, and in 1968 received the Grand Prize of the International Salon of Caricature in Montreal. The second series of *Los Agachados*, which he began in 1967, centered around the campesino Nopalzin, who asked ignorant questions of his friends . . . and eavesdropped on the police. "Nopalzin stood in for the reader, the real object of Los Agachados' pedagogy. . . . Los Agachados kept Nopalzin blithely stupid, but assumed that the readers underwent a more permanent change through hearing what Nopalzin heard" (Rubenstein 158).

32. Dorfman and Mattelart's book appeared first in Chile as *Para Leer al Pato Donald* and responded to the procapitalist ideology of Donald Duck comics that were disseminated across Latin America. Disney tried and failed to prevent the book from appearing in the United States, claiming copyright infringement.

33. "The pen has always doubled for the sword in Latin America," notes Paula K. Speck, and Rius goes one step further "by using the special resources of the comic book form" to fashion a sophisticated satire that entertains but also instructs (113).

34. The upsurge in theory anthologies came in the late 1980s, notes Jeffrey Williams, with 1989 being a watershed year ("Packaging" 280). The sudden appearance of so many anthologies indicates both the arrival and "a kind of *closure* of theory," he suggests, in that theory "has arrived as a fully licensed paradigm" (283).

35. The Appignanesi-Zarate team also produced *Freud for Beginners*.

36. For an overview of the series, see "About Us," For Beginners Books, http://www.forbeginnersbooks.com/aboutus.

37. Once a small company, Icon is now held by Faber and Faber and distributed worldwide by Macmillan Distribution in all markets except Canada, the United States, South Africa, Australia, and New Zealand.

38. In *Fanon for Beginners*, Deborah Wyrick points out that the academic ascension of Fanon probably began in 1978 with the publication of Said's *Orientalism*. Said turns up again in *Arabs and Israeli for Beginners*, as the exemplary Palestinian activist, and we could read Said's *The Question of Palestine*, originally published in 1979 but updated in 1992, as itself a primer for beginners.

39. Harold E. Hinds and Charles M. Tatum note that Rius's leftist commentary on socialist countries and capitalist corruption amounts to a sort of travel literature (80–81). They point out that while Rius identified strongly with socialist and especially Cuban socialism, he offered a balanced account of such and was "never blind to the transgressions of Communist governments" (80). "And while he admired the contemporary Soviet Union, he was clearly critical of government censorship and the brutal invasion of Czechoslovakia" (80). Hinds and Tatum compare his work to that of the nineteenth-century German writer Johann Most, whose book on Marx served to introduce semi-educated workers to Communism. Rius also wrote and illustrated a biography of Che Guevara, titled *ABChe* (Hinds and Tatum 81).

40. Irene Herner's 1979 book *Mitos y monitos: Historietas y fotonovelas en México* (*Myths and the Funnies: Comic Books and Photonovels in Mexico*) was the first major work to appear, an overview of the two genres and an analysis of major character types; the volume emphasizes the author's conviction that comics and *fotonovelas* are bourgeois genres. The fotonovela resembles a comic book but uses photos in place of line drawings.

41. Some commentators on theory have noted a turn away from grand critique and toward a postmodern and ostensibly shallow preoccupation with popular culture (masquerading, according to some, as cultural studies). That is Eagleton's diagnosis in *After Theory*. For Eagleton, theory means Marxist-materialist theory and critique, which began as a critique of middle-class society but gradually became (in his view) that society's ally (24). Theory, according to him, no longer offers any opposition to capitalist orthodoxy, nor does it serve any longer as critical self-reflection (27). He is hardly the only one to link the institutionalization of theory with commodity capitalism or the fading of the political left. Leitch might take a more charitable view, seeing in the contemporary scene of theory evidence of academia's current "disaggregation." "Inevitably," he writes in *Theory Matters*, "the question arises about whether theory, in the new era of cultural studies, isn't just one more example of late postindustrial, post-Fordist capitalist culture—flexibilized, imploded, preoccupied with popular culture, market-oriented, driven by rapid innovation, dedicated to vanguardism and countercultural ideas, and housed comfortably inside the new university. In one sense, how could it be otherwise. But in another sense, projects of cultural critique, rooted in various critical traditions ranging from Marxism to psychoanalysis to such new social movements as women's and civil rights, Third World reparations and environmental justice, invariably promote an ethicopolitics steeped in egalitarian ideas, often setting it at odds with mainstream practices and values" (ix–x).

Writing a decade earlier, Nancy K. Miller offers a positive account of the "efflorescence of personal criticism" in the 1980s, seeing such as having "in part to do with the gradual, and perhaps inevitable waning of enthusiasm for a mode of Theory, whose authority—however variously—depended finally on the theoretical evacuation of the very social subjects producing it" (20).

42. As Nericcio points out, graphic narrative draws not only from literature and the fine arts but also from television and cinema, exhibiting "a conspicuous range" and a

"bastard lineage" (87). Nericcio goes on to call graphic narrative "a mestizo medium," citing Gloria Anzaldúa's expansion of the term and alluding to Latin American, left-leaning illustrated texts like those we are considering. The guides also resemble comics journalism as practiced especially by Joe Sacco, who produced books about political conflict and war zones. On Sacco and comics journalism, see García.

43. These books in turn have links to primers and other earlier material for children designed to support literacy. On matters of genre and audience, see especially Michael Joseph, "Seeing the Visible Book." Joseph's article appears in a special cluster published in the *Children's Literature Association Quarterly* titled "Why Comics Are and Are Not Picture Books," guest edited by Charles Hatfield and Craig Svonkin. In contributions to that symposium, Joseph, Nathalie op de Beeck, and Joseph T. Thomas Jr. all emphasize not just the instability but also the limitations of genre as a concept. Thomas's essay on Shel Silverstein explores the complexities of what we do (and do not) mean by children's literature, while op de Beeck emphasizes the need for skepticism when it comes to "age-based distinctions" in and around genre (474).

44. In 1944, University of Pittsburgh professor W. W. D. Sones reported that between 1935 and 1944 comics "evoked more than a hundred critical articles in educational and nonprofessional journals" (232). Sones himself undertook a series of studies using comic books in educational settings. The 1944 issue of the *Journal of Educational Sociology* was devoted entirely to the question of comics and their use in teaching. There is extensive and interdisciplinary scholarship on the historical and contemporary use of comics in educational contexts. For a sketch of educational comics, and in particular the Classics Illustrated series, see Duncan et al. 336–38.

45. The dominant cultural narrative is that only lately have comics matured into literature, in the form of the graphic novel. Christopher Pizzino contests this account, not so much arguing for comics' legitimacy as underscoring how an ongoing sense of marginality shapes the production, circulation, and reception of imagetexts.

46. As Jan Baetens and Hugo Frey point out, the term *graphic novel* gained industry and popular currency in the 1960s and early 1970s, which would position the genre as nearly simultaneous with the first For Beginners book (1970). After the success of Art Spiegelman's *Maus*, graphic works such as Marjane Satrapi's *Persepolis* have found quick assimilation into the high school and college curriculum. Some titles have migrated into nonhumanities fields, such as Jay Hosler's *The Sandwalk Adventures*, which introduces evolutionary biology by having Charles Darwin talk to follicle mites living in his eyebrows.

47. As Jacobs shows, comics have long modeled and sponsored the sort of multimodal literacy we see in the guides: "the ability to create meaning with and from texts that operate not only in alphabetic form but also in some combination of visual, audio, and spatial forms as well" (3).

48. A comic book series by artist Ryan Dunlavey and writer Fred Van Lente called *Action Philosophers* offers concise and colorful introductions to notable philosophers. Nine issues were published through 2007, when the project folded. A *Publishers Weekly* review of the first three issues declared that "while demonstrating that the lives of philosophers make great tabloid fodder, the comics get the theories right. Totally irreverent and manically imaginative, it's perfect for any bright college kid who likes being a pain in the neck" ("Action Philosophers").

49. Nericcio and Aaron Scott Humphrey have written the only articles about the guides. In their introduction to a special issue of *Modern Fiction Studies* on graphic

narrative, Hillary L. Chute and Marianne DeKoven do mention in passing the "series of exemplary books with such titles as *Introducing Derrida*, *Introducing Feminism*, and *Introducing Hawking*" as perhaps contributing "to the erroneous view that [comic narrative] is a simple medium" (774).

50. Does the dream sequence suggest that Nietzsche is a closet theist?

51. Humphrey undertakes a comparative case study of the For Beginner and Introducing volumes on Derrida and Foucault. He discusses four modes of image-text relation across these sample volumes: arbitrary, parallel, tandem, and fused.

52. Bourdieu does acknowledge that "the new cultural intermediaries" (producers of "cultural programmes on TV and radio" as well as critics writing for newspapers and magazines) "have invented a whole series of genres half-way between legitimate culture and mass production" (323), which might offer better context for the guides.

53. Trask builds on this analysis in the American context, pointing out that the "ironic social style" of postwar academic culture finds expression in the hermeneutics of suspicion and the ongoing bracketing of belief (22).

54. Another Florida colleague, the fiction writer David Leavitt, reported that he was asked to review a proposed manual for creative writing students on theory for "people who hate theory." The proposal made all too obvious its mockery of theory, with tags such as "Theory Disease," "Theory Burnout," "Name-Dropping for Beginners," and so forth. The final section was titled "Life after Theory: Recovering Intelligibility." At Florida, creative writing students do enter the MFA program to write fiction and poetry, not study theory, but as David pointed out in an email to me, today's MFA students are not nearly as "allergic to theory" as past students have been; some are even excited by theory and want to study it. David not only passed on the review but wrote a scathing response.

55. "Theoretical discourse resorts to graphics when it grows impatient with or suspicious of language," notes Bruss. "Indeed, there is a certain pathos in the trust with which it reaches out to those other symbols, as if they were somehow less subject to the vagaries and misreadings to which verbal discourse is heir" (123).

56. See especially the 2015 special issue of *Digital Humanities Quarterly* on the topic of "Comics as Scholarship." In their introduction, Roger Todd Whitson and Anastasia Salter give a useful history of scholarly engagements with and even manifestations as comics. They point to Sousanis's *Unflattening* and note also the 2014 special issue of *Critical Inquiry* on "Comics and Media." A good example of scholarship in comic form is Julie E. Maybee's 2009 *Picturing Hegel: An Illustrated Guide to Hegel's Encyclopaedia Logic*, which uses pictures and diagrams to restage Hegelian logic. As Jason Muir Helms points out in his innovative article "Is This Article a Comic?," also featured in the *DHQ* special issue, scholarly experiments in comic form have various inspirations, among them the emergence of what Gregory Ulmer calls "post-criticism," or using the formal characteristics of the object in one's critique. One could also make the case that scholarship and theory in comic form has an early precedent in the work of Swiss critic and writer Rodolphe Töpffer (1799–1846). Töpffer wrote comic satires as well as theoretical essays on the form.

57. For information, see https://www.sequentialsjournal.net/.

3. Literature for Minors

1. Stiegler approaches the question of the minor differently, warning that the growing tendency to treat legally offending juveniles as adults—thus "denying minority

status to minors" (2)—suggests the disintegration of the generational structure and an abdication of adult (major) responsibility.

2. Deleuze and Guattari propose that Kafka's affection for children and animals animated this challenge to "major" literature.

3. Commenting on Deleuze and Guattari, Flaxman insists that the "minor does not 'belong' to a minority, to a people who have been ethnically or socioeconomically predetermined, because the minor designates a process of becoming, of minorization, that even minorities must undertake" (229–30).

4. Minor status does not require a particular audience or content: "We might as well say that minor no longer designates specific literatures but the revolutionary conditions for everyday literature within the heart of what is called great (or established) literature" (Deleuze and Guattari, *Kafka* 18).

5. We can see an earlier indication of both directions in Bob Dixon's *Catching Them Young: Sex, Race and Class in Children's Fiction* (1977), at once a condemnation of the conservatism of children's literature and a celebration of more progressive materials.

6. Other scholars—such as Karin Westman, Nathalie op de Beeck (in *Suspended Animation*), and Amy Billone—have further enriched our understanding of the ongoing impacts of modernity and modernism, including its preoccupation with Alice and other nineteenth-century "dream children." Reynolds spotlights aesthetic radicality alongside political engagement: "Many children's books offer quirky or critical or alternative visions of the world designed to provide that ultimate response of childhood, 'Why?'" (*Radical Children's Literature* 3). "What we teach when we teach literature to children is not, then, themes and structures," confirms Roderick McGillis, "but rather the desire to examine, analyze, recreate, perform, and understand the forces that shape our own lives. In this sense, the reading of literature and the study of text is both a form of play and a deeply political activity" (206).

7. Tara Forrest explains that both Benjamin and Siegfried Kracauer were influenced by Marcel Proust's distinction between voluntary and involuntary recollection and in the challenges afforded by the latter to conventional historicism. Benjamin's childhood reminiscences, she shows, were shaped by Proust's notion of involuntary memory. On the connections between Benjamin's "weak messianism" and his experimental writing practices, see Gelley, ch. 6.

8. On how Benjamin's ideas support a child-centric approach to literature and education, see Chournazidi.

9. The only difference Mehlman sees between the radio shows and other work is the lack of secondary elaboration in the former. The shows are less edited, he points out, reflecting Benjamin's contractual assignment to speak nonstop for twenty minutes. They are thus the closest thing we have to a psychoanalysis of Benjamin, he thinks (3, 5).

10. Tribunella, "Children's Literature and the Child Flâneur," and "Benjamin, Benson, and the Child's Gaze: Childhood Desire and Pleasure in the David Blaize Books."

11. Esther Leslie provides a compelling account of Benjamin's conception of memory and memory work in relation to cinema and animation.

12. "In preparing his culture to receive and welcome the innovations of modernism, Benjamin enlists a *Kinderbrigade* of fellow urban explorers and innovators," writes Sussman. The children of Benjamin "are already, in their sensibilities, structural anthropologists of mythology, visual cubists, editors of film montage, and jazz musicians, even if, in 1924, Benjamin does not yet venture all these connections" (Sussman 115).

13. I cannot prove that Butler had *Peter Pan* in mind. I do know that in 1997 Biddy Martin published an autobiographical essay called "The Hobo, the Fairy, and the Quarterback," which explores the queer appeal that *Peter Pan* and other favorite texts had for her as a child. In note 6 of that essay, Martin thanks Butler, "who reminded me of the comparison between Peter Pan and Mrs. Darling's kiss during a phone conversation about *Peter Pan*."

14. Richard Wunderlich and Thomas J. Morrissey provide an excellent reception history of *Pinocchio* in the United States, while Emer O'Sullivan uses Collodi's tale to interrogate the idea of a world children's classic.

15. Imitations and "sequels" proliferated at an astonishing rate; for details, see Sigler.

16. Unlike other Golden Age fantasies, however, *Alice* has not been repurposed as self-help. While there is a medical condition called the Alice in Wonderland syndrome, there is thankfully no *Alice* companion to pop-psychological tomes inspired by *Peter Pan* and *The Velveteen Rabbit*.

17. Woolf's first novel, *The Voyage Out*, notes Dusinberre, "gravitates towards *Alice in Wonderland* in many different ways," and her two best-known works, *To the Lighthouse* and *The Waves* "evoke and encapsulate childhood as she claimed Carroll did" (2). There are all kinds of interesting echoes of Carroll in Woolf's novels—passages about looking-glasses and looking-glass worlds, meditations on "mad" assemblies, and more diffuse scenes of play and language play. More generally, Woolf and other modernists were praised for staying close to the heart of childhood and to its fascination with language and rhythm. All of this was bound up with a new interest in child psychology and progressive education.

18. Barzilai continues the *Alice* gaming, describing Lacan's intellectual rivalry with Henri Wallon by casting Lacan as Carroll's White Knight to Wallon's Red Knight.

19. The talk was published as "The Function and Field of Speech and Language in Psychoanalysis" and is included in *Écrits*. Here is the relevant passage: "But we analysts have to deal with slaves who think they are masters, and who find in a language whose mission is universal the support of their servitude, and the bonds of its ambiguity. So much so that, as one might humorously put it, our goal is to restore in them the sovereign freedom displayed by Humpty Dumpty when he reminds Alice that after all he is the master of the signifier, even if he isn't master of the signified in which his being took on its form" (Lacan, *Écrits* 81).

20. Lane also sees Lacan as one step ahead of Deleuze in realizing that Carroll's nonsense "has an internal logic to it, and thus a meaning of its own" (1030).

21. Without discounting Lacan's contribution to the theoretical appreciation of Carroll, we might ask, what happens if we do not privilege Lacan as the key to *Alice* but rather see *Alice* as a key to Lacan? Karen Coats flirts with this possibility in *Looking Glasses and Neverlands*, suggesting that "reading Lacan through *Alice* continues to open our way into a notoriously difficult theory of the subject" (79). If so, it might be because Carroll got there first. Carroll helped to inspire the modernists, the surrealists, and the psychoanalysts. Perhaps Freudian and Lacanian readings of *Alice* work so well because of that history.

22. A number of contributions to this volume attempt to imitate Carroll's playful style but fall flat. The first, the feminist reading, reads like a satire of feminism and recalls Frederick Crews's satires in *The Pooh Perplex*. The book's introduction likewise tries to be playfully profound.

23. Reading the two *Sylvie and Bruno* novels as a kind of confession-reparation on the part of Carroll, Gubar notes that even critics who admire the novels "insist that they should be viewed not as successors to *Alice*" but as something else, including "proto-Modernist experiments (Gattégno, Atherton, Wilson, Purdy), or post-structuralist meditations on textuality (Gordon, Deleuze)" ("Lewis" 372).

24. Jean-Jacques Lecercle writes that "for Deleuze, literature is a constant source of thought experiments" (*Badiou* 3). No wonder Deleuze found Carroll so compelling. Characteristically, he did not apply philosophy to the arts; rather, he tried to extract philosophy from them.

25. Beckman aligns *Alice* with the work of Hannah Arendt on political narration and its capacity to transcend bare life, noting that Arendt "provides us with a strong belief in the importance of narratives at the same time as she insists on the freedom of unpredictability and the introduction of the new"—summed up in the conceit of *becoming* (5).

26. Derrida is quick to acknowledge his own philosophical bestiary or animal menagerie, "the innumerable critics that now overpopulate my texts" (*Animal* 37).

27. The *Alice* section of Zoe Jaques's book on posthuman children's literature counters Derrida's conclusion and suggests that *Alice* "acts as a complex negotiation of the philosophical challenges implicit in an ethical acknowledgement of the gulf between animal and humankind" (44).

28. The *Alice* citation game in theory goes on. In his rejoinder to Deleuze, *Organs without Bodies*, discussing what that phrase might mean, Slavoj Žižek gives the example of the Cheshire Cat in *Alice*, who vanishes bit by bit until only a smile remains.

29. Veronica Schanoes interprets *Alice* in the context of monster studies, pointing to the figurations in Carroll of our dream-child as monster-child also and chalking them up to complicated adult feelings about childhood, ours more than Carroll's.

30. The image of a modified Alice on the collection's cover—with wings and a spikey tail—plus that single, powerful word *curiouser*, speak volumes and evoke queer children past, present, and future. (The Rudd and Coats books also feature *Alice* covers.)

31. Rose treats *Peter Pan* just so, making it represent children's literature and its "impossibility." *Peter Pan* and especially *Alice* are so ostensibly singular that they rise above the general idea or category of children's literature. So too purportedly with *Huck Finn*, at once a classic boy's book and a great—some say *the* great—American novel. Jan Susina beautifully resituates *Alice* as a children's book against this rhetoric of exceptionalism.

32. Nikolajeva also conceives of Pippi as the carnival factor in carnivalesque narrative as imagined by Mikhail Bakhtin ("Misunderstood Tragedy"). Coats is also good on the queerness of Pippi. In an earlier piece, William Moebius treats Pippi and H. A. Rey's Curious George as exemplifying a new enfant terrible type who turns picture-book conventions upside down.

33. Gabrielle Owen similarly reads Rose as a queer theorist.

34. Teresa de Lauretis coined the term *queer theory* in 1991, in a special issue of *differences*. Soon after, she distanced herself from such, saying it had "quickly become a conceptually vacuous creature of the publishing industry" (297). Vacuous or not, queer theory grew and diversified in the 1990s and into the 2000s.

35. Halberstam does acknowledge that not all Pixar films instance "Pixarvolt," his name for this energy. Some Pixar films trend individualistic rather than collectivist;

some even affirm neoliberalism. Nevertheless, Halberstam thinks "the new technologies of children's fantasy . . . offer us the real and compelling possibility of animating revolt" (52).

36. See Sedgwick and Moon's "Divinity: A Dossier. A Performance Piece. A Little-Understood Emotion," included in Sedgwick's *Tendencies*. See also Moon's *A Small Boy and Others*.

37. By order of publication: Rand, *Barbie's Queer Accessories*; Ohi, *Innocence and Rapture: The Erotic Child in Pater, Wilde, James, and Nabokov*; Sammond, *Babes in Tomorrowland*; Mavor, *Reading Boyishly*; Moon, *Darger's Resources*; Chinn, "'I Was a Lesbian Child': Queer Thoughts about Childhood Studies"; and Honeyman, "Trans(cending)gender through Childhood." Many essays in Bruhm and Hurley's *Curiouser* also fit the bill.

38. Catherine Hernandez's *M is for Mustache: A Pride ABC Book* (2015) is part of a new subscription series by the small press Flamingo Rampant producing "feminist, racially-diverse, LGBTQ-positive" picturebooks (https://www.flamingorampant.com/).

39. *Large Fears* was self-published after being funded through Kickstarter. In 2016, YA author Meg Rosoff responded negatively to publicity about Johnson's book, using it to launch a complaint about calls for diversity in children's and young adult literature. Rosoff insisted that there was not a shortage of books for underrepresented children. In the meantime, Johnson and his illustrator, Kendrick Daye, parted ways and the book was only reissued on demand.

40. Along those lines, Huskey considers Kevin Henkes's *Chester's Way* (1988) and the Golden Super Shape Book *The True Story of Wonder Woman* (1995), noting that the queerness of the former "is encoded in the small details of character and image" whereas the "obtrusive lesbianism" of the latter "somehow occupies a blind spot in the reading public's eye: by failing to obscure or acknowledge the forbidden referent, the text requires the reader to hide it for herself" (72).

41. *Louis the Fish* anticipates *Little Lit: Strange Stories for Strange Kids* (2001), the middle volume in the Little Lit series, a comic book anthology project published by *New Yorker* art editor Françoise Mouly and Pulitzer Prize–winning graphic novelist Art Spiegelman. The first entry, by Spiegelman, explores the idea that we are many selves. Maurice Sendak's "Cereal Baby Keller" imagines a child who devours his parents (a trope in Sendak's work), while Ian Falconer and David Sedaris's collaboration "Pretty Ugly" plays on the classic theme of "beauty is cultural." In Claude Ponti's "The Little House That Ran Away from Home," said house gets married to a human couple. Also reproduced are the first strips of Crockett Johnson's Barnaby comic featuring Barnaby's irascible Fairy Godfather, Jackeen J. O'Malley. These are not just strange stories for strange kids; these are stories that push against cultural norms.

42. Howe and Raschka are high-profile figures in American children's literature. Howe is the author of the Bunnicula books and the YA novel *The Misfits*, which inspired GLSEN's annual No Name-Calling Week.

43. Fitzhugh modeled Harriet in part on her friend Marijane Meaker, a prolific author of children's books and lesbian pulp novels.

44. Lenika Cruz remarks that Lemony Snicket's *A Series of Unfortunate Events* was "her first introduction to postmodern literature." And "it was the books' style, not content, I found most compelling of all."

45. *The Miserable Mill* opens with a discussion of literary genres and how they set reader expectations (2).

46. In his forthcoming book, Derritt Mason shows how fans of the hit television program *Glee* use the "It Gets Better" campaign to imagine scenarios in which things actually do not get better for queer kids especially.

47. Cvetkovich explicitly describes her *Depression: A Public Feeling* as queer academic self-help.

48. "It is true, of course, that you never know. A new experience can be extremely pleasurable, or extremely irritating, or somewhere in between, and you never know until you try it. . . . But—and my heart aches as I tell you this—I always know" (*Miserable Mill* 19). Also from the same volume: "Being alive had never seemed lucky before, but as the children considered their terrible time in Sir's care, they were amazed at how many lucky things had actually happened to them" (193). "It *was* lucky," each of them says with a particular point of reference.

49. Tribunella nominates an even earlier candidate for the first gay novel for children: Edward Prime-Stevenson's *Left to Themselves*, a homoromantic boys' adventure tale published the same year as Oscar Wilde's *The Portrait of Dorian Gray*. See Tribunella, "Between," and also the reissued edition of the novel with Tribunella's introduction. As Tribunella underscores, the novel ends happily, unlike many YA novels nearly a century later.

50. As Margaret Galvan details, queer comics have been anthologized in a number of volumes. As valuable as are these collections, Galvan notes, they lift the comics out of their original contexts.

51. In her review for the *Guardian*, Laura Miller praises Bechdel's artistic proficiency but laments the subject matter. "There's a bit too much therapy in *Are You My Mother?*," she concludes, remarking further that psychology "may get at the same truths that art does, but the trip isn't nearly as much fun." Dwight Garner is harsher in the *New York Times*, calling the book "actively dismal," "therapized and flat," with "no real narrative" and "multiple undigested chunks of text."

52. Two examples of Winnicottian influence in queer theory are Michael Snediker's *Queer Optimism* and Nelson's *The Argonauts*, which takes notice of the Winnicottian turn and even cites *Are You My Mother?* in illustration.

53. Winnicott first made this observation at a meeting of the British Psychoanalytical Society, and it quickly became central to his practice and theory.

54. *Are You My Mother?* offers interesting contrast to *Queer: A Graphic History* (2016), a collaboration of Meg-John Barker and Julia Scheele. The publisher of that volume is Icon Books, behind the Introducing graphic guides. The book offers a standard overview of queer terminology, queer studies, and queer politics, beginning with sexology and Freud and running through contemporary queer theory about affect and temporality. The book is thorough, even a little tedious. I would not describe it as whimsical, despite the imagetext form, and there is not much experimentation in terms of design. *Queer: A Graphic History* is about queer theory more than it is queer theory, whereas *Are You My Mother?* meets us somewhere in the middle.

Works Cited

Abate, Michelle Ann. *Raising Your Kids Right: Children's Literature and American Political Conservatism*. Rutgers UP, 2010.

Abate, Michelle Ann, and Gwen Athene Tarbox. Introduction. *Graphic Novels for Children and Young Adults: A Collection of Critical Essays*, edited by Michelle Ann Abate and Gwen Athene Tarbox, UP of Mississippi, 2017, pp. 3–16.

"Action Philosophers Giant-Size Thing Vol. 1." Review of Fred Van Lente and Ryan Dunlavey, *Action Philosophers!*, *Publishers Weekly*, May 1, 2006, https://www.publishersweekly.com/978-0-9778329-0-3. Accessed 20 Mar. 2020.

Adamczak, Bini. *Communism for Kids*. Translated by Jacob Blumenfeld and Sophie Lewis, MIT Press, 2017. First published as *Kommunismus*, Unrast Verlag, 2014.

Adorno, Theodor. *Minima Moralia: Reflections from Damaged Life*. Translated by E. F. N. Jephcott, Verso, 1978.

Agamben, Giorgio. *Infancy and History: The Destruction of Experience*. Translated by Liz Heron, Verso, 1993.

Ahmed, Sarah. *The Promise of Happiness*. Duke UP, 2010.

Alexander, Jonathan. *Writing Youth: Young Adult Fiction as Literacy Sponsorship*. Lexington Books, 2017.

Amasa, Ndofirepi, and Mathebula Thokozani. "Philosophy for Children in South African Schools: Its Role for Citizens-in-Waiting." *South African Journal of Childhood Education*, vol. 1, no. 2, September 2011, pp. 127–42.

Appignanesi, Richard. *Lenin for Beginners*. Illustrated by Oscar Zarate, Pantheon, 1977.

Applebee, Arthur N. *Tradition and Reform in the Teaching of English: A History*. National Council of Teachers in English, 1974.

Aristotle. *Aristotle on His Predecessors: Being the First Book of His Metaphysics.* Translated by A. E. Taylor, reprint edition, Open Court Publishing, 1927.

Armstrong, Louise. *A Child's Guide to Freud.* Illustrated by Whitney Darrow Jr., Simon and Schuster, 1963.

Auerbach, Nina. "Alice in Wonderland: A Curious Child." *Victorian Studies*, vol. 17, no. 1, Sept. 1973, pp. 31–47.

Bache-Wiig, Harald. "Philosophical Homework or Universal Amazement? Jostein Gaarder's *Sophie's World*." *Beyond Babar: The European Tradition in Children's Literature*, edited by Sandra L. Beckett and Maria Nikolajeva, the Children's Literature Association and the Scarecrow P, 2006, pp. 255–76.

Baetans, Jan, and Hugo Frey. *The Graphic Novel: An Introduction*. Cambridge UP, 2015.

Baggett, David, and Shawn E. Klein, editors. *Harry Potter and Philosophy: If Aristotle Ran Hogwarts*. Open Court Publishing, 2004.

Baker, Houston A., Jr. *Blues, Ideology, and Afro-American Literature: A Vernacular Theory*. U of Chicago P, 1984.

Barker, Meg-John, and Julia Scheele. *Queer: A Graphic History*. Icon Books, 2016.

Barthes, Roland. *The Preparation of the Novel. Lecture Courses and Seminars at the Collège de France (1978–1979 and 1979–1980)*. Translated by Kate Briggs, Columbia UP, 2011.

Barzilai, Shuli. *Lacan and the Matter of Origins*. Stanford UP, 1999.

Bayard, Pierre. *How to Talk about Books You Haven't Read*. Translated by Jeffrey Mehlman, Bloomsbury, 2007.

Beauvais, Clémentine. *The Mighty Child: Time and Power in Children's Literature*. John Benjamins Publishing Company, 2015.

———. "The Problem of 'Power': Metacritical Implications of Aetonormativity for Children's Literature Research." *Children's Literature in Education*, vol. 44, no. 1, Mar. 2013, pp. 74–86.

Bechdel, Alison. *Are You My Mother? A Comic Drama*. Houghton Mifflin Harcourt, 2012.

———. *Fun Home: A Family Tragicomic*. Houghton Mifflin Harcourt, 2006.

Beckett, Sandra L. "Michel Tournier Retells the Robinson Crusoe Myth. Friday and Robinson: Life on Speranza Island." *Beyond Babar: The European Tradition in Children's Literature*, edited by Sandra L. Beckett and Maria Nikolajeva, the Children's Literature Association and the Scarecrow P, 2006, pp. 157–89.

Beckett, Sandra L., and Maria Nikolajeva, editors. *Beyond Babar: The European Tradition in Children's Literature*, the Children's Literature Association and the Scarecrow P, 2006.

Beckman, Frida. "Becoming Pawn: *Alice*, Arendt and the New in Narrative." *Journal of Narrative Theory*, vol. 44, no. 1, Winter 2014, pp. 1–28.

Benjamin, Walter. *Radio Benjamin*. Edited by Lecia Rosenthal, translated by Jonathan Lutes, Lisa Harries Schumann, and Diana Reese, Verso, 2014.

Berger, John, and Margaret Busby. Untitled obituary for Glenn Thompson. *The Guardian*, Sept. 2001, www.theguardian.com/news/2001/sep/12/guardianobituaries1. Accessed 2 Sept. 2017.

Berlant, Lauren, and Kathleen Stewart. *The Hundreds*. Duke UP, 2019.

Bernstein, Robin. "The Queerness of Harriet the Spy." *Over the Rainbow: Queer Children's and Young Adult Literature*, edited by Michelle Ann Abate and Kenneth Kidd, U of Michigan P, 2011, pp. 111–20.

Bickford, Tyler. *Schooling New Media: Music, Language & Technology in Children's Culture*. Oxford UP, 2017.

Bignell, Jonathan. *Postmodern Media Culture*. Edinburgh UP, 2000.

Billone, Amy. *The Future of the Nineteenth-Century Dream-Child: Fantasy, Dystopia, Cyberculture*. Routledge, 2016.

Birns, Nicholas. *Theory after Theory: An Intellectual History of Literary Theory from 1950 to the Early Twenty-First Century*. Broadview P, 2010.

Blanchot, Maurice. *The Writing of the Disaster*. Translated by Ann Smock, U of Nebraska P, 1995.

Blumenfeld, Jacob. "The Little Red Book for Children." *New York Times*, www.nytimes.com/2017/05/28/opinion/communism-for-kids-scandal.html. Accessed 3 Nov. 2017.

Bohlmann, Markus P. J. *Misfit Children: An Inquiry into Childhood Belongings*, edited by Markus P. J. Bohlman, Lexington Books, 2017.

Bollert, David. *Plato and Wonder. Extraordinary Times*, IWM Junior Visiting Fellows Conferences, vol. 11, Vienna 2001, http://www.iwm.at/wp-content/uploads/jc-11-131.pdf. Accessed 5 Nov. 2015.

Bourdieu, Pierre. *Distinction: A Social Critique of the Judgment of Taste*. Translated by Richard Nice, Harvard UP, 1998.

Boyne, John. *The Terrible Thing That Happened to Barnaby Brocket*. Illustrated by Oliver Jeffers, Random House, 2012.

Brandt, Deborah. "Sponsors of Literacy." *College Composition and Communication*, vol. 49, no. 2, May 1998, pp. 165–85.

Britzman, Deborah. *A Psychoanalyst in the Classroom: On the Human Condition in Education*. State U of New York P, 2015.

———. "Theory Kindergarten." *Regarding Sedgwick: Essays on Queer Culture and Critical Theory*, edited by Stephen M. Barber and David Clark, Routledge, 2002, pp. 121–42.

Brooker, Will. *Alice's Adventures: Lewis Carroll in Popular Culture*. Continuum, 2005.

Bruhm, Steven, and Natasha Hurley, "Curiouser: On the Queerness of Children." *Curiouser: On the Queerness of Children*, edited by Steven Bruhm and Natasha Hurley, U of Minnesota P, 2004, pp. ix–xxxviii.

Bruss, Elizabeth W. *Beautiful Theories: The Spectacle of Discourse in Contemporary Criticism*. Johns Hopkins UP, 1982.

Burman, Erica. *Developments: Child, Image, Nation*. Routledge, 2008.

Burton, Neel. "A Study of Wonder." *Psychology Today*, www.psychologytoday.com/blog/hide-and-seek/201412/study-wonder. Accessed 5 Nov. 2015.

Butler, Judith. *Gender Trouble: Feminism and the Subversion of Gender Identity.* Routledge, 1990.

———. *The Psychic Life of Power: Theories of Subjection*. Stanford UP, 1997.

Bynum, Terrell Ward. "What Is Philosophy for Children? An Introduction." *Metaphilosophy*, vol. 7, no. 1, Jan. 1976, pp. 1–6.

Campbell, Jill. "Robinson Crusoe through the Ages." *Yale Alumni Magazine*, https://yalealumnimagazine.com/articles/4373-robinson-crusoe-through-the-ages. Accessed 2 Jan. 2019.

Capshaw, Katharine. *Civil Rights Childhood: Picturing Liberation in African American Photobooks*. U of Minnesota P, 2014.

Carpenter, Scott. *Reading Lessons: An Introduction to Theory*. Prentice-Hall, 2000.

Carson, Rachel. *The Sense of Wonder*. Harper & Row, 1965.

Cascardi, Anthony J. *The Cambridge Introduction to Literature and Philosophy.* Cambridge UP, 2014.

Caselli, Daniela. "Attack of the Easter Bunnies: Walter Benjamin's *Youth Hour*." *Parallax*, vol. 22, no. 4, 2016, pp. 459–79.

Castañeda, Claudia. *Figurations: Child, Bodies, Worlds*. Duke UP, 2002.

Chesterton, G. K. "The Library of the Nursery." *Lunacy and Letters*, edited by Dorothy Collins, Sheed & Ward, 1958, pp. 24–26.

Chinn, Sarah. "'I Was a Lesbian Child': Queer Thoughts about Childhood Studies." *The Children's Table: Childhood Studies and the Humanities*, edited by Anna Mae Duane, U of Georgia P, 2013, pp. 149–66.

Chournazidi, Anastasia. "The Pedagogic Role of Children's Literature: Walter Benjamin's Theory in Modern Education." *World Journal of Education Research*, vol. 4, no. 3, 2017, pp. 395–404.

Chute, Hillary L. *Graphic Women: Life Narrative and Contemporary Comics*. Columbia UP, 2010.

Chute, Hillary L., and Marianne DeKoven. "Introduction: Graphic Narrative." *Modern Fiction Studies*, vol. 52, no. 4, Winter 2006, pp. 767–82.

Cixous, Hélène. "Introduction to Lewis Carroll's *Through the Looking-Glass* and *The Hunting of the Snark*." Translated by Marie Maclean. *New Literary History*, vol. 13, no. 2, Winter 1982, pp. 231–51.

Clark, Beverly Lyon. *Kiddie Lit: The Cultural Construction of Children's Literature in America*. Johns Hopkins UP, 2003.

Coats, Karen. *Looking Glasses and Neverlands: Lacan, Desire, and Subjectivity in Children's Literature*. U of Iowa P, 2004.

Cole, Andrew. *The Birth of Theory*. U of Chicago P, 2014.

Costello, Peter R, editor. *Philosophy in Children's Literature*. Lexington Books, 2012.

Cruz, Lenika. "Postmodernism—for Kids." *The Atlantic*, Oct. 23, 2014, www.theatlantic.com/entertainment/archive/2014/10/postmodernism-for-kids/381739/. Accessed 12 June 2015.

Culler, Jonathan. "Bad Writing and Good Philosophy." *Just Being Difficult? Academic Writing in the Public Arena*, edited by Jonathan Culler and Kevin Lamb, Stanford UP, 2003, pp. 43–57.
———. *Framing the Sign: Criticism and Its Institutions*. U of Oklahoma P, 1988.
———. *Literary Theory: A Very Short Introduction*. Oxford UP, 1997.
Culler, Jonathan, and Kevin Lamb, editors. *Just Being Difficult? Academic Writing in the Public Arena*, Stanford UP, 2003.
Cusset, François. *French Theory: How Foucault, Derrida, Deleuze, & Co. Transformed the Intellectual Life of the United States.* Translated by Jeff Fort, U of Minnesota P, 2008.
Cvetkovich, Ann. *Depression: A Public Feeling*. Duke UP, 2012.
———. "Drawing the Archive in Alison Bechdel's *Fun Home*." *Women's Studies Quarterly*, vol. 36, nos. 1 & 2, Spring 2008, pp. 111–28.
Cwi, David. "Competency, the Underprivileged, and Elementary School Philosophy." *Metaphilosophy*, vol. 7, no. 1, Jan. 1976, pp. 76–79.
David, Ron. *Arabs and Israel for Beginners*. Illustrated by Susan David, Writers and Readers Publishing, 1993.
Davies, Merryl Wyn. *Introducing Anthopology*. Illustrated by Piero, edited by Richard Appignanesi, Icon Books, 2002.
Davis, Richard Brian, editor. Alice in Wonderland *and Philosophy: Curiouser and Curiouser*. John Wiley & Sons, 2010.
Deckard, Michael Funk, and Péter Losonczi, editors. *Philosophy Begins in Wonder: An Introduction to Early Modern Philosophy, Theology, and Science*. Wipf & Stock Publications, 2010.
de Lauretis, Teresa. "Queer Theory: Lesbian and Gay Sexualities." *differences: A Journal of Feminist Cultural Studies*, vol. 3, no. 2, 1991, pp. 296–313.
Deleuze, Gilles. *The Logic of Sense*. Edited by Constantin V. Boundas, translated by Mark Lester, with Charles Stivale, Columbia UP, 1990.
Deleuze, Gilles, and Félix Guattari. *Kafka: Toward a Minor Literature*. Translated by Dana Polan, foreword by Réda Bensmaïa, U of Minnesota P, 1986.
———. *What Is Philosophy?* Translated by Hugh Tomlinson and Graham Burchell. Columbia UP, 1994.
de Man, Paul. *The Resistance to Theory*. Foreword by Wlad Godzich, U of Minnesota P, 1986.
Derrida, Jacques. *The Animal That Therefore I Am*. Edited by Marie-Louise Mallet, translated by David Wills, Fordham UP, 2008, pp. 1–51.
———. *The Beast & the Sovereign*. Vol. 2. Edited by Michel Lisse, Marie-Louise Mallet, and Ginette Michaud, translated by Geoffrey Bennington, U of Chicago P, 2011.
———. "Some Statements and Truisms about Neologisms, Newisms, Postisms, Parasitisms, and Other Small Seismisms." *The States of 'Theory': History, Art, and Critical Discourse*, edited by David Carroll, Columbia UP, 1990, pp. 63–94.

Dixon, Bob. *Catching Them Young: Sex, Race and Class in Children's Fiction.* Pluto P, 1977.

Docherty, Thomas. *After Theory: Postmodernism/Postmarxism.* Routledge, 1990.

Doderer, Klaus. "Walter Benjamin and Children's Literature." *"With the Sharpened Axe of Reason": Approaches to Walter Benjamin*, edited by Gerhard Fischer, Berg, 1996, pp. 169–75.

Dorfman, Ariel, and Armand Mattelart. *Para leer al Pato Donald* [*How to Read Donald Duck*]. Editorial Ciencias Sociales, 1974.

Douglas, Kate. *Contesting Childhood: Autobiography, Trauma, and Memory.* Rutgers UP, 2010.

Duane, Anna Mae, editor. *The Children's Table: Childhood Studies and the Humanities.* U of Georgia P, 2013.

Duncan, Randy, Matthew J. Smith, and Paul Levitz. *The Power of Comics: History, Form and Culture.* 2nd ed., preface by Mark Wald, Bloomsbury, 2015.

Durant, Will. *The Story of Philosophy: The Lives and Opinions of the Greater Philosophers.* Simon & Schuster, 1933.

Dusinberre, Juliet. *Alice to the Lighthouse: Children's Books and Radical Experiments in Art.* Macmillan, 1987.

Eagleton, Terry. *After Theory.* Basic Books, 2003.

———. *The Significance of Theory.* Basil Blackwood, 1990.

Eastman, P. D. *Are You My Mother?* Random House, 1960.

Eburne, Jonathan P. *Outsider Theory: Intellectual Histories of Unorthodox Ideas.* U of Minnesota P, 2018.

Edelman, Lee. *No Future: Queer Theory and the Death Drive.* Duke UP, 2004.

Edelstein, Sari. *Adulthood and Other Fictions: American Literature and the Unmaking of Age.* Oxford UP, 2019.

Empson, William. "*Alice in Wonderland*: The Child as Swain." Reprinted in *Aspects of Alice*, edited by Robert Phillips, Penguin, 1971, pp. 400–33.

Erickson, Jon. "Philosophy and Theory." *Journal of Dramatic Theory and Criticism*, vol. 16, no. 1, Fall 2001, pp. 143–48.

Evans, Clyde. "Philosophy with Children: Some Experiences and Some Reflections." *Metaphilosophy*, vol. 7, no. 1, Jan. 1976, pp. 53–69.

Evans, H. M. "Wonder and the Clinical Encounter." *Theoretical Medicine and Bioethics*, vol. 33, no. 2, 2012, pp. 123–36.

Ewers, Hans-Heino. "Children's Literature Research in Germany. A Report." 2002, www.uni-frankfurt.de/~ewers/word-dl/Ewers-Report.doc. Accessed 2 Sept. 2017.

Falconer, Rachel. *The Crossover Novel: Contemporary Children's Fiction and Its Adult Readership.* Routledge, 2009.

Fanon, Frantz. *Black Skin, White Masks.* Translated by Charles Lam Markmann, forewords by Ziauddin Sardar and Homi K. Bhabha, Pluto Press, 1967.

Farson, Richard. *Birthrights.* Macmillan, 1974.

Faulkner, Joanne. "Humanity's Little Scrap Dealers: The Child at Play in Modern Philosophy and Implications for Sexualization Discourse." *Childhood*

Studies and the Practice of Interdisciplinarity: Disciplining the Child, edited by Joanne Faulkner and Magdalena Zolkos, Lexington Books, 2016, pp. 83–101.

———. “Innocence, Evil, and Human Frailty: Potentiality and the Child in the Writings of Giorgio Agamben.” *Angelaki: Journal of the Theoretical Humanities*, vol. 15, no. 2, Aug. 2010, pp. 203–19.

———. “Innocents and Oracles: The Child as a Figure of Knowledge and Critique in the Middle-Class Philosophical Imagination.” *Critical Horizons*, vol. 12, no. 3, 2011, pp. 323–46.

———. “Negotiating Vulnerability through ‘Animal’ and ‘Child.’” *Angelaki: Journal of the Theoretical Humanities*, vol. 16, no. 4, Dec. 2011, pp. 73–85.

Felski, Rita. *The Limits of Critique*. U of Chicago P, 2015.

Feminist Theory, special issue, “The Child and Childhood,” vol. 11, no. 3, December 2010, guest edited by Erica Burman and Jackie Stacey.

Fillingham, Lydia Alix. *Foucault for Beginners*. Illustrated by Moshe Süsser, Writers and Readers Publishing, 1993.

Fitzhugh, Louise. *Harriet the Spy*. Harper & Row, 1964.

———. *Nobody's Family Is Going to Change*. Farrar, Straus and Giroux, 1974.

Fitzsimmons, Rebekah. *The Chronicles of Professionalization: The Expert, the Child, and the Making of American Children's Literature*. Dissertation, University of Florida, 2015.

Flaxman, Gregory. *Gilles Deleuze and the Fabulation of Philosophy*. U of Minnesota P, 2012.

Flynn, Richard. “The Intersection of Children's Literature and Childhood Studies.” *Children's Literature Association Quarterly*, vol. 22, no. 3, Fall 1997, pp. 143–45.

Forrest, Tara. *The Politics of Imagination: Benjamin, Kracauer, Kluge*. Transcript-Verlag, 2007.

Fuss, Diana. “Accounting for Theory in the Undergraduate Classroom.” *Teaching Contemporary Theory to Undergraduates*, edited by Dianne F. Sadoff and William E. Cain, MLA, 1994, pp. 103–13.

———. “Introduction: Human, All Too Human.” *Human, All Too Human*, edited by Diana Fuss, Routledge, 1996, pp. 1–7.

———. “Teaching Theory.” *The Critical Pulse: Thirty-Six Credos by Contemporary Critics*, edited by Jeffrey J. Williams and Heather Steffen, Columbia UP, 2012, pp. 164–72.

Fynsk, Christopher. *Infant Figures*. Stanford UP, 2000.

Gaarder, Jostein. *Sophie's World: A Novel about the History of Philosophy*. Farrar, Straus and Giroux, 2007.

Gallop, Jane. *Anecdotal Theory*. Duke UP, 2002.

Galvan, Margaret. “‘The Lesbian Norman Rockwell’: Alison Bechdel and Queer Grassroots Networks.” *American Literature*, vol. 90, no. 2, June 2018, pp. 407–38.

García, Santiago. *On the Graphic Novel*. Translated by Bruce Campbell. UP of Mississippi, 2010.

Garner, Dwight. "Artist, Draw Thyself (and Your Mother and Therapist)." *New York Times*, May 2, 2012, www.nytimes.com/2012/05/03/books/are-you-my-mother-by-alison-bechdel.html. Accessed 14 Apr. 2018.

Gates, Henry Louis, Jr. *Figures in Black: Words, Signs, and the 'Racial' Self.* 1987. Oxford University Press, 1989.

Gelley, Alexander. *Benjamin's Passages: Dreaming, Awakening.* Fordham UP, 2015.

Gilbert, Jen. *Sexuality in School: The Limits of Education.* U of Minnesota P, 2014.

Gino, Alex. *George.* Scholastic, 2015.

Gittens, Diana. *The Child in Question.* Macmillan, 1998.

Glaser, Edward M. *An Experiment in the Development of Critical Thinking.* Teacher's College P, 1941.

Goh, Irving. *The Reject: Community, Politics, and Religion after the Subject.* Fordham UP, 2015.

Goldschmidt, A. M. E. "*Alice in Wonderland* Psychoanalyzed." *New Oxford Outlook*, May 1933, pp. 69–70.

Gopnik, Alison. *The Philosophical Baby: What Children's Minds Tell Us about Truth, Love, and the Meaning of Life.* Picador, 2009.

Gopnik, Alison, Andrew N. Meltzoff, and Patricia K. Kuhl. *The Scientist in the Crib: What Early Learning Tells Us about the Mind.* William Morrow, 1999.

Graff, Gerald. *Professing Literature: An Institutional History.* U of Chicago P, 1987.

Greyson, Lauren. *Vital Reenchantments: Biophilia, Gaia, Cosmos, and the Affectively Ecological.* Punctum Books, 2019.

Gubar, Marah. *Artful Dodgers: Reconceiving the Golden Age of Children's Literature.* Oxford UP, 2009.

———. *How to Think about Children: Childhood Studies in Academia and Beyond.* Work in progress, cited with permission.

———. "Lewis in Wonderland: The Looking-Glass World of *Sylvie and Bruno*." *Texas Studies in Literature and Language*, vol. 48, no. 4, Winter 2006, pp. 372–94.

———. "On Not Defining Children's Literature." *PMLA*, vol. 126, no. 1, 2011, pp. 209–16.

Guillory, John. *Cultural Capital: The Problem of Literary Canon Formation.* U of Chicago P, 1993.

Haas, Hope J. "The Value of 'Philosophy for Children' within the Piagetian Framework." *Metaphilosophy*, vol. 7, no. 1, Jan. 1976, pp. 70–75.

Halberstam, Jack. *The Queer Art of Failure.* Duke UP, 2011.

Hamilton, Virginia. *The Planet of Junior Brown.* Simon & Schuster, 1971.

Hansen, Sarah. "Infancy, Animality and the Limits of Language." *Journal of Critical Animal Studies*, vol. 9, no. 2, 2011, pp. 167–81.

Harrison, Robert Pogue. *Juvenescence: A Cultural History of Our Age.* U of Chicago P, 2014.

Haynes, Joanna. *Children as Philosophers: Learning through Enquiry and Dialogue in the Primary Classroom*. Routledge, 2002.

Haynes, Joanna, and Karin Murris. *Picturebooks, Pedagogy, and Philosophy*. Routledge, 2012.

Held, David. *Introduction to Critical Theory: Horkheimer to Habermas*. U of California P, 1980.

Held, Jacob M., editor. *Dr. Seuss and Philosophy: Oh, the Thinks You Can Think!* Rowman & Littlefield, 2011.

Helms, Jason Muir. "Is This Article a Comic?" *Comics and Scholarship*, special issue of *Digital Humanities Quarterly*, edited by Roger Todd Whitson and Anastasia Salter, vol. 9, no. 4, 2015, www.digitalhumanities.org/dhq/vol/9/4/000230/000230.html. Accessed 4 Mar. 2017.

Hernandez, Catherine. *M is for Mustache: A Pride ABC Book*. Flamingo Rampart, 2014.

Herner, Irene. *Mitos y monitos: Historietas y fotonovelas en México* [*Myths and the Funnies: Comic Books and Photonovels in Mexico*]. Editorial Nueva Imagen, 1979.

Hill, Katie Rain. *Rethinking Normal*. Simon & Schuster, 2014.

Hinds, Harold E., and Charles M. Tatum. *Not Just for Children: The Mexican Comic Book in the Late 1960s and 1970s*. Greenwood P, 1992.

Hofstadter, Richard. *Anti-Intellectualism in American Life*. Vintage, 1962.

Hoiem, Elizabeth Massa. "From Philosophical Experiment to Adventure Fiction: English Adaptations of French Robinsonades and the Politics of Genre." *Children's Literature*, vol. 46, 2018, pp. 1–29.

Hollingworth, Leta S. *Gifted Children: Their Nature and Nurture*. Macmillan, 1926.

Holmes, Roger W. "The Philosopher's Alice in Wonderland." *Aspects of Alice: Lewis Carroll's Dreamchild as Seen through the Critics' Looking-Glasses, 1865–1917*, edited by Robert Phillips, Penguin, 1981, pp. 199–216.

Honeyman, Susan. "Trans(cending)gender through Childhood." *The Children's Table: Childhood Studies and the Humanities*, edited by Anna Mae Duane, U of Georgia P, 2013, pp. 167–82.

Howe, James. *Otter and Odder: A Love Story*. Illustrated by Chris Raschka. Candlewick P, 2012.

Høyrup, Helene. "Modernism for Children? Cecil Bødker's *Silas and the Black Mare*." *Beyond Babar: The European Tradition in Children's Literature*, edited by Sandra L. Beckett and Maria Nikolajeva, the Children's Literature Association and the Scarecrow P, 2006, pp. 127–56.

Hughes, Felicity A. "Children's Literature: Theory and Practice." *ELH*, vol. 54, no. 3, Autumn 1978, pp. 542–61.

Humphrey, Aaron. "Multimodal Authoring and Authority in Educational Comics: Introducing Derrida and Foucault for Beginners." *Comic and Scholarship*, special issue of *Digital Humanities Quarterly*, guest edited by Roger Todd Whitson and Anastasia Salter, vol. 9, no. 4, 2015, www.digitalhumanities.org/dhq/vol/9/4/000214/000214.html. Accessed 15 Feb. 2017.

Hunt, Caroline. "Young Adult Literature Evades the Theorists." *Children's Literature Association Quarterly*, vol. 21, no. 1, Spring 1996, pp. 4–11.

Hurley, Natasha. "Alice Lost and Found: A Queer Book History." *Textual Transformations in Children's Literature: Adaptations, Translations, Reconsiderations*, edited by Benjamin Lefebvre, Routledge, 2013, pp. 101–25.

———. *Circulating Queerness: Before the Gay and Lesbian Novel*. U of Minnesota P, 2018.

———. "The Perversions of Children's Literature." *Jeunesse: Young People, Texts, Cultures*, vol. 3, no. 2, 2011, pp. 118–32.

Huskey, Melynda. "Queering the Picture Book." *The Lion and the Unicorn*, vol. 26, no. 1, Jan. 2002, pp. 66–77.

Jacobs, Dale. *Graphic Encounters: Comics and the Sponsorship of Multimodal Literacy*. Bloomsbury, 2013.

Jaques, Zoe. *Children's Literature and the Posthuman: Animal, Environment, Cyborg*. Routledge, 2015.

Jaques, Zoe, and Eugene Giddens. *Lewis Carroll's* Alice's Adventures in Wonderland *and* Through the Looking-Glass*: A Publishing History*. Ashgate, 2013.

James, Allison. "Interdisciplinarity—For Better or Worse." *Children's Geographies*, vol. 8, no. 2, May 2010, pp. 215–16.

Jenkins, Christine A., and Michael Cart. *Representing the Rainbow in Young Adult Literature: LBGTQ Content since 1969*. Rowman & Littlefield, 2018.

Jenks, Chris. *Childhood*. Routledge, 1996.

Johnson, Myles E. *Large Fears*. Illustrated by Kendrick Daye, 2015. Self-published.

Johnson, Tony W. *Philosophy for Children: An Approach to Critical Thinking*. Phi Delta Kappa Educational Foundation, 1984.

Johnson, Tony W., and Ronald F. Reed. "Philosophy for Children: Matthew Lipman, Gareth Matthews, and Kieran Egan." *Philosophical Documents in Education*, edited by Tony W. Johnson and Ronald F. Freed, Pearson, 2012, pp. 222–52.

Jones, Katharine. "Getting Rid of Children's Literature." *The Lion and the Unicorn*, vol. 30, no. 3, Sept. 2006, pp. 287–315.

Joseph, Michael. "Seeing the Visible Book: How Graphic Novels Resist Reading." *Why Comics Are and Are Not Picture Books*, special issue of *Children's Literature Association Quarterly*, guest edited by Charles Hatfield and Craig Svonkin, vol. 37, no. 4, Winter 2012, pp. 454–67.

Joy, Louise. *Literature's Children: The Critical Child and the Art of Idealization*. Bloomsbury, 2019.

Kapur, Jyotsna. *Coining for Capital: Movies, Marketing, and the Transformation of Childhood*. Rutgers UP, 2005.

Kashtan, Aaron. *Between Pen and Pixel: Comics, Materiality, and the Book of the Future*. Ohio State UP, 2018.

Kavanagh, Thomas M. Introduction. *The Limits of Theory*, edited by Thomas M. Kavanah, Stanford UP, pp. 1–22.

Kellner, Douglas. *Media Culture: Cultural Studies, Identity and Politics between the Modern and the Postmodern*. Routledge, 1995.

Kennedy, David. "From Outer Space and across the Street: Matthew Lipman's Double Vision." *Childhood & Philosophy*, vol. 7, no. 13, 2011, pp. 49–74.

Kidd, Kenneth. *Freud in Oz: At the Intersections of Psychoanalysis and Children's Literature*. U of Minnesota P, 2011.

———. "Queer Theory's Child and Children's Literature Studies." *PMLA*, vol. 126, no. 1, 2011, pp. 182–88.

Kincaid, James R. *Child-Loving: The Erotic Child and Victorian Culture*. Routledge, 1992.

———. *Erotic Innocence: The Culture of Child Molesting*. Duke UP, 1998.

Kowalski, Dean A. "Horton Hears You, Too! Seuss and Kant on Respecting Persons." *Dr. Seuss and Philosophy: Oh, the Thinks You Can Think!*, edited by Jacob M. Held, Rowman & Littlefield, 2011, pp. 119–31.

Krauss, Ruth. *I Want to Paint My Bathroom Blue*. Illustrated by Maurice Sendak, HarperCollins, 1956.

Lacan, Jacques. *Écrits*. Translated by Alan Sheridan, W. W. Norton, 1977.

———. *My Teaching*. Translated by David Macey, preface by Jacques-Alain Miller, Verso, 2008.

Lambert, Gregg. *Report to the Academy*. Davies Group, 2001.

Lane, Christopher. "Lewis Carroll and Psychoanalysis: Why Nothing Adds Up in Wonderland." *International Journal of Psychoanalysis*, vol. 92, 2011, pp. 1029–45.

Lapouge, Gilles. "Michel Tournier's s'explique." *Lire*, vol. 64, Dec. 1980, pp. 28–46.

Lecercle, Jean-Jacques. *Badiou and Deleuze Read Literature*. Edinburgh UP, 2010.

———. *Philosophy through the Looking Glass*. Open Court, 1985.

Leclaire, Serge. *A Child Is Being Killed: On Primary Narcissism and the Death Drive*. Translated by Marie-Claude Hays, Stanford UP, 1997.

Le Doeuff, Michèle. *The Philosophical Imaginary*. Translated by Colin Gordon, Stanford UP, 1989.

Leitch, Vincent B. *Theory Matters*. Routledge, 2003.

Lekachman, Robert. *Capitalism for Beginners*. Illustrated by Borin Van Loon, Pantheon, 1981.

Leslie, Esther. *Hollywood Flatlands: Animation, Critical Theory and the Avant-Garde*. Verso, 2002.

Lesnik-Oberstein, Karín. *Children's Literature: Criticism and the Fictional Child*. Clarendon Press, 1994.

———. *On Having One's Own Child: Reproductive Technologies and the Cultural Construction of Childhood*. Karnac, 2008.

Lesnik-Oberstein, Karín, and Stephen Thomson. "What Is Queer Theory Doing with the Child?" *Parallax*, vol. 8, no. 1, 2002, pp. 35–46.

Lewis, Lizzie. "SAPERE P4C school data." Received by Kenneth Kidd, 23 Nov. 2016.

Lewis, Tyson E. "A Constellation of Childhood." *Childhood & Philosophy*, vol. 3, no. 6, 2007, pp. 175–85.

———. "King of the Wild Things: Children and the Passionate Attachments of the Anthropological Machine." *Philosophy in Children's Literature*, edited by Peter R. Costello, Lexington Books, 2012, pp. 285–300.

Lipman, Matthew. *Harry Stottlemeier's Discovery*. Institute for the Advancement of Philosophy for Children, 1974.

———. "Philosophy for Children." *Metaphilosophy*, vol. 7, no. 1, Jan. 1976, pp. 17–39.

———. *Philosophy Goes to School*. Temple UP, 1988.

Lipman, Matthew, and Ann Margaret Sharp. *Wondering at the World: Instruction Manual to Accompany* Kio and Gus. UP of America, 1986.

Lipman, Matthew, Ann Margaret Sharp, and Frederick S. Oscanyan. *Philosophical Inquiry: An Instructional Manual to Accompany* Harry Stottlemeier's Discovery. 2nd ed., UP of America, 1977.

———. *Philosophy in the Classroom*. Institute for the Advancement of Philosophy for Children, 1977.

———. *Philosophy in the Classroom*. 2nd ed. Philadelphia: Temple UP, 1980.

Litvak, Joseph. *Strange Gourmets: Sophistication, Theory, and the Novel*. Duke UP, 1997.

Lone, Jana Mohr. *The Philosophical Child*. Rowman & Littlefield, 2012.

Love, Jessica. *Julián Is a Mermaid*. Candlewick, 2018.

Lyotard, Jean-François. "A Bizarre Partner." *Postmodern Fables*, translated by Georges Van Den Abbeele, U of Minnesota P, 1997, pp. 123–47.

———. *The Inhuman: Reflections on Time*. Translated by Geoffrey Bennington and Rachel Bowlby, Polity Press, 1991.

———. *Libidinal Economy*. Translated by Iain Hamilton Grant, Indiana UP, 1993.

———. *The Postmodern Explained: Correspondence 1982–1985*. Translation edited by Julian Pefanis and Morgan Thomas, translated by Don Barry, Bernadette Maher, Julian Pefanis, Virginia Spate, and Morgan Thomas, afterword by Wlad Godzich, U of Minnesota P, 2003.

Mallan, Kerry. "Queer." *Keywords for Children's Literature*, edited by Philip Nel and Lissa Paul, NYUP, 2011, pp. 186–89.

Marcus, Leonard. *Minders of Make-Believe: Idealists, Entrepreneurs, and the Shaping of American Children's Literature*. Houghton Mifflin, 2008.

Margolin, Leslie. *Goodness Personified: The Emergence of Gifted Children*. Aldine De Gruyter, 1994.

Martin, Biddy. "The Hobo, the Fairy, and the Quarterback." *Femininity Played Straight: The Significance of Being Lesbian*, edited by Biddy Martin. Routledge, 1997, pp. 33–44.

Mason, Derritt. *Queer Anxieties of Young Adult Literature and Culture*. UP of Mississippi, forthcoming.

Matthews, Gareth B. *Dialogues with Children*. Harvard UP, 1984.

———. "Philosophy and Children's Literature." *Metaphilosophy*, vol. 7, no. 1, Jan. 1976, pp. 7–16.

———. *Philosophy and the Young Child*. Harvard UP, 1980.

———. "Philosophy as Child's Play." Seventeenth Annual Children's Literature Association Conference, 31 May–3 June 1990, San Diego State University, San Diego, Calif.

———. *The Philosophy of Childhood*. Harvard UP, 1994.

———. *Socratic Perplexity and the Nature of Philosophy*. Oxford UP, 1999.

Mavor, Carol. *Reading Boyishly: Roland Barthes, J. M. Barrie, Jacques Henri Lartigue, Marcel Proust, and D. W. Winnicott*. Duke UP, 2007.

May, Leila S. "Wittgenstein's Reflection in Lewis Carroll's Looking-Glass." *Philosophy and Literature*, vol. 31, 2007, pp. 79–94.

Maybee, Julie E. *Picturing Hegel: An Illustrated Guide to Hegel's Encyclopaedia Logic*. Lexington Books, 2009.

McCarty, Marietta. *Little Big Minds: Sharing Philosophy with Kids*. Jeremy P. Tarcher, 2006.

McGillis, Roderick. *The Nimble Reader: Literary Theory and Children's Literature*. Twayne Publishers, 1996.

McHale, Brian. *The Cambridge Introduction to Postmodernism*. Cambridge UP, 2015.

McLaughlin, Jeff, editor. *Comics as Philosophy*. UP of Mississippi, 2005.

———. *Graphic Novels as Philosophy*. UP of Mississippi, 2017.

McLaughlin, Thomas. *Street Smarts and Critical Theory: Listening to the Vernacular*. U of Wisconsin P, 1996.

McQuillan, Martin, Graeme MacDonald, Robin Purves, and Stephen Thomson, editors. *Post-Theory: New Directions in Criticism*. Edinburgh UP, 1999.

Mehlman, Jeffrey. *Walter Benjamin for Children: An Essay on His Radio Years*. U of Chicago P, 1993.

Meskin, Aaron. "The Philosophy of Comics." *Philosophy Compass*, vol. 6, 2011, pp. 854–64.

———. "What Is the Philosophy of Comics?" *Comics Forum*, March 26, 2019, www.comicsforum.org/2012/03/26/what-is-the-philosophy-of-comics-by-aaron-meskin/. Accessed 3 May 2019.

Meskin, Aaron, and Roy T. Cook, editors. *The Art of Comics: A Philosophical Approach*. Wiley-Blackwell, 2012.

Michals, Teresa. *Books for Children, Books for Adults: Age and the Novel from Defoe to James*. Cambridge UP, 2014.

Mickenberg, Julia L. *Learning from the Left: Children's Literature, the Cold War, and Radical Politics in the United States*. Oxford UP, 2006.

Mickenberg, Julia L., and Philip Nel. *Tales for Little Rebels*. NYUP, 2010.

Miller, Carl F. "Horton Hears Badiou!: Ethics and an Understanding of Dr. Seuss's *Horton Hears a Who!*" *Philosophy in Children's Literature*, edited by Peter R. Costello, Lexington Books, 2012, pp. 83–100.

Miller, Laura. "Are You My Mother? by Alison Bechdel—Review." *The Guardian*, www.theguardian.com/books/2012/may/24/are-you-my-mother-alison-bechdel-review. Accessed 6 Apr. 2018.

Miller, Nancy K. *Getting Personal: Feminist Occasions and Other Autobiographical Acts*. Routledge, 1991.

Mills, Claudia, editor. *Ethics and Children's Literature*. Ashgate, 2014.

———. Introduction. *Ethics and Children's Literature*, edited by Claudia Mills, Ashgate, 2014, pp. 1–12.

Mintz, Steven. *Huck's Raft: A History of American Childhood*. Harvard UP, 2004.

———. *The Prime of Life: A History of Modern Adulthood*. Harvard UP, 2015.

Mitchell, W. J. T. Introduction. *Against Theory: Literary Studies and the New Pragmatism*, edited by W. J. T. Mitchell, U of Chicago P, 1982, pp. 1–10.

———. *Picture Theory: Essays on Verbal and Visual Representation*. U of Chicago P, 1994.

Moebius, William. "*L'Enfant Terrible* Comes of Age." *Notebooks in Cultural Analysis: An Annual Review*. Vol. 2, edited by Norman F. Cantor, Duke UP, pp. 32–50.

Moon, Michael. *Darger's Resources*. Duke UP, 2012.

———. *A Small Boy and Others: Imitation and Initiation in American Culture from Henry James to Andy Warhol*. Duke UP, 1998.

Muñoz, José Esteban. *Cruising Utopia: The Then and There of Queer Futurity*. NYUP, 2009.

Murris, Karin. "The Philosophy for Children Curriculum, Narrativity and Higher-Order Thinking." Philosophy of Education Society of Great Britain Annual Conference, New College, Oxford, 2012. Conference presentation.

———. "Philosophy with Children, the Stingray, and the Educative Value of Disequilibrium." *Journal of Philosophy of Education*, vol. 42, nos. 3 & 4, 2008, pp. 667–85.

———. *The Posthuman Child: Educational Transformations through Philosophy with Picturebooks*. Routledge, 2016.

Murris, Karin, and Steve Bramall, Shirley Egley, Maughn Gregory, Joanna Haynes, and Steve Williams. "What Philosophy with Children Is Not: Responses to Some Critics and Constructive Suggestions for Dialogue about the Role of P4C in Higher Education." www.scribd.com/document/231811215/MurrisSymposium-What-Philosophy-With-Children-is-Not-Responses-to-Some-Critics-and-Constructive-Suggestions-for-Dialogue-About-the-Role-of-P4C-in-Higher-Education. Accessed 19 Nov. 2016.

Nel, Philip. *Was the Cat in the Hat Black? The Hidden Racism of Children's Literature and the Need for Diverse Books*. Oxford UP, 2017.

Nelson, Claudia. *Precocious Children & Childish Adults: Age Inversion in Victorian Literature*. Johns Hopkins UP, 2012.

Nelson, Maggie. *The Argonauts*. Graywolf P, 2015.

Nericcio, William Anthony. "Artif[r]acture: Virulent Pictures, Graphic Narrative, and the Ideology of the Visual." *Mosaic*, vol. 28, no. 4, Dec. 1995, pp. 79–109.

Nietzsche, Friedrich. *Thus Spoke Zarathustra: A Book for Everyone and No One.* Translated and introduced by R. J. Hollingdale. Penguin, 1961.

Nikolajeva, Maria. *Children's Literature Comes of Age: Toward a New Aesthetic.* New York: Garland, 1996.

———. "Exit Children's Literature." *The Lion and the Unicorn*, vol. 22, no. 2, 1998, pp. 221–36.

———. "A Misunderstood Tragedy: Astrid Lindgren's Pippi Longstocking Books." *Beyond Babar: The European Tradition in Children's Literature*, edited by Sandra L. Beckett and Maria Nikolajeva, the Children's Literature Association and the Scarecrow P, 2006, pp. 49–74.

———. *Power, Voice and Subjectivity in Literature for Young Readers*. Routledge, 2010.

Nodelman, Perry. *The Hidden Adult: Defining Children's Literature*. Johns Hopkins UP, 2008.

———. *Words about Pictures: The Narrative Art of Children's Picture Books*. U of Georgia P, 1988.

Norberg, Jakob. "Adorno's Advice: Minima Moralia and the Critique of Liberalism." *PMLA*, vol. 126, no. 2, 2011, pp. 398–411.

Norris, Christopher. *The Contest of Faculties: Philosophy and Theory after Deconstruction*. Methuen, 1985.

Nussbaum, Martha C. *Love's Knowledge: Essays on Philosophy and Literature.* Oxford UP, 1990.

Ogata, Amy F. *Designing the Creative Child: Playthings and Places in Midcentury America*. U of Minnesota P, 2013.

Ohi, Kevin. *Innocence and Rapture: The Erotic Child in Pater, Wilde, James, and Nabokov.* Palgrave Macmillan, 2005.

O'Malley, Andrew. *Children's Literature, Popular Culture, and Robinson Crusoe.* Palgrave Macmillan, 2012.

op de Beeck, Nathalie. "On Comics-Style Picture Books and Picture-Bookish Comics." *Why Comics Are and Are Not Picture Books*, special issue of *Children's Literature Association Quarterly*, edited by Charles Hatfield and Craig Svonkin, vol. 37, no. 4, Winter 2012, pp. 468–76.

———. *Suspended Animation: Children's Picture Books and the Fairy Tale of Modernity*. U of Minnesota P, 2010.

O'Sullivan, Emer. *Comparative Children's Literature*. Routledge, 2005.

Owen, Gabrielle. "Queer Theory Wrestles the 'Real' Child: Impossibility, Identity, and Language in Jacqueline Rose's *The Case of Peter Pan*." *Children's Literature Association Quarterly*, vol. 35, no. 3, Fall 2010, pp. 255–73.

Palumbo-Liu, David. "The Morality of Form; or, What's 'Bad' about 'Bad Writing'?" *Just Being Difficult? Academic Writing in the Public Arena*, edited by Jonathan Culler and Kevin Lamb, Stanford UP, 2003, pp. 171–80.

Paris, Leslie. "Children's Liberation: Children's Rights in the Wake of 1960s Social Movements." Canadian Historical Association Conference, Vancouver, BC, June 2008. Conference presentation.

Park, Alice. "Baby Einsteins: Not So Smart After All." *Time*, Monday, Aug. 6, 2007, http://content.time.com/time/health/article/0,8599,1650352,00.html. Accessed 16 Nov. 2015.

Parker, Robert Dale. *How to Interpret Literature: Critical Theory for Literary and Cultural Studies*. Oxford UP, 2011.

Parkes, Christopher. *Children's Literature and Capitalism: Fictions of Social Mobility in Britain, 1850–1914*. Palgrave, 2012.

Payne, Michael. "What Difference Has Theory Made? From Freud to Adam Phillips." *College Literature*, vol. 32, no. 2, Spring 2015, pp. 1–15.

Payne, Michael, and John Schad, editors. *Life. After. Theory*. Continuum, 2003.

Pfitzer, Gregory M. *Picturing the Past: Illustrated Histories and the American Imagination, 1840–1900*. Smithsonian Institution P, 2002.

Phillips, Richard. *Mapping Men and Empire: A Geography of Adventure*. Routledge, 1997.

Pickering, Samuel F., Jr. *John Locke and Children's Books in Eighteenth-Century England*. U of Tennessee P, 1981.

Pieper, Joseph. *Leisure: The Basis of Culture*. Ignatius P, 2009.

Pitcher, George. "Wittgenstein, Nonsense, and Lewis Carroll." *Massachusetts Review*, vol. 6, no. 3, 1965, pp. 591–611.

Pizzino, Christopher. *Arresting Development: Comics at the Boundaries of Literature*. U of Texas P, 2016.

Plato. *The Dialogues of Plato*. Translated by Benjamin Jowett, vol. 4, Clarendon Press, 1892.

Polonsky, Ami. *Gracefully Grayson*. Hyperion, 2014.

Potts, Jason, and Daniel Stout. "Introduction: On the Side." *Theory Aside*, edited by Jason Potts and Daniel Stout, Duke UP, 2014, pp. 1–25.

Pratt, David. *Bob the Book*. Chelsea Station Editions, 2010.

Priego, Ernesto. "A History of Mankind for Beginners." *Críticas*, April 1, 2002, www.criticasmagazine.com/article/CA201136.html. Accessed 18 June 2018.

Prime-Stevenson, Edward. *Left to Themselves*. Introduction and notes by Eric L. Tribunella, Valancourt, 2016.

Pritchard, Michael S. *Philosophical Adventures with Children*. UP of America, 1985.

Pugh, Tison. *Innocence, Heterosexuality, and the Queerness of Children's Literature*. Routledge, 2011.

Qvortrup, Jens, William A. Corsaro, and Michael-Sebastian Honig, editors. *The Palgrave Handbook of Childhood Studies*. Palgrave Macmillan, 2009.

Rabaté, Jean-Michel. *The Future of Theory*. Blackwell, 2002.

Rand, Erica. *Barbie's Queer Accessories*. Duke UP, 1995.

Rauch, Alan. *Useful Knowledge: The Victorians, Morality, and the March of Intellect*. Duke UP, 2001.

Ray, Robert B. "Cinephelia as a Method." *For the Love of Cinema: Teaching Our Passion In and Outside of the Classroom*, edited by David T. Johnson and Rashna Wadia Richards, Indiana UP, 2017, pp. 27–49.

Redfield, Marc. *Theory at Yale: The Strange Case of Deconstruction in America*. Fordham UP, 2016.

Reé, Jonathan. *Witcraft: The Invention of Philosophy in English*. Allen Lane, 2019.

Reynolds, Kimberley. *Left Out: The Forgotten Tradition of Radical Publishing for Children in 1910–1949*. Oxford UP, 2016.

———. *Radical Children's Literature: Future Visions and Aesthetic Transformations in Juvenile Fiction*. Palgrave, 2007.

Reynolds, Kimberley, Jane Rosen, and Michael Rosen, editors. *Reading and Rebellion: An Anthology of Radical Writing for Children, 1900–1960*. Oxford UP, 2018.

Rio, Eduardo del. *Cuba for Beginners*. Pathfinder P, 1970.

Rius. *Marx for Beginners*. Translated by Richard Appignanesi, Pantheon, 1976.

Rodowick, D. N. *Elegy for Theory*. Harvard UP, 2014.

Ronell, Avital. "The Unrelenting Creepiness of Childhood." *The ÜberReader: Selected Works of Avital Ronell*, edited by Diane Davis, U of Illinois P, 2008, pp. 101–27.

Rose, Jacqueline. *The Case of Peter Pan, or The Impossibility of Children's Fiction*. U of Pennsylvania P, 1984.

Rosenthal, Lecia. "Walter Benjamin on the Radio: An Introduction." *Radio Benjamin*, edited by Lecia Rosenthal, translated by Jonathan Lutes with Lisa Harries Schumann and Diana K. Reese, Verso, 2014, pp. ix–xxix.

Rosenthal, Lynne. "*Misunderstood*: A Victorian Children's Book for Adults." *Children's Literature*, vol. 1, 1974, pp. 94–102.

Rosmarin, Adena. "On the Theory of 'Against Theory.'" *Against Theory: Literary Studies and the New Pragmatism*, edited by W. J. T. Mitchell, U of Chicago P, 1982, pp. 80–88.

Roth, Matthue. *My First Kafka: Runaways, Rodents, and Giant Bugs*. Illustrated by Rohan Daniel Easton. One Peace Books, 2014.

Rubenstein, Anne. *Bad Language, Naked Ladies & Other Threats to the Nation: A Political History of Comic Books in México*. Duke UP, 1998.

Rubin, Joan Shelley. *The Making of Middlebrow Culture*. U of North Carolina P, 1992.

Rudd, David. *Reading the Child in Children's Literature: An Heretical Approach*. Palgrave Macmillan, 2013.

Said, Edward W. *Beginnings: Intention and Method*. Columbia UP, 1975.

Sainsbury, Lisa. "'But the Soldier's Remains Were Gone': Thought Experiments in Children's Literature." *Children's Literature in Education*, vol. 48, 2017, pp. 152–68.

———. *Ethics in British Children's Literature: Unexamined Life*. Bloomsbury, 2013.

Saint-Amour, Paul K. "Weak Theory, Weak Modernism." *Modernism/modernity*, vol. 25, no. 3, Sept. 2018, pp. 437–59.

Salzani, Carlo. "Experience and Play: Walter Benjamin and the Prelapsarian Child." *Walter Benjamin and the Architecture of Modernity*, edited by Andrew Benjamin and Charles Rice, re.press, 2009, pp. 175–200.

Sammond, Nicholas. *Babes in Tomorrowland: Walt Disney and the Making of the American Child, 1930–1960*. Duke UP, 2005.

Sánchez-Eppler, Karen. *Dependent States: The Child's Part in Nineteenth-Century American Culture*. U of Chicago P, 2005.

Sanders, Joe Sutliff. *A Literature of Questions: Nonfiction for the Critical Child*. U of Minnesota P, 2018.

———. "Reinventing Subjectivity: China Miéville's *Un Lun Dun* and the Child Reader." *Extrapolation*, vol. 50, no. 2, 2009, pp. 293–306.

Sautet, Marc. *Nietzsche for Beginners*. Illustrated by Patrick Boussignac, Writers and Readers Publishing, 1990.

Schanoes, Veronica. "Queen Alice and the Monstrous Child: Alice through the Looking-Glass." *Children's Literature*, vol. 45, 2017, pp. 1–20.

Schmidt, Gary D. *Making Americans: Children's Literature from 1930 to 1960*. U of Iowa P, 2013.

Schuman, Rebecca. "Kafka at Bedtime." *Jewish Review of Books*, Winter 2014, https://jewishreviewofbooks.com/articles/622/kafka-at-bedtime/. Accessed 3 April 2018.

Schwebel, Sara L. *Child-Sized History: Fictions of the Past in U. S. Classrooms*. Vanderbilt UP, 2011.

Scotto, Thomas. *Jerome by Heart*. Illustrated by Olivier Tellec, translated by Claudia Zoe Bedrick and Karin Snelson, Enchanted Books, 2018.

Sedgwick, Eve Kosofsky. "Paranoid Reading and Reparative Reading; or, You're So Paranoid, You Probably Think This Introduction Is about You." *Novel Gazing: Queer Readings in Fiction*, edited by Eve Kosofsky Sedgwick, Duke UP, 1997, pp. 1–37.

———. *Tendencies*. Duke UP, 1993.

Sedgwick, Eve Kosofsky, and Adam Frank. "Shame in the Cybernetic Fold: Reading Silvan Tomkins." *Shame and Its Sisters: A Silvan Tomkins Reader*, edited by Eve Kosofsky Sedgwick and Adam Frank, biographical sketch by Irving E. Alexander, Duke UP, 1995, pp. 1–28.

Sharpe, Christina. *In the Wake: On Blackness and Being*. Duke UP, 2016.

Shavit, Zohar. *The Poetics of Children's Literature*. U of Georgia P, 1986.

Sheldon, Rebekah. *The Child to Come: Life after the Human Catastrophe*. U of Minnesota P, 2016.

Shuttleworth, Sally. *The Mind of the Child: Child Development in Literature, Science, and Medicine, 1840–1900*. Oxford UP, 2010.

Sigler, Carolyn, editor. *Alternative Alices: Visions and Revisions of Lewis Carroll's* Alice *Books*. UP of Kentucky, 1998.

Simon, Roger I. "The Fear of Theory." Roger I. Simon, *Teaching against the Grain: Texts for a Possibility of Pedagogy*, Bergin & Garvey P, 1992, pp. 79–100.

Small, David. *Imogene's Antlers*. Crown Publishers, 1985.

Smith, Randall B. "'If Philosophy Begins in Wonder': Aquinas, Creation, and Wonder." *Communio*, vol. 41, Spring 2014, pp. 92–111.

Smith, Victoria Ford. *Between Generations: Collaborative Authorship in the Golden Age of Children's Literature.* UP of Mississippi, 2017.
Snediker, Michael D. *Queer Optimism: Lyric Personhood and Other Felicitous Persuasions.* U of Minnesota P, 2009.
Snicket, Lemony. *The Bad Beginning. A Series of Unfortunate Events, Book the First.* Illustrated by Brett Helquist, HarperCollins, 1999.
———. *The Grim Grotto. A Series of Unfortunate Events, Book the Eleventh.* Illustrated by Brett Helquist, HarperCollins, 2004.
———. *The Miserable Mill. A Series of Unfortunate Events, Book the Fourth.* Illustrated by Brett Helquist, HarperCollins, 2000.
Sones, W. W. D. "The Comics and Instructional Method." *Journal of Educational Sociology*, vol. 18, 1944, pp. 232–40.
Sosnoski, James. "Students as Theorists: Collaborative Hypertextbooks." *Practicing Theory in Introductory College Literature Courses*, edited by James A. Cahalan and David B. Downing, National Council of Teachers of English, 1991, pp. 271–90.
Sousanis, Nick. *Unflattening.* Harvard UP, 2015.
Speck, Paula K. "Rius for Beginners: A Study in Comicbook Satire." *Studies in Latin American Popular Culture*, vol. 1, 1982, pp. 113–35.
Spellman, Margaret Boyle. *The Evolution of Winnicott's Thinking: Examining the Growth of Psychoanalytic Thought over Three Generations.* Karnac, 2013.
Spiegelman, Art, and Françoise Mouly. *Little Lit: Strange Stories for Strange Kids.* RAW Junior, 2001.
Steedman, Carolyn. *Strange Dislocations: Childhood and the Idea of Human Interiority, 1780–1930.* Virago, 1995.
Stein, Jordan Alexander. *Avidly Reads Theory.* NYUP, 2019.
Stiegler, Bernard. *Taking Care of Youth and the Generations.* Translated by Stephen Barker, Stanford UP, 2010.
Stockton, Kathryn Bond. *The Queer Child, or Growing Sideways in the Twentieth Century.* Duke UP, 2009.
Sundmark, Björn. "The Child Robinsonade." *Child Autonomy and Child Governance in Children's Literature: Where Children Rule*, edited by Christopher Kelen and Björn Sundmark, Routledge, 2016, pp. 84–95.
Susina, Jan. *The Place of Lewis Carroll in Children's Literature.* Routledge, 2010.
Sussman, Henry. *Around the Book: Systems and Literacy.* Fordham UP, 2011.
Thacker, Deborah. "Disdain or Ignorance? Literary Theory and the Absence of Children's Literature." *The Lion and the Unicorn*, vol. 24, no. 1, Jan. 2000, pp. 1–17.
Thomas, Joseph T., Jr. "The Panel as Page and the Page as Panel: Uncle Shelby and the Case of the Twin *ABZ* Books." *Why Comics Are and Are Not Picture Books*, special issue of *Children's Literature Association Quarterly*, edited by Charles Hatfield and Craig Svonkin, vol. 37, no. 4, Winter 2012, pp. 477–88.
Todres, Jonathan, and Sara Higinbotham. *Human Rights in Children's Literature: Imagination and the Narrative of Law.* Oxford UP, 2016.

Trask, Michael. *Camp Sites: Sex, Politics, and Academic Style in Postwar America*. Stanford UP, 2013.

Tribunella, Eric L. "Benjamin, Benson, and the Child's Gaze: Childhood Desire and Pleasure in the David Blaize Books." *Pedagogy, Culture & Society*, vol. 24, no. 4, 2016, pp. 505–15.

———. "Between Boys: Edward Stevenson's *Left to Themselves* (1891) and the Birth of Gay Children's Literature." *Children's Literature Association Quarterly*, vol. 37, no. 4, Winter 2012, pp. 374–88.

———. "Children's Literature and the Child Flânuer." *Children's Literature*, vol. 38, 2010, pp. 64–91.

Turner, Susan M., and Gareth B. Matthews, editors. *The Philosopher's Child: Critical Perspectives in the Western Tradition*. U of Rochester P, 1998.

Ulanowicz, Anastasia. *Second-Generation Memory and Contemporary Children's Literature: Ghost Images*. Routledge, 2013.

Ulmer, Gregory L. "The Object of Post-Criticism." *The Anti-Aesthetic: Essays on Postmodern Culture*, edited by Hal Foster, Bay P, 2002, pp. 83–100.

UNESCO. *Philosophy, a School of Freedom: Teaching Philosophy and Learning to Philosophize*. Coordinated by Moufida Goucha, 2007. http://unesdoc.unesco.org/images/0015/001541/154173e.pdf. Accessed 19 March 2020.

UN General Assembly. *Convention on the Rights of the Child*, 20 November 1989, https://www.ohchr.org/en/professionalinterest/pages/crc.aspx.

van Loon, Hendrik Willem. *The Story of Mankind*. H. Liveright, 1921.

Vansieleghem, Nancy. "Listening to Dialogue." *Studies in Philosophy and Education*, vol. 25, nos. 1 & 2, 2006, pp. 175–90.

Wall, John. *Ethics in Light of Childhood*. Georgetown UP, 2010.

Wannamaker, Annette. "A 'Heap of Meaning': Objects, Aesthetics and the Posthuman Child in Janne Teller's Y.A. Novel *Nothing*." *The Lion and the Unicorn*, vol. 39, no. 1, Jan. 2015, pp. 82–99.

Warner, Michael. "Styles of Intellectual Publics." *Just Being Difficult? Academic Writing in the Public Arena*, edited by Jonathan Culler and Kevin Lamb, Stanford UP, 2003, pp. 106–25.

Wartenberg, Thomas E. *Big Ideas for Little Kids: Teaching Philosophy through Children's Literature*. Rowman & Littlefield, 2009.

———. Foreword. *Philosophy in Children's Literature*, edited by Peter R. Costello, Lexington Books, 2012, pp. ix–xi.

Watkins, Evan. *Work Time: English Departments and the Circulation of Cultural Value*. Stanford UP, 1989.

Wegner, Phillip E. "Greimas Avec Lacan; Or, From the Symbolic to the Real in Dialectical Criticism." *Criticism*, vol. 51, no. 2, Spring 2009, pp. 211–45.

Weikle-Mills, Courtney. *Imaginary Citizens: Child Readers and the Limits of American Independence, 1640–1868*. Johns Hopkins UP, 2013.

Weinstone, Ann. "Science Fiction as a Young Person's First Queer Theory." *Science Fiction Studies*, vol. 26, no. 1, pp. 41–48.

Weld, Sara Pankenier. *Voiceless Vanguard: The Infantilist Aesthetic of the Russian Avante-Garde*. Northwestern UP, 2014.

Wenzel, Robert. "The Most Dangerous Book on Economics Ever Written for Kids." *Economic Policy Journal*, https://www.economicpolicyjournal.com/2017/05/the-most-dangerous-book-on-economics.html. Accessed 13 March 2020.

Westman, Karin. Introduction. *Children's Literature and Modernism*, special issue of *Children's Literature Association Quarterly*, edited by Karin Westman, vol. 32, no. 4, 2007, pp. 283–86.

Whitson, Roger Todd, and Anastasia Salter. "Introducing: Comics and the Digital Humanities." *Comics and the Digital Humanities*, special issue of *Digital Humanities Quarterly*, edited by Roger Todd Whitson and Anastasia Salter, vol. 9, no. 4, 2015, www.digitalhumanities.org/dhq/vol/9/4/000210/000210.html. Accessed 14 Feb. 2017.

Wilkie-Stibbs, Christine. *The Outside Child in and out of the Book*. Routledge, 2008.

Williams, Jeffrey J. "Packaging Theory." *College English*, vol. 56, no. 3, Mar. 1994, pp. 280–99.

Williams, Raymond. *Keywords: A Vocabulary of Culture and Society*. Rev. ed. Oxford UP, 1983.

Winnicott, D. W. *Playing and Reality*. Routledge, 1989.

Woodhouse, Barbara Bennett. *Hidden in Plain Sight: The Tragedy of Children's Rights from Ben Franklin to Lionel Tate*. Princeton UP, 2008.

Woodson, Jacqueline. "The Pain of the Watermelon Joke." *New York Times*, www.nytimes.com/2014/11/29/opinion/the-pain-of-the-watermelon-joke.html. Accessed 18 May 2018.

Wunderlich, Richard, and Thomas J. Morrissey. *Pinocchio Goes Postmodern: Perils of a Puppet in the United States*. Routledge, 2008.

Wyile, Andrea Schwenke. "'Astonishment Is Thinking': Graphic Metaphor and Its Philosophical Consequence in Mahler's *Poèmes* and Lemieux's *Stormy Night*." *The Lion and the Unicorn*, vol. 37, no. 3, Sept. 2013, pp. 277–300.

Wyness, Michael. *Childhood and Society*. 2nd ed. Palgrave, 2012.

Wyrick, Deborah. *Fanon for Beginners*. Illustrated by Deborah Wyrick. Writers and Readers Publishing, 1998.

Yorinks, Arthur. *Louis the Fish*. Illustrated by Richard Egielski, Farrar, Straus and Giroux, 1980.

Yoshitake, Shinsuke. *Can I Build Another Me?* Thames & Hudson Ltd., 2015.

Young, Eugene B. "Carroll, Lewis." Eugene B. Young, with Gary Genosoko and Janelle Watson, *The Deleuze and Guattari Dictionary*, Bloomsbury, 2013, pp. 57–58.

Zipes, Jack. "Walter Benjamin, Children's Literature, and the Children's Public Sphere: An Introduction to New Trends in West and East Germany." *Germanic Review: Literature, Culture, Theory*, vol. 63, no. 1, 1988, pp. 2–5.

Žižek, Slavoj. *Organs without Bodies: On Deleuze and Consequences*. Routledge, 2004.

Index

Kenneth B. Kidd is Professor of English at the University of Florida. He is the author of *Making American Boys: Boyology and the Feral Tale* and *Freud in Oz: At the Intersections of Psychoanalysis and Children's Literature*. He is also co-editor (with Derritt Mason) of *Queer as Camp: Essays on Summer, Style, and Sexuality* (Fordham).

Printed in the USA
CPSIA information can be obtained
at www.ICGtesting.com
JSHW021942141223
53817JS00009B/20

9 780823 289608